Getting Started in

Annuities

The Getting Started in Series

Getting Started in
Annuities

Gordon K. Williamson

John Wiley & Sons, Inc.

New York • Chichester • Weinheim • Brisbane • Singapore • Toronto

Published by John Wiley & Sons, Inc.
Published simultaneously in Canada.

This publication is designed to provide accurate and authoritative information in regard to the subject matter covered. It is sold with the understanding that the publisher is not engaged in rendering professional services. If professional advice or other expert assistance is required, the services of a competent professional person should be sought.

Library of Congress Cataloging-in-Publication Data:
Williamson, Gordon K.
    Getting started in annuities / Gordon Williamson.
        p.   cm.—(Getting started in series)
    Includes index.
    ISBN 0-471-28303-7 (pbk. : alk. paper)
    1. Annuities.   2. Insurance, Life.   I. Title.   II. Series:
    Getting started in.
    HG8790.W553   1998
    368.3'7—dc21   98-22785

Printed in the United States of America.

10 9 8 7

Contents

Introduction

J ust since the beginning of the 1990s, hundreds of billions of dollars have been invested in annuities. The popularity of this tax-advantaged investment has increased dramatically since their introduction close to 50 years ago; other forms of annuities have been around for over a century. There are literally tens of millions of investors who own one or more annuities. Since the beginning of the decade, there have been several years where the growth rate of annuities has been greater than that of mutual funds.

Annuities provide tax-deferred growth guarantees, professional management, safety, flexibility, growth, and the option of having a monthly income stream that you cannot outlive. This investment vehicle allows you to choose how your money will be invested. Investment choices range from a fixed-rate guarantee, similar to a bank certificate of deposit, to aggressive growth, similar to a mutual fund.

With an annuity, you decide not only how your money is to be invested, but for how long. You can lock in a rate of return that ranges from three months up to 10 years, or invest in a portfolio of stocks, bonds, or money market instruments for any period. A feature that all annuities possess is that you are never required to take out any money during your or your spouse's lifetime. Yet you can take out part of your interest, growth, and principal at any time. Any account balance that remains after your death passes free of probate to your heirs.

There is no limit to the amount of money that can be invested in an annuity. You can invest a single, lump-sum amount, or make periodic or sporadic investments. Annuities can be used as a general investment or within a qualified retirement plan. This investment can be utilized by young and old, single investors as well as couples, trusts or businesses.

The appeal of annuities is broad. Some annuities are extremely safe and conservative; others range from moderate-risk to quite risky, offering the potential for high returns. With an annuity you can target a certain segment, such as Pacific Basin or emerging markets stocks, or stick with more traditional areas such as government bonds or growth stocks.

In this book you will learn what annuities are, how they work, their advantages and disadvantages, the different ways to make contributions and withdrawals, alternatives to annuities, how fixed-rate annuities compare to certificates of deposit, how variable annuities compare to mutual funds, the effect of 1997 tax law changes, and historical performance figures for several variable annuity categories, as well as which annuities are appropriate for you, based on your age, risk level, and time horizon.

This is the fourth book ever written about annuities; I am the author of three of those books (all of which are published by John Wiley & Sons, Inc.). This book provides updated tables (through December 31, 1997) and discusses new changes in light of recent tax legislation, particularly in the areas of estate planning and the Roth IRA. I think you will find this book easy to understand and follow.

Chapter

What an Annuity Is and How It Works

DEFINITIONS

An annuity is an investment you make through an insurance company. It represents a contractual relationship between you and the company. And, although offered by only the insurance industry, annuities have little, if anything, in common with insurance coverage. Annuities are marketed and sold through insurance agencies, banks, savings and loan (S&L) institutions, brokerage firms, financial planners, and *investment advisers*.

 investment adviser organization or individual that provides professional advice on a wide range of investments, including annuities.

When you purchase, or invest in, an annuity you are given certain assurances by the insurance company. These promises depend on the company issuing the contract (the investment) and the type of annuity chosen. There are three ways to categorize an annuity: (1) how the money is invested (fixed-rate or variable), (2) when income is desired (immediate or deferred), and (3) if additional monies can be added to the investment (flexible-premium or single-premium).

How the Money Is Invested

A *fixed-rate annuity* is very similar to a bank certificate of deposit (CD). The investor is assured of a guaranteed rate of return for a specified period of time. Usually, the longer the period of time, the greater the rate of interest. Just like a bank, an insurance company may offer a rate of return that is more or less competitive than its peers offer. Rates may be locked in for one to 10 years, depending on the annuity contract.

fixed-rate annuity   investor receives a set rate of return.

A *variable annuity* is similar to a mutual fund family. The investor selects from one or more different investment *portfolios*, called *subaccounts*. Portfolio choices may range from ultraconservative (a money market account) to quite aggressive (Pacific Basin stocks). The investor decides how the money should be allocated and can make changes at any time.

variable annuity   no set rate of return, but choice of one or more *portfolios* (*subaccounts*).

portfolio   collection of securities owned by an individual or institution (such as a variable annuity *subaccount*).

subaccount   variable annuity investment choice(s), may include a combination of stocks, bonds, and money market securities.

When Income Is Desired

The investor (known as the *contract owner*), decides if and when income from an annuity is needed. An *immediate annuity* is for an individual or couple who wants to start receiving monthly, quarterly, semiannual, or annual tax-advantaged checks. A *deferred annuity*, which is the most popular type of annuity, is structured so that the investment grows and compounds, tax-deferred, indefinitely. At some point in the future, the contract owner may decide to start making withdrawals.

contract owner the person or entity that owns the annuity. Most of the time, the contract owner is the one who made the investment. The annuity contract is between the insurer (the issuer of the contract) and the contract owner.

immediate annuity a type of fixed-rate or variable annuity wherein money starts to be paid to the contract owner or annuitant either right away or within a month, quarter, or year. Immediate annuities are designed for people who need income on a regular basis.

deferred annuity there are two types of annuities, deferred and immediate; deferred annuities are the more popular of the two. Under a deferred annuity, the investment grows and compounds tax-deferred. Income, growth, and/or principal are withdrawn at some time in the future by the contract owner or heirs.

Adding Money to an Annuity

If the annuity contract allows you to add money to your existing contract, the annuity is referred to as having a *flexible premium*. Virtually all variable annuities are flexible-premium. If the contract allows only a single, onetime investment, it is referred to as having a *single premium*. Almost all fixed-rate annuities are single-premium. Investors who want to add money would have to fill out a new application and accept the then-current interest rate(s). There is no disadvantage to having two or more single-premium annuities.

flexible premium   when you invest in an annuity, the money being invested is sometimes referred to as the premium. A flexible premium means that additional monies can be added at any time in the future to the same annuity contract. Flexible premiums are extremely common with variable annuities but rare with fixed-rate annuities.

single premium   a lump sum of money that is used to purchase an annuity. Most fixed-rate annuities have a single premium since the contract owner is locking in a set rate of return for a specific period, similar to a bank CD.

FOUR PARTIES TO AN ANNUITY

There are always four parties to each annuity: the insurer, the contract owner, the annuitant, and the beneficiary. Oftentimes, the contract owner and the annuitant are the same person.

The Insurer

Whether you invest in an annuity through your local bank, financial planner, brokerage firm, or anyone else who is licensed to sell this product, the agreement is always between you and an insurance company. There are over two thousand insurance companies in the United States; several hundred of these insurers deal in annuities.

The insurance company you choose, known as the insurer, invests your money according to how you fill out the application and the type of annuity offered (i.e., fixed-rate or variable, immediate or deferred, flexible- or single-premium). In the case of a fixed-rate annuity, probably the only option is the duration (e.g., one, two, three, five, seven, or 10 years). The interest rate guaranteed for the period selected will not be on the application, because such rates can change daily, weekly, or monthly. A phone call to the company or a talk with your adviser will quickly tell you the current rates for the different periods of time. In the case of a variable annuity application, your biggest decisions will probably be choosing which subaccounts (very similar to funds within a mutual fund family) and what percentage or dollar amount of your investment will go into the portfolios selected (e.g., 50 percent in growth, 20 percent in high-yield bonds, and 30 percent in global stocks).

The insurer is always an insurance company. In addition to placing the money, the company makes certain promises. These assurances and the terms of the agreement are contained within the *annuity contract*. The contract details what can and cannot be done. Items such as adding more money, making withdrawals, cancellation penalties, and guarantees are all spelled out.

annuity contract an investment in an annuity represents a contractual agreement between the investor (who is usually the contract owner) and the insurer (the insurance company that issues the agreement, known as the annuity contract. The annuity contract contains certain guarantees, assurances, descriptions, terms, and potential penalty provisions.

The Contract Owner

Those who invest in annuities are known as contract owners. It is their money; they decide among the different options being offered. Contract owners have the right and ability to add more money, terminate the agreement, withdraw part or all of the money, or change the parties named in the contract.

When the contract owner enters into an agreement, he or she must be aware of all the terms. If the contract owner decides to make additions, withdrawals, or a complete liquidation, there may be restrictions or penalties.

The contract owner can be an individual, couple, trust, corporation, or partnership. The only requirement is that the owner must be an adult or legal entity. A minor can be the owner as long as the policy lists the minor's custodian (e.g., "Mrs. Sally Adams, custodian for the benefit of Johnny Adams").

Since the contract owner controls this investment, he or she can gift or will part or all of the contract to anyone or any entity at any time.

The Annuitant

If there is one party to the annuity that is difficult to understand, it is the annuitant. The best way to understand the purpose of the annuitant is by analogy. When you purchase life insurance an insured party is named. The life insurance policy continues in force until the owner terminates the contract or fails to make any required premium payments, or the insured dies.

An annuity's terms remain in force until the contract owner makes a change or the person named in the contract as *annuitant* dies. Thus, the annuitant is like the insured in a life insurance policy. However, unlike the death of the insured in a life insurance policy, the death of the annuitant does not necessarily mean the contract is about to come to an end.

> **annuitant**   the "measuring life" of the annuity contract; similar to the "insured" in a life insurance policy. Every annuity contract must include an annuitant. The annuitant has no voice or control over the investment or its disposition. The death of the annuitant may trigger certain insurance company guarantees if the money was invested in a variable annuity.

Looked at another way, the annuitant is simply the "measuring life." The annuitant, like an insured, has no voice or control of the contract. There is only one situation in which the annuitant can benefit from an annuity, known as *annuitization* and explained in detail in Chapter 3. The annuitant does not have the power to make withdrawals or deposits, change the names of the parties to the agreement, or terminate the con-

tract. And just as is the case when you purchase life insurance on someone else (the insured), the annuitant must usually sign the contract.

> **annuitization** the even distribution of both principal
> and interest over a period of time.

The person you name as the annuitant (the "insured") can be anyone: yourself, your spouse, parent, child, relative, friend, or neighbor. The
only qualification is that the named annuitant is actually a person (i.e.,
not a living trust, corporation, partnership, etc.) currently living who is
under a certain age. The maximum age of the proposed annuitant depends on the insurance company. Most companies require that the annuitant be under the age of 75 when the contract is initially signed. Other
companies set a maximum age of 70, 80, or 85. It is important to note that
the contract (the investment) usually stays in force after the annuitant
reaches this maximum age.

Most annuities allow the contract owner to change the annuitant at
any time. The only stipulation is that the new annuitant must have been
alive when the contract was originally set up. Some contracts allow you to
name a *coannuitant*. The naming of a coannuitant could result in the contract lasting even longer since any *forced annuitization* or *contract termination* could be postponed until the death of the second annuitant.

> **coannuitant** a second "measuring life," somewhat
> similar to a second-to-die life insurance policy. Naming a
> coannuitant means the death of one annuitant will not
> trigger a possible forced distribution of the annuity. Only
> a small number of insurers include a coannuitant option
> as part of the annuity application.

> **forced annuitization** some contracts require
> distribution or orderly liquidation once the annuitant
> reaches a certain age, typically 80 or 85.

contract termination   if the contract is "annuitant–driven," the death of the annuitant may require liquidation within five years.

The Beneficiary

In a life insurance policy, the status of the beneficiary is of little value until the death of a certain individual. In the case of an annuity, the beneficiary is awaiting the death of the annuitant. And, like the beneficiary of a life insurance policy, the beneficiary of an annuity has no voice in the control or management of the policy. The only way in which the beneficiary can prosper from an annuity is upon the death of the annuitant.

The named beneficiary(s) can be a spouse, children, friends, relatives, neighbors, trusts, corporations, or partnerships. The annuity application allows for multiple beneficiary designations of varying or similar proportions (e.g., 25 percent to Mary Jones, 15 percent to Jack Jones, 10 percent to Edward Smith, and 50 percent to the Nelson Family Trust).

In the case of a married couple, it is quite common for the contract owner to be one spouse and the annuitant to be the other spouse. (*Note:* A few companies allow co-ownership, in which case both spouses could be owners.) This type of multiple titling is to protect the assets of the couple in the case of the untimely death of the annuitant. After all, if the annuitant were to die before the couple they would not want the annuity proceeds to go to a charity or child named as beneficiary while one or both spouses were still alive.

A single person, widow, or widower will usually name oneself as the contract owner and annuitant, while listing a loved one or entity (e.g., living trust, charity, corporation, etc.) as the beneficiary. By making such an election, the individual retains complete control and dominion over the investment during his or her lifetime. Upon the death of the annuitant the money will automatically pass to the intended heir.

The contract owner can change the beneficiary or beneficiaries at any time; consent by the existing beneficiary(s) is not necessary. You do not need to notify someone that he or she has been listed as a beneficiary of your annuity; similarly, you do not have to tell anyone of removal as an intended beneficiary.

One Person Can Have Multiple Titles

At the time you invest in an annuity the insurance company needs to know the name of the owner(s), annuitant, and beneficiary(s). As previously mentioned, the owner(s) and beneficiary(s) do not have to be people—they can be entities; only the annuitant, the "measuring life," has to be a natural person.

As pointed out above, the same person can hold multiple titles. Thus, you could be the contract owner and beneficiary of your own contract. Or, you could be the owner, annuitant, and beneficiary. In fact, any combination you can think of is acceptable. Keep in mind that if you choose an entity (living trust, corporation, etc.), the entity can be only the contract owner and/or beneficiary; a living individual under a certain age (not a couple) must be named as the annuitant. Also remember that the insurer is always an insurance company; in order for you to change insurers you must change insurance companies.

HOW THE CONTRACT IS "DRIVEN"

In the past, all annuity contracts were "*annuitant–driven*," meaning that certain provisions or sections of the annuity contract came into being if the annuitant died, reached a certain age, or became disabled. Provisions such as waiver of any insurance company penalty, the death benefit, IRS penalty, and/or the required annuitization or distribution of the contract became effective based on what happened to the annuitant.

 annuitant–driven　for a majority of annuity contracts, provisions come into being if the annuitant dies, reaches a certain age, or becomes disabled.

Today, a growing minority of annuity contracts are "*owner–driven*," meaning that the provisions listed in the previous paragraph are based on whether something happens to the contract owner (i.e., death, disability, or reaching a certain age). A few annuity contracts have a provision that some sections or terms of the contract can come into being if *either* the owner, co-owner, or annuitant dies, reaches the age of annuitization, or becomes disabled. Such "either/or" substitutes make the annuity contract more flexible and usually more appealing.

owner–driven for a minority of annuity contracts, the policy stays in force until the contract owner dies.

EXAMPLE OF A FIXED-RATE ANNUITY

Suppose you have $5000 to invest and decide that you want the safety and predictability offered by a fixed-rate annuity. You contact your investment adviser and he or she goes about shopping for a contract that provides a competitive rate of return for the number of years that interest you, and includes provisions or features that are deemed to be important. You have told your adviser that one of your chief concerns is locking in a guaranteed rate of return for three years (you are uncertain as to the future direction of interest rates and therefore do not want to commit to a five-, seven-, or 10-year lock-in rate).

After contacting a number of issuers, your adviser has narrowed the selection process down to two possible candidates. Both contracts offer the same comparatively high rate of return for a three-year period. However, one of the contracts allows for up to a 10 percent annual free withdrawal, based on 10 percent of the contract's current value ($5000 plus all accumulated interest), not the original principal ($5000 in this example). Furthermore, the same insurer's product has a five-year penalty schedule versus six years for the other annuity. Therefore, it is decided that the contract with the more liberal withdrawal provision and shorter-term penalty will be selected.

EXAMPLE OF A VARIABLE ANNUITY

Suppose you have $20,000 to invest in a variable annuity. The variable annuity that you are going to invest in offers eight investment options: (1) aggressive growth, (2) growth, (3) growth and income, (4) balanced, (5) high-yield bonds, (6) government securities, (7) foreign stocks, and (8) money market. You decide to invest the money as follows: $5000 in the growth portfolio, $7000 in balanced, and $8000 in foreign stocks. The only other decision you need to make is who the parties will be.

Continuing with this same example, further suppose that you are married and have two children, ages 16 and 23; you are 57 and your wife is 52. You and your spouse decide that both of you will be the joint owners and that your wife will be the beneficiary and you will be the annuitant.

Several years pass and your $20,000 investment is now worth $50,000. You die and the question becomes what happens to the variable annuity investment. Since your wife is the beneficiary, she has a choice: She can either terminate the investment and immediately receive a check for $50,000 (she will have to send the insurance company a certified copy of the death certificate and a written request for the distribution), or she can continue on with the investment indefinitely. Let us suppose she decides to keep the investment intact, thereby avoiding any taxable event.

As the sole owner of this investment the surviving spouse (the wife) must now decide who will be the new annuitant and beneficiary. She decides to name herself as the annuitant and the two children as beneficiaries (each to receive 50 percent of the contract's value upon her death). At this point, the investment (contract) will continue until the surviving spouse makes a change or dies. If no changes are made between now and her death, the children will automatically inherit the annuity upon their mother's death. Prior to death, the mother could drop one or both children as the beneficiary(s) or change the percentage that one or both will later receive—all without the knowledge of the kids.

WAYS TO STRUCTURE AN ANNUITY CONTRACT

In order to protect yourself and your loved ones, consideration should be given to *who* is named *what* when filling out an annuity application. The contract's provisions (flexibility) plus the investor's objectives will dictate who is named the contract owner, annuitant, and beneficiary. Some specific examples may be helpful:

Naming Your Spouse as the Beneficiary

If you want your surviving spouse to have the option of continuing the contract upon your death, he or she should be named the beneficiary. Naturally, such spouse would then have complete control and *disposition* over the investment after the death of annuity (or owner if the contract were "owner driven").

 disposition the power to decide the distribution of the investment.

Naming the Same Person as Owner and Annuitant

Most of the time, the owner and the annuitant are the same person. There may be certain circumstances when you would want them to be different. Check the ramifications as to what happens at the death of one or the other. Some contracts pay the death benefit when either the annuitant or the owner dies; other contracts pay upon the death of the owner and still others pay only upon the death of the annuitant.

Any distributions resulting from the death of the owner are exempt from the 10 percent IRS pre-59$\frac{1}{2}$ penalty. However, if the annuitant is different from the owner and the annuitant dies, and the contract requires distribution if either the owner or the annuitant dies, *and* the beneficiary is not a spouse and is under age 59$\frac{1}{2}$, then the 10 percent IRS penalty does apply to the *taxable* portion of the distribution.

Joint Ownership

A joint owner or co-owner has equal rights to the investment as the owner. No annuity change or distribution can occur without the consent of both owners. With a number of contracts, a distribution is triggered upon the death of either owner and will be paid as stipulated in the contract.

Nonnatural Ownership

If a nonnatural party (e.g., a trust or partnership) owns the annuity, the death benefit will be triggered upon the death of the annuitant. The death benefit would then have to be paid out over a period of five years or less unless the beneficiary annuitized the contract. Naming a nonnatural entity as the owner results in less tax-planning flexibility.

Owner–Driven versus Annuitant–Driven Contract

Most contracts are annuitant–driven; however, a number of contracts are owner–driven. It is important to know how your contract works because the value and distribution at death may be impacted (or altered) depending on who dies first.

Chapter

2

Types of Annuities

As mentioned in the previous chapter, there are three ways to categorize or describe an annuity. One of those ways deals with income and when, if ever, it is received. Another classification has to do with how your money is invested. The third way to describe an annuity is whether additional investments can be made under the same contract (money added to the original investment or premium).

IMMEDIATE ANNUITIES . . . I NEED MONEY NOW

If you purchase an immediate annuity, you are instructing the company to start sending you checks as soon as possible. Immediate annuities are designed for individuals or couples who want to rely on receiving a specific amount of money. The money may be the person or couple's sole source of income or merely a supplement to other monies coming in. The check can be used for anything you wish; after all, it is your money.

The checks can be sent either monthly, quarterly, semiannually, or annually. The amount of each check will not fluctuate if you use a fixed-rate contract since in that case the insurance company guarantees a set rate of return. If a variable annuity is chosen, the amount of each check will be different depending on the performance of the underlying investments (e.g., the growth, international bond, balanced, and/or foreign stock portfolios you selected).

The amount of each check you receive will depend on the amount deposited with the insurance company, how many years of income you want, how the money is invested, and the competitiveness of the insurer.

Obviously, the more you invest and the shorter the period of distribution, the larger the check.

If you plan on having checks sent to you for only three or four years, using a fixed-rate annuity is probably the best choice. If the expected time horizon is five years or longer, then a variable annuity is the better choice for most people.

DEFERRED ANNUITIES . . . I WANT TO SAVE

Most people who purchase an annuity do so because they want their money to grow. These same people may or may not ever need an income stream. They are attracted to deferred annuities (which are either fixed-rate or variable) because this type of annuity provides them with the flexibility of having growth for a short or long period of time and later, if so desired, receiving income through either sporadic or scheduled annuity withdrawals.

Investors who purchase bank CDs do so because they want the interest income or because they plan on rolling over the interest and matured CD into another CD. Deferred annuities can be structured in a similar fashion. The owner of the annuity can request that a certain amount of income be sent to him or her annually. In the alternative, part or all of the principal can also be sent out at any time. However, in most cases, the owner of the annuity simply has the principal and any appreciation automatically reinvested, similar to someone who invests in a CD or money market fund.

Deferred annuities can offer a great deal of flexibility. Anything earned in the account can be taken out, or can be automatically reinvested, thereby providing an even greater return. The contract owner also has the ability, subject to possible costs (in the early years of the investment), to terminate the investment or simply withdraw part of the principal.

FIXED-RATE ANNUITIES . . . I WANT GUARANTEES

Besides determining if, how, and when income and/or principal is to be received, we must also determine how our money is going to be invested. A fixed-rate annuity or a fixed-rate subaccount in a variable annuity provides the contract owner with a guaranteed rate of return; it is very similar in concept to a bank CD.

When you purchase a CD from a financial institution, the amount of interest you receive or are credited depends on how long you are willing to commit your money and what institution you deposit it with. A fixed-rate annuity operates in the same way. Just like banks, some insurance companies simply offer higher rates than others. And just like banks, insurers offer fixed-rate annuities or fixed-rate subaccounts with different maturities.

The most common maturities for annuities are one, three, or five years. When you invest in a CD, the rate of return is usually locked in for a specific period of time. The same thing is true for a fixed-rate annuity; your rate of return is guaranteed for the contract period. You receive this rate whether the stock market goes up, interest rates go down, the insurance company has a profitable year, or it has a losing year.

Usually when you invest in a fixed-rate annuity, the longer you are willing to commit your money, the higher the interest rate you will receive. The interest you are credited with can be either sent to you annually or reinvested so that you can take advantage of *compound interest*.

compound interest   interest already earned is reinvested so that a larger amount is earning interest.

Fixed-rate annuities are most popular with people who want assurances as to the safety of their principal. These people also want to know exactly what they can expect in the way of interest on their money. Fixed-rate annuities, since they provide guarantees as to principal and rate of return, are ideal investment candidates for very conservative investors or anyone who wants to know exactly what he or she will have at the end of a specific period of time.

VARIABLE ANNUITIES . . .
FOR INVESTMENT FLEXIBILITY

Not every individual or couple wants a set rate of return. After all, if someone guarantees you a "floor," the "ceiling" is probably not far away. Variable annuities offer an alternative to those investments that pay a set rate of return. When you invest in a variable annuity you are, in a sense, captain of your own ship, for investing in a variable annuity is similar to investing in a mutual fund family; while you have a wide array of options to choose from, neither the mutual fund family nor the insurance company offering the annuity will tell you how to invest your money. They do not directly share in any profits you make and they will not absorb any of your losses. The same thing is true when you buy a stock, bond, or mutual fund. If that security goes up 35 percent in one year, you get to keep the entire gain. On the other hand, if that same investment falls by 16 percent, no one comes to your rescue.

As an example, if you had $40,000 to invest in an annuity you might opt for the following: $7000 in a balanced portfolio, $13,000 in a growth and income position, $10,000 in a government securities account, and $10,000 in international equities. Your only limitations would be the investment options being offered by the variable annuity and the amount of money you are willing to put in any one position. You could put all the money in one specific portfolio.

If you were investing in a mutual fund family and this group did not offer a gold fund, you could not invest in metals. You would have to either look at other mutual fund groups or set aside some money and go into a second fund family. The same thing is true with a variable annuity; you are limited by the investment choices offered by that company. If you do not like all of its choices, choose a different insurer.

The type of annuity selected—fixed or variable—depends on the features the investor is looking for. Individuals or couples who want a set rate of return and the satisfaction of knowing that their principal can never erode will opt for a fixed-rate annuity (or a split annuity, which is explained in Appendix E). The investor who realizes that gains and losses may occur but wants investment flexibility by having the opportunity of moving monies among a "family of funds" will be attracted to a variable annuity.

SINGLE PREMIUM

Fixed-rate annuities (similar to a bank CD) almost always only allow a single premium (a onetime investment) because interest rates are constantly changing. It would be unfair to invest in an annuity and lock in a return of X percent for the next year or more and then several weeks later expect the same rate of return for new money even though interest rates had declined. Similarly, if rates have increased, the investor would want the then–higher rate for any new money.

A contract owner who likes a particular company or the general provisions of a specific annuity contract can "add" money by filling out another application, thereby having a second contract. The new contract may or may not offer the same interest rate that is guaranteed for the same or different period of time.

FLEXIBLE PREMIUM

Variable annuities, on the other hand, almost always allow additional monies to be added to the same contract (a flexible premium), just like adding money to a mutual fund or mutual fund family. Since the investor chooses from one or more of the contract's investment options (e.g., growth and income, small company growth, government bonds, etc.), any and all investment risk is borne by the investor and not the insurance company. This is quite different from a fixed-rate annuity wherein the insurer bears all of the investment risk.

WHICH ANNUITY IS BEST FOR YOU?

By far the most important decision the annuity investor makes is how the money is to be invested. Turning a deferred annuity into an immediate annuity (for someone who might now need income) is easy. And, since there are several hundred different annuity contracts and options offered, it should be of little concern whether your annuity is single- or flexible-premium.

Both fixed-rate and variable annuities are popular. Literally tens of billions of dollars are invested in each type of annuity every year. What type of annuity *you* invest in should depend on the following factors: (1) your time horizon, (2) any existing investments you already own, (3) categories that have historically been good performers, (4) your goals and objectives, as well as (5) your risk tolerance level. Each of these five points will be addressed.

Time Horizon

The more time you are willing to live with an investment, the more you should concentrate on equity instruments. All investments that have existed in the past and all of those that exist today can be broken down into one of two categories: equity or debt instruments. An *equity vehicle* represents partial or complete ownership of an asset. Equity instruments include ownership in any of the following: stocks, real estate, a business interest, oil, any metal, and certain types of variable annuity portfolios (e.g., aggressive growth, growth, growth and income, international stocks).

> **equity vehicle** all investments fall into one of two categories: equity or debt. When you own an equity, you own part or all of the asset. Examples include real estate, common stock, preferred stock, variable annuity subaccounts, and mutual funds that invest in stocks, as well as collectibles (rare coins, stamps, etc.) and metals.

Debt instruments are those investments in which you have loaned someone else the use of your money. Examples of debt obligations include: second trust deeds, all types of bonds, government securities, bank CDs, money market accounts, savings accounts, as well as fixed-rate annuities and certain categories of variable annuity subaccounts (e.g., government bonds, corporate bonds, money market, and the bond portion of a balanced fund).

> **debt instruments** IOUs of an individual, partnership, company, municipality, or national government. Examples of debt instruments include trust deeds, notes (short-term IOUs), and bank CDs, as well as corporate, municipal, and U.S. government bonds. When you buy (or invest in) a debt instrument, you are lending your money to an entity or a person. In return for the use of your money, the borrower (the bank, corporation, government, etc.) agrees to pay you interest plus your principal at some future date.

If your time horizon for investing is one or two years, then fixed-rate annuities are almost certainly your best choice. Only a somewhat optimistic or aggressive contract owner who was looking at a commitment of two years or less would choose a variable annuity and then select one or more stock or long-term bond portfolios. If your time horizon is three or more years, then variable annuities should be considered.

Existing Investments

If your current investments are mostly comprised of debt instruments, then equity options (growth, growth and income, international stocks, metals, aggressive growth) within a variable annuity should be viewed as serious candidates. Conversely, if most of your holdings are in equity vehicles, such as stocks or real estate, then a guaranteed fixed-rate or one or more of the debt portfolio options (i.e., government bonds, money market, high-yield) within a variable annuity should be reviewed.

One of the key fundamentals of successful investing has always been *diversification*. No matter how good the debt or equity market looks, no matter how positive or negative the press or financial gurus appear, the marketplace can always change suddenly. Therefore, you do not want to have all of your assets in any one category. As an investor, your concern is not only to maximize returns, but also to be able to sleep at night.

diversification choosing a mix of conservative and aggressive investments to balance market highs and lows; the policy of all variable annuities to spread investments among a number of different securities to reduce the risk inherent in investing.

Historically Good Performers

Look at those generic categories of investments that have historically done well over long periods of time. A time frame of 15 years or more is recommended. True, your investment horizon may be a fraction of this, but keep in mind two points: (1) 15 years includes good as well as bad times, and (2) bad results cannot be hidden when studying the long term. Even the investor looking at a one- or two-year holding period should ask, "Do I want something that does phenomenally one out of every five years, or do I want something that has a very good return in eight or nine out of every ten years?" Unless you are a gambler, the answer is obvious.

Throughout history, *equity has outperformed debt*. The longer the time frame reviewed, the better equity vehicles look. Stocks have outperformed bonds in every decade over the past half century. Put another way, would you rather have loaned Henry Ford or Bill Gates the money to start their companies, or would you rather have given them money in return for a piece of the action?

A 65-year-old retired couple should realize that one or both of them will most likely live at least 20 more years. Since this is the case, and we know that equities have almost always outperformed bonds when looking at a 10-year or more horizon, our emphasis should be in this area.

Figures 2.1 to 2.5, courtesy of the Institute of Business & Finance, show the frequency with which U.S. stocks, as measured by the S&P 500, have outperformed U.S. bonds, as measured by 20-year U.S. Treasury bonds.

The conservative investor may say that stocks are too risky. True, the day-to-day or year-to-year volatility of equities can be quite disturbing. However, it is also true that the medium- and long-term effects of inflation and the resulting diminished purchasing power of a fixed income are even more devastating. At least with an equity there is a better than 50–50 chance that its value will go up. In fact, over the past half century, equities have shown positive returns three out of every four years. In the case of

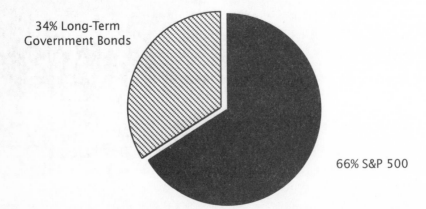

FIGURE 2.1 The better performer—S&P 500 versus government bonds, one-year holding periods (1947–1996). Over the past 50 years, stocks have outperformed bonds the majority of the time. The S&P 500 outperformed long-term government bonds in 33 of the past 50 years (66 percent of the time).

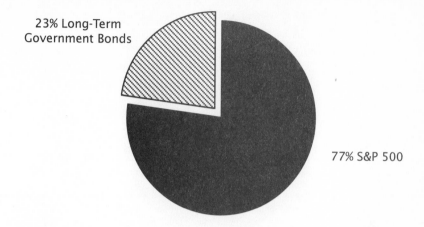

FIGURE 2.2 The better performer—S&P 500 versus government bonds, three-year holding periods (1947–1996). During the majority of three-year holding periods, small stocks outperformed large stocks, and both categories of stocks outperformed government bonds. The S&P 500 outperformed government bonds in 37 of the 48 most recent three-year holding periods (77 percent of the time).

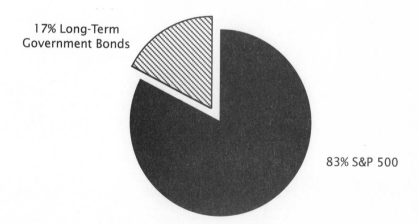

FIGURE 2.3 The better performer—S&P 500 versus government bonds, five-year holding periods (1947–1996). The common belief about long-term bonds is that they are safer than stocks. However, there have been extensive periods of time when long-term government bonds have been more volatile than common stocks. The S&P 500 outperformed government bonds in 38 of the 46 most recent five-year holding periods (83 percent of the time).

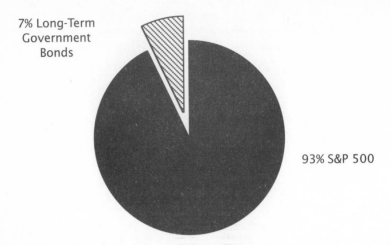

7% Long-Term
Government
Bonds

93% S&P 500

FIGURE 2.4   The better performer—S&P 500 versus government bonds, 10-year holding periods (1947–1996). The case for stocks instead of bonds and for medium-term bonds instead of long-term bonds becomes very convincing over longer holding periods. The S&P 500 outperformed government bonds in 38 of the 41 most recent 10-year holding periods (93 percent of the time).

0% Long-Term
Government
Bonds

100% S&P 500

FIGURE 2.5   The better performer—S&P 500 versus government bonds, 15- and 20-year holding periods (1947–1996). During the past half century, there has not been a period of 13 years or longer when bonds did better than stocks.

inflation, what do you think are the chances that the cost of goods and services will go *down* during the next one, three, five, or 10 years? The answer is "not likely." The last time we had deflation was 1954 when the *consumer price index* (CPI) dropped by one-half percent.

consumer price index (CPI)   the most commonly used yardstick to measure the rate of inflation in the United States.

Goals and Objectives

Commonly expressed goals are to "retire comfortably," "send a child through college," and "buy a house." Your personal goals may be more or less lofty or complex than those just mentioned. Whatever your goals are, it is important to turn them into a dollar *investment objective*. That is, if the goal is to retire comfortably, your definition of "comfortably" may mean that you need investments that can earn $1000 a month, or maybe you need at least $15,000 every two weeks.

investment objective   goal (e.g., long-term capital growth, current income, etc.) that the investor and subaccount pursue together.

Once you know your existing holdings and the dollar amount needed upon, say, retirement, then it is easy to calculate what is needed (e.g., if you assume that you can safely get a 9 percent return on an investment and your objective is $54,000 per year, then you will need a nest egg of approximately $600,000 that averages a 9 percent yield annually).

If you have reviewed your goals, objectives, and existing holdings, it becomes relatively easy to see what types of investments you should focus on. If your $93,000 must grow to $600,000 in a dozen years or less, then it is almost certain that equities must be used (one or more of the moderate or aggressive options within a variable annuity). If time is on your side and the $93,000 can grow to the needed $600,000 over, say, 25 to 30 years, then you can be conservative and use fixed-rate annuities or one of the safer options offered within a variable annuity (a money market port-folio, government securities, etc.).

Whatever annual growth rate you are projecting (e.g., 6 percent to 8 percent for bonds and 11 percent to 15 percent for equities), do not forget to factor in inflation. Thus, a bond portfolio compounding at 7 percent a year has a real growth rate of about 4 percent (7 percent minus 3 percent for inflation). If you do not factor in an inflation rate, you may miss your goal by a wide margin. As an example, a 7 percent return means that a portfolio doubles about every 10 years. At the end of two doubling periods (just over 10 years each in this example), a hypothetical $100,000 would grow to $400,000 ($100,000 times 2 equals $200,000; $200,000 times 2 equals $400,000). However, once a 3 percent rate of inflation is factored in, 7 percent drops down to a real return of 4 percent. If a portfolio averages 4 percent per year, at the end of 20 years $100,000 has grown to only $220,000.

Risk Tolerance Level

Talking about debt versus equity instruments or hearing how XYZ averaged 19 percent over each of the past 10 years is fine, but if you cannot live with the investment because of its volatility or perceived risk, then you should not be in that type of investment.

No investment is worthwhile if you stay awake at night worrying about it. If you do not already know or are uncertain about your risk level, contact your financial adviser. These professionals usually have some type of questionnaire that you can answer; once completed, the results will be a good indication of which investments are proper for you and which should be avoided. If you do not deal with a financial adviser, try the following test. Your score, and what it means, is shown at the end of the questionnaire.

TEST FOR DETERMINING YOUR RISK LEVEL

1. "One should invest for the long term, five to 10 years or more. The final result is more important than daily, monthly, or annual fluctuations in value."—(10 points) I totally disagree; (20) I am willing to accept some volatility, but not loss of principal; (30) I could accept a moderate amount of yearly fluctuation in return for a good *total* return; (40) I would accept an occasional negative year if the final results were good; (50) I agree.

2. Rank the importance of current income.—(10 points) Current income is critical, and the exact amount must be known; (20) income is important, but I am willing to have the amount vary each period; (30) income is fairly important, but other aspects of investing are also of concern; (40) only a modest amount of income is needed; (50) current income is unimportant.

3. Rank the amount of loss (based on the investment's current value) you could tolerate in a single quarter.—(10 points) None; (20) a little, but over a year's time the total value of the investment should not decline; (30) consistency of total return is more important than trying to get big gains; (40) one or two quarters of negative returns is the price you must pay when looking at the total picture; (50) a single quarter's or year's loss is unimportant.

4. Rank the importance of beating inflation.—(10 points) Factors such as preservation of principal and current income are much more important; (20) I am willing to have only a little variance in my returns, *on a quarterly basis only*, in order to have at least a partial hedge against inflation; (30) I could accept some annual volatility in order to offset inflation; (40) I consider inflation to be important, but have mixed feelings about how much volatility I could accept from one year to the next; (50) the long-term effects of inflation are devastating and should not be ignored by anyone.

5. Rank the importance of beating the stock market over any given two-to-three-year period.—(10 points) Irrelevant; (20) a small concern; (30) fairly important; (40) very important; (50) absolutely critical.

Add up your score from the five questions. Your risk tolerance level, as defined by your total point score, is as follows: 0–50 points = extremely conservative; 50–100 points = somewhat conservative; 100–150 points = moderate; 150–200 points = somewhat aggressive; 200–250 points = very aggressive.

SAMPLE PORTFOLIOS

Listed below are sample portfolios that would be appropriate for the five different risk levels described in the previous paragraph. The percentage figures represent portions of one's entire portfolio, excluding any direct or indirect ownership of real estate (i.e., personal residence, income-producing property, real estate investment trusts, etc.). How much of each investment category should be inside an annuity will depend on your current and projected tax bracket, your time horizon, whether you are income-oriented, plus the likelihood that you would have to tap into an investment during the next five to ten years. *Notes:* (1) municipal bonds are not an option within an annuity; (2) a sector or specialty fund typically invests in a single industry or a single country.

Extremely Conservative

Investment Category

Money market	15 percent
Two- to three-year fixed-rate/bank CD	15 percent
Intermediate-term bonds	15 percent
Long-term bonds	10 percent
High-yield bonds	15 percent
Balanced	10 percent
Utilities	10 percent
Real estate fund/subaccount	10 percent

A three-category alternative to this eight-category portfolio is: 35 percent money market, 25 percent high-yield bonds, and 40 percent balanced (stocks and bonds).

Somewhat Conservative

Investment Category

Money market	10 percent
Intermediate-term bonds	10 percent
High-yield bonds	20 percent
Balanced	20 percent
Utilities	15 percent
Real estate fund/subaccount	10 percent
Growth and income	10 percent
Growth	5 percent

A three-category alternative to this eight-category portfolio is: 20 percent money market, 20 percent high-yield bonds, and 60 percent balanced.

Moderate

Investment Category

Money market	5 percent
High-yield bonds	15 percent
Real estate fund/subaccount	10 percent
Equity-income	15 percent
Growth and income	20 percent
Growth	10 percent
Small-company growth	10 percent
Foreign stock	15 percent

A three-category alternative to this eight-category portfolio is: 10 percent money market, 50 percent equity-income stocks, and 40 percent global stocks (U.S. and foreign).

Somewhat Aggressive

Investment Category

Real estate fund/subaccount	10 percent
Equity-income	10 percent
Growth and income	10 percent
Growth	15 percent
Small-company growth	20 percent
Foreign stock	15 percent
Emerging markets	10 percent
Aggressive growth	10 percent

A three-category alternative to this eight-category portfolio is: 35 percent growth and income, 30 percent small-company growth, and 35 percent global stock.

Very Aggressive

Investment Category

Growth and income	10 percent
Growth	10 percent
Small-company growth	15 percent
Foreign stock	10 percent
Emerging markets	20 percent
Aggressive growth	15 percent
Industry group sector	10 percent
Single-country sector	10 percent

A three-category alternative to this eight-category portfolio is: 30 percent growth, 40 percent aggressive growth, and 30 percent emerging markets.

DIVERSIFICATION

Everyone has heard the expression, "Don't put all your eggs in one basket"; the advice is also applicable to investing. No matter how much we like investment X, if a third of our net worth is already in X, we probably should not add any more to this investment. After all, there is more than one good investment.

Since there is no single investment category that is the top performer every year, it makes sense to diversify into several fundamentally good categories. By using proper diversification, we have an excellent chance to be number one with a portion of our portfolio every year. Babe Ruth hit more home runs than almost anyone else, but he also struck out more. As investors, we should be content consistently hitting doubles and triples.

The percentage of your holdings that should be in a fixed-rate subaccount or one or more subaccounts within a variable account will depend on a combination of several items: time, current holdings, what you are trying to accomplish with this particular pot of money, and your risk level. In general, cautious investors will be attracted to fixed-rate annuities; moderate or average risk takers, as well as aggressive buyers will opt for a variable annuity.

Due to its flexibility, the variable annuity will end up being the answer for most people. Even the conservative investor could go into a variable and focus on the more traditional portfolios such as a balanced, government securities, or high-yield bond subaccount. The moderate or aggressive investor could buy the same variable annuity and divide money among a growth, growth and income, and international securities subaccount.

Chapter

Advantages
of Annuities

T here are positive aspects to every single investment. This does not mean that it is necessarily appropriate for our temperament or current condition. All investments also have disadvantages; there is no perfect investment. This chapter covers the many different advantages of owning an annuity. The following chapter will detail the disadvantages.

Annuities, which have been around for over a hundred years, provide more features than virtually any other investment. These traits include: security of your investment, safety of the industry, financial clout, the use of outside rating services, tax-deferred growth, tax-free exchanges, performance, professional management, no commission charge to the client, withdrawal options, a guaranteed death benefit, and avoidance of probate.

SAFETY

One of the benefits of a fixed-rate annuity is that your principal is guaranteed every day. You can terminate the contract after being in it for only a day, month, year, or decade and always be assured that you will get back at least 100 percent of your principal. There are very few investments that can use the phrase "principal guaranteed at all times." In fact, the only other types of investments that can legitimately make this claim are accounts of up to $100,000 at financial institutions insured by the Federal

Deposit Insurance Corporation (FDIC) and certain types of life insurance contracts. Interest from U.S. government securities is guaranteed, but the face value of such securities is only guaranteed if the T-bill, T-note, or T-bond is held until maturity.

Not only is your principal guaranteed in a fixed-rate annuity at all times, but so is the interest rate (for the specified period of time described in the contract). A large number of variable annuities have a fixed-rate investment option that would provide the same guaranteed rate of return.

When you invest money in a variable annuity, the insurance company sends the money to a money management company. Depending on which investments you selected on the application, the money manager may be either a mutual fund company or a division within the insurance company. In either case, your money is not commingled with the general account of the insurer (as it almost always is in the case of fixed-rate annuities or the fixed-rate investment option within a variable annuity). Since there is no commingling, investors need not be concerned about how well the insurance company manages its own portfolio or even if the company later becomes financially troubled or bankrupt. The best way to explain this relieving bit of information is by analogy.

Suppose you invested some money with a stock brokerage firm and a year later discovered that it was going bankrupt. The stocks, bonds, and money market account you had at this firm would not be in jeopardy because you did not invest *in* the brokerage firm, you merely invested *with* them. The same thing is true with variable annuities. The few people who have lost money in annuities due to the parent company's financial troubles were those who invested in fixed-rate annuities, not variable annuities. This is because *most fixed-rate annuity accounts are commingled* with the general account of the insurer; if the parent company makes poor investment choices, the investors can end up suffering.

The value of a variable annuity can fluctuate daily. Principal is not guaranteed on a day-to-day basis; principal is secured via the guaranteed death benefit (see later in chapter). Furthermore, the rate of return in a variable annuity is not guaranteed either (again, the one exception being if one opts for the fixed-rate subaccount).

You may wonder why fixed-rate accounts have such strong guarantees and variable subaccounts do not. Keep in mind that in a variable annuity *you* decide which type of portfolio(s) to go into and with what dollar amount(s). And, just like mutual funds, real estate, and individual stocks or bonds, you have the potential to make or lose a modest or large amount of money. In a fixed-rate annuity, the insurer decides how the money is to be invested. In order to maintain a very high level of safety, fixed-rate annuity assets are invested in government securities, corporate bonds, money market instruments, and high-quality mortgages.

FINANCIAL CLOUT

There are over two thousand different life insurance companies in the United States. Collectively, these companies own, control, or manage more assets than *all of the banks in the world combined*. The insurance industry of North America owns, controls, or manages more assets than *all of the oil companies in the world combined*.

During the Great Depression, it was not the government that bailed out the banking industry, it was U.S. insurance companies. If there were ever a financial collapse in this nation, the insurance industry would be next to last—second only to the government—to fold. And this is only true because the government has taxing power and, of course, the ability to print money. If the insurance industry were ever to collapse, we would look back at the Great Depression as a walk in the park in comparison.

STATE LEGAL RESERVE POOLS

Virtually every state requires that any insurer doing business in the state must become part of the state's legal *reserve pool*. This pool protects annuity investors as well as those who purchase other life insurance products or policies.

 reserve pool   system of insurance companies that assumes the liabilities of a defunct member company.

The reserve pool operates in a straightforward manner. If an insurance company goes out of business, the remaining insurers must assume the liabilities and obligations of the now-defunct insurer. The liability assumed by any one insurance company depends on how much business it does in that particular state. If insurance company LMN sells 2 percent of all insurance and annuities issued in that state, then LMN must accept 2 percent of any bankrupt insurer's obligations for that state.

If your state has a legal reserve system (only a few states do not have such a system), it may be useful to find out how it works. The system and its extent of coverage can vary from state to state. Nevertheless, if an insurance company wishes to do business in a state that has such a reserve it must join the pool. Insurers who do not join such systems will be banned from the state by the insurance commissioner.

Again, keep in mind that this form of protection is really designed for fixed-rate annuities or investors who opt for the fixed-rate (guaranteed) option within a variable annuity. However, variable annuities are also protected. The only thing the variable annuity investor has to worry about is how well the underlying portfolios perform—in short, the stock, bond, metals, and/or real estate markets; what happens to the insurance company has no real impact on the value or security of the investment(s).

RATING SERVICES

Even though annuities have close to a perfect track record, some companies are safer than others. During the past few years we have read that some insurers have troubled portfolios that contained large amounts of junk bonds and poor real estate holdings. And, even though no one has ever *had* to lose a dime in a fixed-rate annuity, these developments have caused some alarm. It is for this reason that more and more people are concerned about the quality of their insurance companies.

The best-known annuity rating service is A.M. Best. The A.M. Best Company is a neutral, unbiased source that rates insurance companies for their current financial soundness and ability to pay future insurance and annuity claims. A.M. Best, an Oldwick, New Jersey, company, has been in the business since 1899. Their job is somewhat similar to Moody's and Standard & Poor's, two well–known stock and bond rating services.

The highest rating an insurance company can receive is A++ (superior); the second highest rating is A+ (excellent). Most investors should stick with companies that have an A++ or A+ rating. There are several dozen companies that have one of these two ratings.

Keep in mind that you do not give up anything by using a highly rated company. Unlike junk bond investors, who take a higher risk for the chance of getting a perceived higher return, the annuity investor gets very little, if any, extra return by buying a fixed-rate annuity from a lesser-rated company.

Savvy insurance advisers look for a second rating. These advisers will recommend annuities and insurance products to their clients only if the insurer has a top rating from A.M. Best and either Moody's, Standard & Poor's, or Duff & Phelps. These different rating services are described in Chapter 11.

If you are investing in a variable annuity, the rating of the insurance company is usually of little importance. The reason for this apparent lack of concern is because when you invest in a variable annuity, you are not investing in the assets of the insurance company, so your fate is not tied to the solvency of the insurer. Money invested in a variable annuity is automatically turned over to the different portfolio managers of the subaccounts. It is the performance of your subaccounts that determines the safety and return on your investment. These portfolio managers are not buying securities issued by the insurer.

As mentioned earlier, when you invest in a fixed-rate annuity, your money is almost always commingled with what is referred to as the insurance company's *general account*, which includes money from other sources. The insurance company's goal is to get the highest return possible, while maintaining an overall high level of safety. Once in a great while, a small percentage of the higher-yielding investments do not perform well and the result is a loss. In extreme cases, this can affect the contract owners' value, liquidity, and/or rate of return.

general account   pool of money from fixed-rate annuity investors and other sources.

Poor investment performance for an extremely small percentage of the insurance industry made headline news in the late 1980s and very early 1990s. Since then, regulators, rating services, and insurance company money managers have become much more conservative. Today, the chance of a highly-rated insurer having financial trouble is a fraction of 1 percent.

A small number of fixed-rate annuity issuers segregate the investors' money. In these limited cases, whatever might happen to the general account of the insurer would not impact the value, rate of return, or liquidity of the annuity investors.

TAX-DEFERRED GROWTH

One of the chief reasons why tens of millions of people around the world are attracted to annuities is because money in an annuity grows and compounds tax-deferred. Unlike municipal (tax-free) bonds, there is nowhere on your tax return to indicate the value, interest, yield, or growth of your fixed-rate or variable annuity.

The only time you pay taxes on your annuity is if you withdraw growth or interest from the account. For example, if someone invested $20,000 in a variable annuity and the contract was now worth $55,000, the first $35,000 taken out would be taxable; the remaining $20,000 would not be taxed since this is considered a return of principal and the IRS never taxes return of principal.

The interest or growth is taxable in the year in which it is withdrawn and only on the amount actually received. Continuing the aforementioned example, if the insurer withdrew $6000 from the annuity that had grown from $20,000 to $55,000, only the $6000 would be taxed. Subsequent redemptions would be taxed in the year of distribution; the final $20,000, in this example, would not be taxed since that represents the original principal. As a side note, you cannot claim that the first money withdrawn was contributed dollars and therefore not taxable. The IRS no longer allows this option for contracts purchased after 1981.

What Happens at Death

Participants in annuities purchased before 1981 can opt to withdraw principal first and growth/interest later. By utilizing such a strategy, no taxes would be paid on any of the redemptions until such cumulative withdrawals equaled the contract owner's contributions (principal).

The avoidance of income taxes can last indefinitely. The death of the annuitant would normally mean that the contract is terminated. However, if one spouse is named as the annuitant and the other spouse is named as the beneficiary the contract can continue. The surviving spouse has the option of liquidating part or all of the investment without cost, fee, or penalty by either the IRS or the issuer (the insurance company). Withdrawals or complete liquidations could trigger an *income tax event* to the extent that any monies received by the survivor were considered growth or interest.

 income tax event when a sale of a security or other asset is made, there is a potential income tax event since the item is usually sold for either a profit or a loss. In the case of annuities, any withdrawal of income or growth is reported to the IRS, and taxes are due on the gain.

The surviving spouse does not have to terminate the contract upon the death of the other spouse in this example. The remaining spouse can take over the investment and postpone any income tax event. The contract would then continue until the death of the surviving spouse. If the remaining spouse later remarries and names the new spouse as the beneficiary, the tax deferral could last until the death of both of these spouses.

Sooner or later, all spouses will die. Upon the death of the final spouse, the nonspousal beneficiary(s) are entitled to the proceeds. These beneficiaries have four choices:

1. Pay taxes immediately.
2. Make withdrawals during the next five years, paying taxes along the way.
3. Wait up to five years, make a complete liquidation, and then pay taxes.
4. Annuitize (have the orderly distribution of the entire investment over a period of time) and pay some taxes with each withdrawal.

Each of these four options is discussed below by use of the same example.

Let us suppose that Mary and John Smith bought an annuity in 1990 for $40,000. John dies in 1994 and Mary dies in 1997; the children inherit an annuity that is now worth $100,000. The beneficiaries could withdraw the entire $100,000 and pay income taxes on the $60,000 gain. A taxable event would occur in the calendar year in which the $60,000 was received. Estate (inheritance) tax liability would depend on the net value of the deceased parents' estate; there is no estate tax if the value of the estate is $625,000 or less ($1,250,000 if both spouses die at the same time). As a side note, the $625,000 individual lifetime exclusion is being slowly increased to $1,000,000 per person by the year 2006.

The children, or whoever the beneficiaries are, do not have to take the proceeds from the annuity upon death of the final spouse. They have the option of making withdrawals systematically or sporadically during the next five years. Odd or similar amounts can be taken out at any time. Any amount withdrawn would be taxed in the year in which it was received. If the children took out $15,000 in 1997, then taxes would be due on $15,000 worth of income received for the 1997 calendar year. If $10,000 more was taken out in 1998, taxes would be due on that amount for the 1998 calendar year. If this option is used, the only IRS requirement is that the contract must be completely liquidated within five years after the death of the final spouse. In our example of $40,000 growing to $100,000, the final $40,000 withdrawn would not be taxed since it is still considered a return of principal.

The third option is to let the $100,000 contract continue to grow and compound tax-deferred for up to five years. At the end of five years, let us suppose that the contract is worth $165,000. The beneficiaries would be required to liquidate the entire investment and pay taxes on the difference between the amount withdrawn and the principal ($165,000 minus $40,000 equals taxes due on $125,000 gain). The beneficiaries do not have to wait five years to make a complete liquidation. The entire amount can be withdrawn at any time during this five-year period.

The fourth option is annuitization. This concept will be fully discussed in Chapter 5. Briefly, annuitization must be chosen by the beneficiary within 12 months after the death of the surviving spouse or single person. Annuitization simply means that the beneficiary will receive a specific amount each month until the beneficiary's share, plus any accumulating interest or growth, has been completely withdrawn. These withdrawals have a certain tax benefit: the IRS considers each check a partial return of principal (subject to the exclusion ratio) and therefore not taxable.

TAX-FREE EXCHANGES

Sometimes you go into one investment and later discover that it is not what you wanted or its quality has changed. One of the advantages of annuities is that you can change companies for whatever reason you like. You simply have your money moved from one annuity to another.

This move is known as a *1035 exchange* and is named after the Internal Revenue Code (IRC) section that allows such exchanges. These moves are also known as *tax-free exchanges* since you do not pay any taxes even though a change has been made. Always keep in mind that the only time you pay taxes on the growth or interest in an annuity is when you make withdrawals or a complete liquidation (you never pay taxes on withdrawals of principal).

> **1035 exchange**   also known as a *tax-free exchange*, the transfer of an investment from one annuity company to another; such a transfer is not taxed.

In order for you to take advantage of a tax-free exchange, the money from one insurer must go directly to another insurance company. You cannot have the check sent to you first. The IRS allows such 1035 exchanges because the money is never seen or touched by anyone except the insurers.

Tax-free exchanges are easy to do. First, you find a new annuity (company) you want to have the contract moved to, and fill out the application along with a separate form identified as a "1035 exchange request." You then send these two forms in, along with your existing contract, to the new company. The new insurer takes care of the rest. If you cannot find your existing contract, which is usually a few dozen pages in length, you simply fill out a "lost contract form" and send it to the company you want your assets transferred to.

You do not have to contact the person who sold you the original annuity. The "lost contract form" and "1035 exchange request" are each less than a page in length. You can make a tax-free exchange at any time. You are not limited by number of exchanges per year. Furthermore, you can transfer part or all of the contract; however, a large number of companies do not permit partial transfers.

Although 1035 exchanges are straightforward and do not trigger an IRS penalty or tax, they may include a penalty by the insurance company. Whether an insurance company penalty will occur depends on the specifics of the contract. Normally, no penalties occur if the money has stayed with the original issuer for a certain number of years. With some companies this period of time is one year or less; however, most insurers have a penalty schedule that lasts for five to eight years. A few policies have a penalty that never completely disappears.

The penalties briefly described above will be fully explained in the next chapter. The following chapter will also show you the different ways in which the penalty can be avoided.

PERFORMANCE

Fixed-Rate Annuities

Fixed-rate contracts offer you a set rate of return for a specified period of time; the rate is guaranteed for this period. The interest rate you are guaranteed varies depending on the annuity you choose and the period of time selected. Some insurance companies are more competitive than others. With a little comparison shopping, you can often get a rate that is equal to or higher than a bank CD or money market account.

Variable Annuities

Since variable annuities offer several different investment choices (known as subaccounts or portfolios) ranging from conservative to aggressive, the selection process is more difficult. You can simplify the decision-making process by first deciding what you are trying to do with your money.

For instance, if you are looking for a variable annuity that offers a growth and income account as well as an international securities portfolio, you could limit your adviser's research to insurers that offer at least these two types of subaccounts. The adviser could then study these particular annuities for any performance or risk concerns that are important to you.

The important thing to remember about both fixed-rate subaccounts and other subaccount choices is that they can offer some tremendous benefits without sacrificing performance. Fixed-rate accounts offer similar or higher rates than other investments that have comparable safety (e.g., bank CDs, T-bills, money market accounts). Other subaccounts (growth, government securities, corporate bonds, etc.) within variable annuities can equal or exceed the performance of the highest-rated mutual funds. Performance comparisons between mutual funds and variable annuities are shown in Appendix C.

PROFESSIONAL MANAGEMENT

One of the difficult parts about dealing with stockbrokers is that no one ranks their performance. If you ask brokers how they have done for their clients, they will all tell you "great." There is no source or agency to dispute such claims. But, if all brokers have done a fantastic job for their clients, why have so many people lost money?

The truth is that millions of people have lost money with their stockbrokers, financial planners, accountants, etc. It is equally true that lots of people have lost money in most types of mutual funds and variable annuities. But you have a much better chance with a mutual fund or variable annuity because of professional management. More often than not, a loss is a result of investor impatience or *short-term* moves in the stock or bond markets.

With variable annuities, you can easily track performance. There are several independent sources that track the performance of annuities. Some of these outside rating services are: Morningstar, Lipper Analytical Services, VARDS, and Standard & Poor's. Some magazines and periodicals, such as the *Wall Street Journal*, *Investment Advisor*, and *Money*, also run articles periodically that discuss annuities and chart their performance. *Barron's* includes performance figures weekly.

NO COMMISSION OR SALES CHARGES

Whether you invest in a fixed-rate or a variable annuity, 100 percent of your money goes to work for you from day one. You pay no commission when you go into an annuity. Furthermore, you do not pay a commission when you withdraw part of the account or liquidate the entire contract. There is usually a surrender charge (0–8 percent) imposed on withdrawals that exceed the free withdrawal privilege (typically 10 percent), a charge that disappears in time (0–10 years). Less than 2 percent of all insurers charge an upfront commission.

The broker or adviser you deal with gets paid a commission from the insurance company. Bypassing your stockbroker, insurance agent, or financial planner does not benefit you in the least. The insurance company will either keep the commission or pay it out to one of its producers. It should not make any difference to you anyway; all of your money is being invested.

Since the insurance company pays the commission, it is in your best interest to make sure that someone who can later help out receives the fee. By ensuring that your agent or adviser receives the fee, you obligate him or her to answer any questions or facilitate any changes you might have now or in the future. This broker can also research other companies if your annuity somehow becomes shaky or fails to perform as expected. The best person to help you out is a Certified Fund Specialist (CFS). The CFS program concentrates on mutual funds and annuities. CFS graduates are well-versed in these areas and must maintain their knowledge by fulfilling annual continuing education requirements. For the name of a CFS in your area, telephone the Institute of Business & Finance at 800-848-2029.

Annuities are sometimes referred to as *no-load* or commission-free since any commission paid almost always comes directly out of the insurance company's pocket. The commission normally ranges from 1 to 6 percent; the exact amount depends on the type of annuity and the penalty period. The most common rate paid by the annuity company is 4 percent. Some annuities are truly no-load and no commission is paid to anyone or kept by the insurer.

no-load   an investment that does not charge the investor a commission fee.

The insurance company is safely able to pay a commission out of its own pocket because the great majority of annuities, both fixed-rate and variable, have what is referred to as a "back-end penalty" or *contingent deferred sales load* (CDSL) that lasts from one to 10 years, depending on the company and the specific product. A small number of companies have a CDSL or CDSC (contingent deferred sales charge) that never disappears. At the other extreme, a small percentage of the annuities offered are truly no-load; investors can make withdrawals of growth or principal at any time without any insurance company back-end penalty or charge.

Sending your money directly into the insurance company will not save you anything. A much better strategy is to make sure that your representative, whether at a bank, savings and loan, brokerage firm, insurance agency, or financial planning group, knows that you are going through him or her and that you expect quality service and advice in the future.

> **contingent deferred sales load (CDSL)**   commission incurred by the investor when liquidating part or all of an investment. Also known as a *back-end load*, a CDSL can be avoided by withdrawing less than a certain amount each year (usually 10 percent of the money invested), death of the annuitant or owner (depending on how the contract is worded), or by keeping the money with the insurer for a specified number of years, which can range from one to 10 years but is usually in the five-to-seven-year range.

WITHDRAWAL OPTIONS

The good news is that you can always take out part or all of your money at any time from a fixed-rate or variable annuity. The bad news is that the withdrawal may be subject to a penalty.

Most annuities allow withdrawals of up to 10 percent per year without cost, fee, or penalty. The free withdrawal is usually based on a percentage of your principal, not current value. Thus, if Jane Smith initially invests $20,000 in an annuity and later adds $30,000, she can withdraw up to $5000 each year, *after the first year*, without any cost. This is the maximum even though her account may have a current value of $90,000. Some companies calculate the free withdrawal based on *the greater of* current value or principal contribution(s). In such a case, Jane could withdraw $9000 (10 percent of $90,000).

A few companies allow withdrawals of up to 15 percent per year. Still other companies allow free withdrawals of growth at any time or 10 percent to 15 percent based on the current value of the contract (which would be principal plus growth). Whatever rate your company allows, keep in mind two points: (1) Close to 75 percent of all people who invest in an annuity never take any money out and (2) the restrictions on withdrawals eventually disappear. Such withdrawal restrictions, which generally last about five to seven years, do not apply to a truly no-load annuity. A no-load annuity will usually allow withdrawals of any amount, at any time, without cost or penalty.

The restrictions referred to above simply mean that you can take out more than, say, 10 percent per year, but you will pay a penalty. The amount of penalty depends on the type of contract you have and the insurance company you use. Some annuities let you take out all of your growth (or accumulated interest) at any time. Other annuities impose a penalty for excess withdrawals during the first five to seven years. The following example assumes that the penalty (or CDSL) ends in five years.

Suppose that you invested $500,000 in the GHI annuity and the account is currently worth $800,000. As with most companies, GHI allows free annual withdrawals of up to 10 percent, based on the value of *original* contribution(s). In this case you could take out $50,000 each year without penalty during the penalty period. At the end of five years, you could withdraw as much as you wanted from GHI without cost.

But, let us suppose during the first few years of the investment you needed $70,000 quickly. GHI would allow you to take out $50,000 during that year without cost. The remaining $20,000 you needed would be subject to a penalty. If this request was made during the second year of the investment, the penalty would probably be in the 5 percent range. The penalty is imposed on only the excess amount—the amount above the free withdrawal. In this example, 5 percent, or $1000, would be charged (5 percent of $20,000). You would end up getting $69,000 of the $70,000 withdrawn.

There are ways to avoid any and all penalties. These strategies and examples are detailed in the next chapter. For purposes of this section, remember that: (1) The penalty normally completely disappears after a certain number of years, (2) you can make withdrawals up to a certain amount every year without penalty, and (3) the great majority of people who own annuities never make withdrawals.

ANNUITIZATION

Annuitization provides for the even distribution of both principal and interest (or growth) over a period of time. The advantage that annuitization offers over other forms of liquidation or withdrawal is that disbursements are tax-favored; systematic and sporadic withdrawals are not. Most annuity contracts allow annuitization. When a contract is annuitized, the contract owner decides whether to receive checks on a monthly, quarterly, semiannual, or annual basis. You may annuitize a fixed-rate or a variable contract. The disadvantage of annuitization is that the process, once started, usually cannot be altered (see "Flexible Annuitization" section later in this chapter for possible exception with a few companies).

A further potential disadvantage for annuitizing a variable annuity is that the amount of each check will vary; how much it varies will depend on which subaccount(s) you have selected and the dollar amount allocated to each of those investments (subaccounts). For the variable annuity owner, the investment risk and reward, even during annuitization, are borne by the recipient of the checks (usually the contract owner/annuitant), and not the insurer. Over time, a stock-oriented contract that is annuitized should provide a higher income stream than a bond, fixed-rate, or money market contract that is annuitized.

The more aggressively the money is invested (something decided by the contract owner/annuitant prior to and during annuitization), the less predictable the income stream. Conversely, if the contract owner chooses short-term bond, utility, and/or money market subaccounts (assuming such options exist with the contract), the more predictable the amount will be from check to check. During annuitization, most contracts allow the investor to change subaccounts. Whether changes should be made will depend on the available investment options within the contract, the investor's then-current risk level, the amount of patience the investor has to weather the ups and downs of the marketplace, plus the desire for possibly getting more income.

A further potential disadvantage for annuitizing a fixed-rate annuity is that the rate of return during annuitization may be artificially low. The amount of each monthly, quarterly, or annual check will depend on the competitiveness of the insurer, the level of current interest rates, the amount of principal that is to be annuitized, and the duration of the withdrawals. Each of these points is discussed below.

Competition

When you shop for a money market or savings account, the rate offered by institutions will vary, and some companies are more competitive than others. The same is true in the case of annuitization. Some insurance companies may offer very attractive yields during the accumulation (growth) period, but poor returns during disbursement (annuitization).

Current Interest Rates

The amount of each check you receive upon annuitization of a fixed-rate contract will be level; it will not go up or down with interest rates, the stock market, or the economy. The figure will be quoted on a per $1000 basis. For example, if you have a $13,000 contract, the insurer may quote you something like "eight dollars per thousand per month for the remainder of your life." What this means is that if you choose this company, you will be getting a check every month for exactly $104 ($8 times 13), or $1248 annually for as many years as you live. If you live for 80 more years, the insurance company must send you those $104 monthly checks for the next 80 years.

If and when you decide to annuitize part or all of your investment, the amount you receive monthly, quarterly, or annually will depend somewhat on interest rates at the time the contract is annuitized. If the insurer can take your money and invest it in a conservative manner such that it results in a high return to the company, a large portion of this would be passed on to you. The amount of your check will stay level, no matter how lucky or unsuccessful the insurer is in its own portfolio.

Principal to Be Distributed

The next point, amount of principal to be annuitized, is self-explanatory. Obviously, the larger amount of capital that is to be returned to you, plus interest that is accumulating on the still-to-be-dispersed amounts, the greater each check will be.

Period of Annuitization

Almost as obvious is the duration of the checks. Someone who wants to annuitize $40,000 over a five-year period will get greater monthly checks than someone who wants to annuitize the same amount over a 10-year horizon. What makes the duration a little tricky is the fact that annuitization does not have to be for a specific number of years. You can opt for one of the lifetime annuitization options, in which case income would last until death.

At the time of application, an annuity payment mode is selected: monthly, quarterly, semiannual, or annual. The first annuity payment must be made no later than the end of the modal period selected. For example, if a contract is issued with a monthly mode on September 15, the first payment must be made on or before October 15.

Many people annuitize over three to 10 years or longer. Other contract owners want an income stream that will continue for the remainder of their lives. Still others want monthly checks to continue during the lifetimes of two people such as a married couple, father and daughter, or two friends. And finally, a few people want the checks to last for a lifetime, theirs or someone else's, with a minimum guarantee of at least, say, 10 years. Each of the options mentioned in this paragraph is discussed below.

THE EXCLUSION RATIO

Upon annuitization of a variable or fixed-rate contract, an *exclusion ratio* is determined by the insurer, using tables provided by the IRS. This ratio, or formula, is used by the IRS in determining the amount of each check received that is considered a return of capital, and therefore not taxed, and the amount that is considered growth and/or interest, which is fully taxed.

 exclusion ratio   the proportion of an annuitized payment that is a return of capital and therefore not taxed.

The exclusion ratio varies depending on the life expectancy of the annuitant, based on mortality tables, or the set number of years opted for by the contract owner. The longer the expected period, the smaller the exclusion ratio becomes.

The portion of each income distribution that is subject to taxes is determined by a formula. The calculation is based on the total projected amount the investor or annuitant is expected to receive, based on a life expectancy, also known as a mortality table. If annuitization is to take place over a specified number of years, say five to fifteen, then the amount of existing interest or growth, plus projected amounts over that period certain, are calculated.

The total amount of income or growth referred to in the preceding paragraph, plus principal, is referred to as the *expected return*. More importantly, once an expected return is determined, the next step is to calculate the percentage of the amount that was invested in the contract.

 expected return   the projected or assumed rate of growth.

For example, if an investor contributed $100,000 into an annuity, and the projected expected return was $300,000 ($100,000 of principal plus $200,000 of growth), one-third of the total expected return represents money paid in by the contract owner and is therefore not subject to income taxes. This "return of principal" is also known as the exclusion ratio. In this particular example, the exclusion ratio is 33.33 percent (one-third of the total).

Once this percentage figure is calculated, it is used each year to determine how much of the annual payments should be classified as a return of capital (not taxable) and how much should be regarded as taxable income (accumulated growth and/or interest). Once the total of all payments representing "return of capital dollars" over the years equals the principal, then these tax-favored payments end. Any future distributions thereafter would be fully taxable. The exclusion ratio would change almost every month if a variable contract were annuitized, since the performance of the stock and bond markets cannot be predicted.

If you opt for annuitization, the amount of each check received depends on the amount in the investment and the period of time in which it is expected to be distributed. The shorter the time frame, the greater the amount of each check and the larger the exclusion ratio. This is because the investment has less time to grow and compound. If there is relatively little growth or income that has accumulated in the account, then most of each check received during annuitization will be considered a return of principal and not taxable.

Thus, annuitization over five years could result in an exclusion ratio of close to 85 percent (literally 85 percent of all distributions made would not be taxable). The same size contract annuitized over eight years would have more time for accumulation on the undistributed balance and may have an exclusion ratio of only 40 percent to 60 percent.

When you make a single contribution or a series of contributions into a variable annuity it is referred to as the "accumulation period"; you are acquiring *accumulation units*. Just like shares of a mutual fund, accumulation units in a variable annuity have a specific price "per share" but fluctuate in value thereafter. In the case of a mutual fund or variable annuity, the changing values will correspond to the performance of the investment portfolio(s) you choose.

accumulation units   similar to shares in a mutual fund; price per unit will depend on performance of portfolio.

When you want to start making withdrawals from a variable annuity, either sporadically, under a systematic withdrawal program, or by annuitizing part or all of the contract, accumulation units are converted to annuity units. An *annuity unit* is a value the insurer uses when it calculates the amount of income to be paid out monthly, quarterly, semiannually, or annually.

annuity unit   annuitizing a contract converts accumulation units into annuity units, which are used to calculate the amount of income to be paid out.

If annuitization is chosen, the factors used by the insurance company to determine the number of annuity units are: (1) the period over which the payments are expected to last (one of the lifetime options), (2) the number of guaranteed payments (e.g., "lifetime with 10 year certain" or "complete annuitization over exactly five years"), (3) the interest or growth rate projected by the insurer (this would depend on the general level of interest rates if a fixed-rate annuity contract were to be annuitized or on the projected total return of the stock and/or bond markets if a variable annuity contract were annuitized), and (4) any administrative expenses to be incorporated into the unit calculations.

Focusing for a moment on the third item above, the interest or growth rate projected by the insurer, if the company projects a high interest or growth rate, the annuity unit will have a greater value than it would with a lower rate. Interest or growth rates are normally predicted annually to determine the projected investment return for that particular year.

Once a specific form of annuitization is selected, the calculated number of annuity units remains constant over the payment period. If you are invested in a variable account, the annuity unit's value will fluctuate, just as it did during the accumulation period. The value will continue to vary according to the performance of the underlying investment portfolio. Therefore, the amounts of periodic payments will also fluctuate.

Keep in mind that you do not have to annuitize your entire contract. A specific portion of the investment could be annuitized and the exclusion ratio would only apply to that portion. Also remember that you do not ever have to annuitize with most companies.

Example of How the Exclusion Ratio Works

Imagine that you have $100,000 to invest and you decide on a fixed-rate annuity. Further assume that you need as much current income as possible for the next five years. You therefore decide to annuitize your contract and request monthly checks. During the next 60 months (five years), approximately 85 percent of each check you receive will be considered a return of capital and therefore not taxed (according to IRS tables). The remaining approximately 15 percent is considered income and taxed. Once all of the excluded amounts total $100,000, all remaining checks are considered to be 100 percent comprised of income and therefore taxed as ordinary income.

If, in the example above, you were sent monthly checks of $2100, you would be taxed on only approximately 15 percent of this amount until you received your 57th check. Eighty-five percent, the exclusion ratio in this example, of $2100 equals $1785, and $100,000 divided by $1785 equals 56. At the end of the 56th check, all $100,000 of principal will have been returned, and all remaining checks are considered gravy and therefore completely taxed.

If you do not understand annuitization, do not be overly concerned. Most brokers and financial advisers are not completely comfortable with this topic. If and when you decide to annuitize your contract (investment), a representative from the insurance company can explain all of the options available to you over the phone, and will be happy to answer any questions you might have about this complex subject. Perhaps most importantly, only a small percentage of annuity owners ever end up annuitizing.

ANNUITIZATION OPTIONS

Just prior to annuitization, you must select a period of time over which annuitization will take place. Depending on the insurer, annuitization can take place over one of the following periods: (1) life only, (2) joint and last survivor, (3) lifetime with period certain, (4) set number of years, or (5) specific dollar amount.

Life Only

Under the lifetime option, checks continue to be received until the death of the annuitant (the measuring life). At the time of annuitization you may decide to list the annuitant as yourself, your spouse, child, friend, or neighbor. The only requirement is that the person you choose is currently living and that the named annuitant signs the annuitization agreement.

All of the lifetime options share a common characteristic; while the insurer is hoping that one or both measuring lives (annuitants) die soon, the investor hopes that the annuitant(s) live for another 100 years. At the death of the annuitant(s), the balance of your account automatically goes to the *insurance company*, not to your heirs.

If you want your beneficiary to get the balance of the account, you should either list him or her as a coannuitant or opt for a period certain (i.e., complete disbursement of principal and interest over a 3, 5, 10, 15, 20, etc., period of time). By choosing a period certain, you prevent the insurance company from benefiting from a premature death.

Joint and Last Survivor

The joint and last survivor option is usually chosen by a married couple or someone who provides support for another. Under this plan, checks are not stalled or altered after the death of the first person. The same amount continues to be sent out until the death of the survivor, regardless of whether that survivor is your spouse, son, daughter, friend, or other. Some annuity contracts are structured so that the survivor receives less after the death of the first person; in such a case, annuity payments would most likely be higher (than a contract whose benefit does not decrease) while both parties were alive.

Under this option, one could say that the insurance company is hoping for the speedy death of two people; the death of one of the parties named does not do it any good. This last survivor option is ideal for a husband or wife who wants to make sure that one's spouse continues to get regular income after one's death.

Lifetime with Period Certain

A few people who choose one of the lifetime annuitization options want a certain minimum guarantee. Under this alternative, checks continue until the measuring life (the annuitant) dies; if death occurs during a period certain, checks continue until the period ends.

As an example, if you choose your lifetime with a 10-year period certain and you die during the next 10 years, checks would continue to be sent to your beneficiary(s) until the remainder of the 10 years is up. The period certain, 10 years in this example, does not begin when the annuitant dies. It is measured from the date of the original annuitization. Thus, if you died after having received monthly checks for seven years, your beneficiary would receive the same monthly checks for three more years.

If you favor a lifetime option, keep in mind that each option will not provide the same monthly check. Annuity issuers set their rates (amount they will pay you per $1000 invested) based largely on life expectancy tables. If you are age 70, you will receive much more money each month than a 40-year-old who wishes to annuitize the same amount. The 40-year-old, who has a much longer life expectancy, will almost certainly receive a cumulative sum far greater than the 70-year-old. A 75-year-old who chooses "life only" will receive more income each month than a 75-year-old who chooses "life only with 10-year period certain" or "joint and last survivor." *The longer the potential payout period may last, the lower the payment.*

A quick summary of the lifetime options may be in order. Under all of the life options just described, the balance of the account, no matter how small or large, eventually reverts to the insurer unless the contract states otherwise (some contracts will send a check representing the present value of the expected remaining income stream to the beneficiary named in the contract). If, instead, a set number of years is chosen, such as annuitization over three to 20 years, all capital (principal) plus accumulated interest is dispersed over the term selected, whether the annuitant is alive or deceased.

Set Number of Years

The person annuitizing the fixed-rate or variable contract can request that the contract be liquidated over a specific number of years, as long as the period selected is for at least three years (an IRS requirement). Annuitizing over a set number of years could be a good strategy for an individual, couple, or estate that will need current income for, say, 5, 8, 15, 20, or 30 years and/or until other sources of income or assets become available (i.e., a pension plan, repayment of a debt, a trust is turned over to the beneficiary, etc.).

Specific Dollar Amount

Although not very common, some contracts allow annuitization to be based on a specific dollar figure being sent out each period for as long as the money lasts (principal plus any ongoing growth or interest that is compounding). Such an option could be suitable for the investor who has a specific plan in mind (e.g., "I want $750 per month for as long as possible and as soon as the money runs out, I will tap into my IRA account").

Summary of Annuitization Options

The "life only" option means that payments continue until the annuitant dies, whether the annuitant lives a few weeks or for several more decades. "Joint and last survivor" means that the income stream continues as long as either party is alive (e.g., a surviving spouse, friend, sibling, etc.). "Lifetime with period certain" means that the income stream lasts for at least a specified number of years, usually 5, 10, 15, or 20 years, even if the annuitant dies tomorrow or next year. "Set number of years" means that payments last for a specific period, whether the annuitant is young or old, lives or dies. The final option, "specific dollar amount," is designed for someone who wants a set dollar figure each period, knowing that the income stream may last for a few years or several decades, depending on the amount of principal, how much is being requested each period, and the performance of the remaining principal.

FLEXIBLE ANNUITIZATION

Until recently, once annuitization began, the variable annuity contract owner had no access to principal, interest, or growth except through periodic payments. Now some companies, including Minnesota Mutual, Keyport Life, Hartford, and Equitable, have begun offering a product that can be immediately annuitized while still allowing for additional withdrawals that may equal up to the entire account balance.

Unlike traditional variable annuities that have an annuitization option that guarantees income for life, investors in these new products must earmark the number of years during which they will receive periodic payments. Once annuitization begins, the contract owner can cash out the remaining balance at any time. Other product designs allow partial withdrawals once the investor signs on.

GUARANTEED DEATH BENEFIT

Your principal is guaranteed every day in a fixed-rate annuity. A *guaranteed death benefit* is of no added benefit for an investment that carries such an assurance. Thus, this section deals with *variable* annuities only.

> **guaranteed death benefit**   the beneficiary receives the greater of the principal or the value of the account as of the date of the annuitant's death.

When you invest in a variable annuity it almost always contains a guaranteed death benefit. The guarantee works as follows: The beneficiary will receive the greater of the principal, plus any ongoing additions, or the value of the account as of the annuitant's date of death. Some contracts are owner–driven and any death benefit may be predicated on the owner's death.

This guaranteed death benefit makes the variable annuity an ideal investment for an older couple who want a high income stream or growth to offset inflation. One spouse can name oneself as the annuitant and invest in one or more of the stock or bond subaccounts, knowing that upon his or her death, the survivor will get back the greater of the amount invested or current value, minus any previous withdrawals.

As an example, suppose that Mr. and Mrs. Jones invest $400,000 in a variable annuity and Mr. Jones names himself as the annuitant. He also feels lucky and decides to put the entire $400,000 into the aggressive stock portfolio (subaccount). A few months or years later there is a stock market crash, recession, depression, and/or other terrible events. The account drops in value to $5000; the Joneses have lost $395,000. But have they? Later, Mr. Jones dies. Mrs. Jones then receives $400,000 as the beneficiary, even though the account on the date of Mr. Jones's death is worth approximately $5000.

The guaranteed death benefit is based on the greater of all contributions (investments made by the owner) or value on the date of the annuitant's death. Suppose in the above example that during their lifetimes the $400,000 grew to $1,200,000, dropped to $50,000, went up to $870,000, and then fell to $750,000 on the date of Mr. Jones's death. Mrs. Jones would be entitled to $750,000. She is not entitled to the peak value of the account during the annuitant's lifetime.

Finishing the example, if the Joneses originally invested $400,000 and then later added another $500,000, the minimum death benefit would be $900,000, reduced by any withdrawals made from the account. It would not be fair to expect the insurance company to reimburse you for money you had taken out before the annuitant's death (or owner's death if the contract was owner–driven).

The guaranteed death benefit lasts until you terminate the contract, you annuitize the investment, or the annuitant reaches the age of annuitization. This age of annuitization depends on the company you use, but it is normally age 75, 80, or 85. You may wish to change annuitants if your annuitant is close to reaching this maximum age of annuitization. Many companies allow such changes. Keep in mind that the contract owner must make the substitution and get the signature of the new annuitant. Such substitutions could go on indefinitely. A number of contracts never require annuitization, regardless of age.

ENHANCED DEATH BENEFIT

A growing minority of variable annuities have what is referred to as an "enhanced" guaranteed death benefit. The most common of these enhancements provides for a death benefit that is the greater of the contract value on the date of death *or* the principal (plus any additions) compounding at 5 percent per year (capped at 200 percent of principal contribution). This 5 percent compounding of principal, plus any additions, typically stops compounding once the owner (or annuitant in some contracts) reaches a specific age, usually age 80. Using an owner–driven contract, let us go through an example of this enhancement.

John invested $50,000 in a variable annuity when he was 30; at age 40 he added an additional $30,000 (the minimum guaranteed death benefit at this point would be $80,000). At age 50, John dies and the contract is inherited by his spouse, Sally. At the date of death the contract was worth only $60,000. Yet Sally would inherit $50,000 compounding at 5 percent annually for 20 years ($50,000 multiplied by a factor of 2.65 equals $132,500) plus $30,000 compounding at 5 percent for 10 years ($30,000 multiplied by a factor of 1.63 equals $48,900). Adding these two figures together ($48,900 plus $132,500) would result in a death benefit of $181,400. However, since there is a 200 percent cap, Sally will receive a contract valued at $160,000 ($50,000 plus $30,000 equals $80,000; 200 percent of $80,000 is $160,000). And, although $160,000 is not as good as $181,400, it is still quite a bit better than the investment's $60,000 value on the date of John's death.

Continuing with the same example, but altering it slightly, suppose that on John's death the variable contract was worth $300,000. In this case, Sally would be entitled to $300,000 (which would be a larger figure than the enhanced death benefit).

A few variable annuity contracts have an enhanced death benefit that is based on the highest anniversary value or principal contribution(s), whichever is greater. Thus, if the annuity contract began on August 17, 1998, with $100,000 and then was worth $90,000 on August 17, 1999, $130,000 on August 17, 2000, $110,000 on August 17, 2001, and $97,000 on June 5, 2002, the date of death, the beneficiary would be entitled to the peak anniversary value, $130,000 in this example (and not the peak value at the end of a calendar year or some peak value on a date other than August 17 in this example).

AVOIDANCE OF PROBATE

Probate is a messy, lengthy, and expensive process. It took over 15 years to probate the estate of Howard Hughes, and over 10 years in the case of Marilyn Monroe. The lawyers who probated John Wayne's estate made so much money in the process that they closed down their firm once the Duke's estate was finally closed.

probate   a term that means "prove the will." This legal proceeding takes place even if the deceased did not leave a will. Probate can be an expensive, time-consuming, and frustrating event. The typical probate takes well over a year; the cost of probate is based on the value of the decedent's gross estate and can be tens of thousands of dollars, or more. Annuities, qualified retirement accounts (i.e., IRAs, Keoghs, pension plans, etc.), and assets held in joint tenancy with rights of survivorship pass free of probate and are not considered part of the probatable estate.

The amount you will spend on probate and executor (the person who settles your estate after you are gone) fees depends on the gross value of your estate (e.g., the value of all of your assets, including boats, cars, stocks, bank accounts, and real estate, *not* reduced by any outstanding mortgages or debts). In California, an estate that has a gross value of

$100,000 will pay court-ordered fees of $6300. Probate and executor fees increase as the size of your estate increases.

Table 3.1 shows the statutory probate fees for the state of California. Some states have fees that are even greater. The fees are based on the gross value of your estate (you cannot deduct any liens or mortgages), not its net value.

These fees will probably be much higher than you think since: (1) your estate will probably increase in value between now and the date of death, and (2) the lawyer who probates the estate can always petition the court for any additional or extraordinary fees.

Probate fees are not something you can generally negotiate. In most states, they are based on a set schedule. The only fees that can be negotiated are those of the executor. Perhaps the only somewhat positive thing that can be said about probate fees are that they reduce the size of your estate when determining any estate tax liability.

Fortunately, at least the value of your annuity will not be included when the gross estate is being valued for probate purposes. All annuities avoid probate unless the named beneficiary is the annuitant's estate (or owner's estate in the case of an owner–driven contract). The beneficiary receives the investment immediately without cost, fee, or commission.

TABLE 3.1 California Statutory Probate Fees	
Estate's Gross Value	Probate Fee
$ 100,000	$ 6,300
200,000	10,300
300,000	14,300
400,000	18,300
500,000	22,300
600,000	26,300
700,000	30,300
800,000	34,300
900,000	38,300
1,000,000	42,300
2,000,000	62,300
3,000,000	82,300

Equally important, there is no delay. The beneficiary can get the money within a few days after the annuitant's death. The only requirement is that the beneficiary needs to send in a written request to the annuity company, along with a certified copy of the death certificate.

Estate Taxes

The value of the annuity is included in the decedent's estate for estate tax purposes, regardless of how the fixed-rate or variable annuity contract is worded. Annuities can avoid the delays and expense of probate, but not the cost of estate taxes. However, each of us does have a $625,000 lifetime exclusion (increased to $1,000,000 over the next several years). This means that each of us can leave up to $625,000 (or whatever the increased figure is) without any federal estate tax liability.

There are a few points to keep in mind about the lifetime exclusion. First, the exclusion is based on the estate's net size, meaning its gross value minus liens, mortgages, debts, and estate-settlement charges. Second, the exclusion is cumulative and includes any and all assets bequeathed to someone other than a spouse. Third, gifts and inheritances to a spouse are never subject to estate or gift taxes, regardless of the amount. Fourth, the exclusion is not $625,000 to $1,000,000 per donee (the person receiving the gift or inheritance); the exclusion is per *donor* (the person making the gift or inheritance).

Gifts

Speaking of gifts, in addition to the lifetime exclusion, you may gift up to $10,000 per year without having to file a federal gift tax return or paying any gift taxes and without eating into your $625,000 to $1,000,000 lifetime exclusion. And, unlike the lifetime exclusion, the annual $10,000 gift limit is per donee (the person receiving the gift), not per donor (the person making the gift). This means a person can make an unlimited number of gifts to as many people as he or she desires and as long as no single person receives more than $10,000 worth of gifts during the year, there would be no gift tax liability and no gift tax return to be filed.

The $10,000 becomes $20,000 per year if you are married and both spouses are making the gift. There is also no dollar limit per donee if the money is used for medical or educational purposes. (*Note:* Make sure the check is made out to the facility and not the individual.) Finally, the

$10,000 annual exclusion ($20,000 per couple) is slowly being increased beginning in 1998 in order to offset the effects of inflation. Such increases, however, will only be in $1000 increments. So, depending on annual increases in the consumer price index (CPI), it may take several years' worth of inflation before the $10,000 annual limit is increased to $11,000 and so on.

TOLL-FREE TELEPHONE NUMBER

Most annuities have an 800 number. This means you can phone and find out the value of your subaccount(s) anytime during normal business hours. Some annuity companies have automated services that allow you to phone any day at any time and find out the value of your contract as well as any recent activity (e.g., a liquidation or addition of new money).

SUMMARY OF BENEFITS

Annuities have advantages unheard of with other investments. They are issued by the safest financial industry in the world. Investors can sleep comfortably knowing that their money has been matched by reserve requirements that exceed 100 percent of the amount invested.

If we are concerned about the safety of our money, we can consult outside rating services. Growth of money in an annuity is always tax-deferred; such deferral is not used to calculate whether one's Social Security benefits are taxable. If we ever become dissatisfied with our annuity, we can always move it to another company without any IRS penalty or tax. The performance of our annuity depends on the locked-in rate or performance of the chosen subaccount(s). We always have the ongoing advantage of professional management that oversees the portfolio's holdings daily.

Whatever we invest in, 100 percent of the money goes to work immediately, without commission. Money can be taken out of an annuity at any time for any reason. Certain withdrawal options are also tax-advantaged. Our principal is always guaranteed in a fixed-rate annuity; in the case of variable annuities, an investment that could make us substantially more money than a fixed-rate account, there is usually a guaranteed death benefit. And finally, this investment vehicle passes quickly to our beneficiary; it avoids the costs and delays of probate.

When you invest in an annuity you have hired professional management. Individually, you and I cannot afford to hire the same money managers as the Kennedys and Rockefellers, but *collectively* we can hire even better performers. By hiring professionals to manage our money we do not have to worry about the day-to-day fluctuations in the stock and bond markets or wonder if the securities purchased are about to be downgraded. A money management team takes care of all of this, leaving the investor to focus on the risks and rewards of his or her life.

Chapter

Disadvantages of Annuities

T he previous chapter focused on the many advantages of both fixed-rate and variable annuities. Up to now, annuities look like a near-perfect investment. Before you rush out and invest all of your money in an annuity, read this chapter to find out the negative points. Fortunately, the disadvantages of annuities are few; most of them will not apply to you. The disadvantages of annuities are: (1) potential IRS penalty and taxes, (2) potential insurance company penalty, and (3) the ongoing expenses of variable annuities.

IRS PENALTY

No matter what type of annuity you purchase, it is subject to a 10 percent IRS penalty for withdrawals of growth or income made prior to age 59½. No penalty is imposed on one's principal. There are four ways in which this 10 percent penalty can be avoided: (1) death of the annuitant (or owner if the contract is owner–driven), (2) disability of the contract owner, (3) annuitization, or (4) the contract owner reaching age 59½ or older.

It does not matter how old the annuitant (and/or owner, depending on the wording of the contract) is; if he or she dies, all IRS penalties are waived. Disability, the second way in which the IRS penalty is waived, is defined in Section 72 of the Internal Revenue Code. Keep in mind that with most contracts, it must be the death or disability of the annuitant, not the contract owner or beneficiary. But some contracts are owner–driven, meaning that the death or disability of the owner will waive any IRS penalties.

Annuitization will also avoid any penalty, but annuitization must be elected by the contract owner within one year after investing in the annuity; the age of the owner is unimportant. Annuitization is the orderly process of receiving back your investment, plus interest and/or growth over a certain period of time. It provides for tax-advantaged distributions and is discussed in Chapters 3 and 5. The final way in which the 10 percent IRS penalty can be avoided is the contract owner being age $59^{1}/_{2}$ or older.

It is because of the potential IRS penalty that annuities are not recommended for younger people unless the investment is part of a retirement plan such as an IRA, Keogh, pension, or profit-sharing plan. Annuities inside a retirement plan is a debatable strategy that is discussed in Appendix F. The one other exception would be if someone feels that she will not need to touch these funds unless an unexpected emergency arises. Annuities are ideal candidates for the investor who is near or past age $59^{1}/_{2}$.

The contract owner(s) can be any age ranging from just born to over 110 (unless the contract is owner–driven). Despite the IRS penalty, annuities can still make sense for a young individual or couple, depending on how soon the money is withdrawn from the account and the assumed rate of growth.

As an example, suppose that Susan Anderson, age 25, invests $10,000 in a variable annuity that ends up giving her an average annual compound rate of return of 15 percent. At this rate of return, her $10,000 will more than double and be worth $20,113 in five years. Let us further suppose that at the end of five years she wants to withdraw her $20,113. Before she receives her $20,113, she would have to pay a 10 percent penalty on the $10,113 growth portion of her annuity. A 10 percent penalty on $10,113 equals $1011. Susan would receive $19,102 but would still be subject to income taxes on the $10,113 worth of growth and/or income.

The income tax liability is not reduced by the amount of the penalty. That is why Susan would be subject to ordinary income tax on the $10,113 gross figure, not the $9102 after-penalty amount. Based on Susan's state and federal tax bracket combined, a hypothetical 33 percent for our example, she would pay $3337 in state and federal income taxes. Her net proceeds would be $15,765 based on the following calculation:

$10,113 (gross profit) minus $1011 in penalties minus $3337 in taxes (on the growth) plus her original investment of $10,000, which is not subject to taxes or penalties.

The example detailed above assumes somewhat of a worst-case situation: an annuity contract that is subject to a 10 percent IRS penalty. Remember that this penalty does not apply to any contract owner (investor) who is age 59½ or older. The penalty can also be waived by the death or disability of the annuitant and/or contract owner.

ORDINARY INCOME TAXES

An investment in an annuity means that your money will grow and compound tax-deferred, *not tax-free*. Any and all income tax liability can be postponed indefinitely. The previous chapter noted that the death of one spouse would not trigger income taxes if the beneficiary were the surviving spouse. Taxes can be further deferred if the surviving spouse remarries, naming himself or herself the beneficiary and the new partner the annuitant. When the final spouse dies, the beneficiaries can postpone taxes for up to an additional five years. Taxes are due in the year in which income or growth is received; the IRS does not tax a return of principal, even if it is going to an heir. The amount of taxes due is based on the heir's tax bracket. No annuity distribution qualifies for capital gains treatment. The taxable portion is always considered "ordinary income."

As you can see, at some time, perhaps not during your lifetime, income taxes will have to be paid. There is no *step-up in basis* or other technique to completely avoid taxes forever. Fortunately, this negative of eventually having to pay taxes is not all bad. Since you are the owner of the annuity, *you decide when withdrawals are to be made*. Hopefully, you will take money out in only those years when you are in a lower tax bracket. Obviously, it is much better to pay income taxes at a 15 percent rather than a 28 percent rate. To illustrate the advantage of tax-deferred growth versus an investment that grows at the same rate but is fully taxed each year, let us look at an example.

step-up in basis   the unrealized appreciation on an inherited asset is not taxed (see page 67).

Ordinary Income Tax Example

Suppose you and your neighbor each have $1 million to invest and you are both in a 33 percent tax bracket, state and federal combined. You have both decided on an investment that should average 12 percent per year. Your neighbor invests the entire $1 million in a growth and income mutual fund; you invest your $1 million in a growth and income portfolio within a variable annuity. Assuming a 24-year time horizon and a 15 percent pretax rate of return, the final numbers are quite impressive for the variable annuity owner.

At the end of 24 years, the annuity owner has amassed over $16 million. After paying income taxes of $5 million, you net a little over $11 million. Your neighbor, who was paying income taxes every year for 24 years, ends up netting approximately $6,829,000. It's easy to see the $4+ million advantage offered by the annuity.

The case for the annuity owner becomes even stronger if some of the withdrawals are made when you are in a lower tax bracket. This would be a strong possibility since *you* decide what year liquidations are made.

The annuity investor looks even better if we assume a set of older owners who are receiving Social Security benefits, since almost all of these benefits can end up being taxable. This Social Security tax, wherein up to 85 percent of your benefits become taxable, kicks in if you have an adjusted gross income of at least $25,000 (single) or $32,000 (married). The formula used to determine the $25,000 and $32,000 levels includes all sources of income, including interest from tax-free bonds *and* Social Security payments. The formula does *not* include the deferred growth or income within an annuity.

Partial Withdrawals Can Result in High Taxation

Assume you are under age 59½, you invested $100,000 a year ago in an annuity that is now worth $120,000, the variable annuity contract includes an 8 percent declining surrender-rate penalty schedule (which is now 7 percent since the contract is in its second year), and you now want to take out $20,000. In this very specific example, over half of the money you want to take out would be eaten up by taxes and penalties. Here is the math:

Withdrawal from the annuity	$20,000
Income taxes, at 40 percent (state and federal combined)	– 8,000
7 percent back-end load or penalty (year two of the contract)	– 700
10 percent IRS penalty under age 59½	– 2,000
Net left over	$ 9,300

Withdrawals are 100 percent taxable until all earnings are taken out unless the contract is annuitized; withdrawals of principal are not taxable since they are considered a return of principal. Ten percent of principal, $10,000 in this example, can usually be taken out each year without any insurance company penalty; some companies assess a penalty on earnings as well as growth during the penalty period.

Annuity Aggregation Rule

The *annuity aggregation rule* applies to multiple annuity contracts established after October 21, 1988, that are *issued by the same company, to the same policyholder, within 12 months* of each other. If two or more contracts are issued by the same insurer to the same person (contract owner), distributions from either contract would be combined together for income tax purposes. The resulting tax liability could be greater than what would have happened had the second contract been purchased from another insurance company. An example will clarify this tax situation.

annuity aggregation rule   distributions are combined for tax purposes if a person owns two or more contracts from one insurer.

The example below assumes the following: (1) person A invests $100,000 in one annuity or invests $50,000 in each of two annuities offered by the same company and the second purchase is within 12 months of the first (so that the annuity aggregation rule applies); (2) person B invests $50,000 with the ABC annuity company and $50,000 with the XYZ annuity company; (3) all portfolios grow at a hypothetical 8 percent annual return; (4) $85,691 is withdrawn by person A and person B at the end of the seventh contract year; and (5) the 1997 tax rates used are for a single individual.

Activity	Person A	Person B ABC	XYZ
Money invested ($100,000 each for A and B)	$100,000	$50,000	$50,000
Value in seven years (*Note:* $85,691 × 2 = $171,382)	$171,382	$85,691	$85,691
$85,691 withdrawal	−$85,691	−$85,691	0
Remaining balance in account(s)	$85,691	0	$85,691
Taxable amount	$71,382	$35,691	0
Taxes due	$17,131	$ 6,789	0

As you can see, person B comes out ahead with a tax liability that is much less than person A ($6789 versus $17,131). Phrased another way, person B gets to keep much more of the $85,691 withdrawal ($85,691 minus $6789 versus $85,691 minus $17,131). The remaining balance(s) for person A and person B are identical ($85,691), even though person B now has only one remaining contract (the other was completely liquidated due to the withdrawal).

What happens later, however, can greatly mitigate or even eliminate any concern over the annuity aggregation rule. If person A were to eliminate the remaining balance, there would be no tax liability ($85,691 is less than the original $100,000 principal investment). In fact, person A would be entitled to a tax loss of over $14,000 ($100,000 minus $85,691 equals $14,309). Person B would have a tax liability if the remaining balance were liquidated. The tax liability for person B would be based on a $35,691 gain ($85,691 minus $50,000 equals $35,691). Thus, the annuity aggregation rule should be a concern under certain withdrawal circumstances only.

Tax Deferral and Stepped-Up Basis

Even though most investors understand the benefits of tax deferral, few fully appreciate the significant benefit of stepped-up basis. Most assets receive a step-up in tax basis to fair market value at the time of death (annuities and retirement accounts do not get a step-up in basis). Tax deferral on the unrealized and untaxed appreciation becomes tax forgiveness. Unfortunately, a stepped-up basis takes place only through inheritance (when the owner of the asset dies).

To better understand what a step-up in basis means, let us go through a quick example. Suppose Joe Jones buys a stock or piece of real estate for $100,000 and at the time of his death the asset is worth $900,000. The heir receives that asset as if it cost $900,000 (even though Joe Jones paid only $100,000 for it). When the heir later sells the asset, his or her cost basis is $900,000—any gain or loss is calculated based on the heir having "paid" $900,000. This means that if the heir later sells the asset for $950,000, there will be taxes due on only the $50,000 gain. If the heir sells it for exactly $900,000, no taxes are due since there is considered to be zero profit ($900,000 minus $900,000 equals 0). If the heir sells the asset for $870,000, there would be a $30,000 *loss* that the heir could use to offset other gains (or a small amount of ordinary income each year)!

Unfortunately, annuities and retirement accounts do not qualify for a step-up in basis, irrespective of how long the asset (or account) was held by the now-deceased or the new owner (the heir or beneficiary). The same thing is true with gifts. If you receive securities, real estate, or whatever, as a gift, the cost-basis of the asset does not increase due to any passage of time or death of the person who made the gift.

Table 4.1 compares the benefit of tax deferral and stepped-up basis. The illustration assumes that $10,000 earns a 10 percent annual compound return for 20 years. It shows the impact of several different holding periods.

The table is comprised of five columns: Column 1 lists different holding periods or events; column 2 shows the amount that $10,000 would grow to under the different holding periods shown in column 1; column 3 shows the *after-tax* annual compound return for the 20-year period based on the events described in column 1; column 4 shows the effective tax for the different situations (the effective rate is reduced the longer the holding period is, and is 0 percent when there is a step-up in basis); and column 5 shows the *pretax* rates of return that would be necessary under each of the situations described in column 1 to equal the ending value of $67,300 (the figure one would receive if there was a step-up in basis). It is assumed that a 33 percent long-term capital gains rate (state and federal tax rates combined) is used for every situation that results in a taxable event (meaning every line except the last line).

		After-Tax Annual Compound Return	Effective Tax Rate	Pretax Rate of Return Required to Equal No Taxes
TABLE 4.1 Tax Deferral versus Stepped-Up Basis				
Holding Period/Event	Ending Value			
Taxed annually	$36,666	6.7%	33%	14.9%
Sold and taxed every three years	$37,900	6.9%	31%	14.4%
Sold and taxed every five years	$39,400	7.1%	29%	13.8%
Sold and taxed every 10 years	$42,800	7.5%	25%	12.9%
Sold and taxed every 20 years	$48,400	8.2%	18%	11.9%
Never taxed (stepped-up basis in 20 years)	$67,300	10.0%	0%	10.0%

As you can see, there is a big difference between avoiding taxes (the step-up value of $10,000 growing to $67,300 when the original owner dies after owning the investment for 20 years and never having sold it) versus holding the asset for three to 20 years and then selling it.

It could be argued that a professional money manager could justify a 100 percent taxable event every three or more years because a higher rate of return (higher than the 10 percent annual compound rate assumed for all holding periods) might be obtained in a different investment. However, it order to justify such a sale(s), the adviser would have to earn a 49 percent higher (14.9 percent versus 10 percent) pretax return *every year* compared to the after-tax return of 10 percent (14.9 percent minus 10 percent equals 4.9 percent; 4.9 percent divided by 10 percent equals 49 percent).

STATE PREMIUM TAX

Some states charge a premium tax if and when the contract is annuitized (see Chapter 3 for a discussion of annuitization). It is a charge that is based on the value of the investment at the time of annuitization. The charge may be up to 3.5 percent of the value of the contract. The entire tax is deducted before the first check is sent out. Prior to annuitizing any contract, check with your financial or tax adviser to find out if your state has such a tax and, if so, the rate.

INSURANCE COMPANY PENALTY

The previous sections dealt with the potential IRS penalty and income taxes. Regardless of whether this penalty and/or taxes is applicable to you, you must also be aware of any potential annuity penalty imposed by the *insurer*. This insurance company penalty applies only if you take out more than a certain amount of money from your contract within a set number of years (a few companies have no such penalty). The number of years ranges from zero to ten years, with four years being the most common for fixed-rate annuities and eight years for variable annuities. A very small number of companies impose a penalty that disappears only when the contract is annuitized or there is death. The penalty is based on a schedule that is often published in the sales literature and is always included as part of the annuity contract. It is referred to as a contingent deferred sales charge (CDSC), back-end load, or surrender charge.

As you may recall, when you invest in an annuity you can make annual withdrawals of 10 percent to 15 percent per year, after the first year. The 10 to 15 percent is usually based on principal, but some companies calculate a dollar figure that is based on a percentage of principal and all accumulated growth up to that point in time. With most companies, if you skip one or more years, the figure does not accumulate (e.g., if you take nothing out during the first two years you cannot, without penalty, take out 30 percent the following year). Several companies allow you to take out accumulated growth at any time without penalty, even during the first year.

The insurance company penalty occurs if you take out an amount in excess of the free withdrawal privilege. As an example, if you invested $90,000 in an annuity, you could withdraw $9000 per year without penalty. At the end of a set number of years you could withdraw any amount without penalty. But, let us suppose that during the fourth year of the contract you needed $15,000. The amount in excess of the free withdrawal, $6000 ($15,000 needed minus the $9000 allowed), would be subject to a penalty. The amount of the penalty varies, depending on your company's penalty schedule, but would probably be approximately 4 percent in this example. Based on a 4 percent penalty, $240 would be subtracted from your withdrawal request (4 percent of $6000). The initial $15,000 request would result in a net amount of $14,760 to the investor.

One of the items your adviser should be looking at when shopping for an annuity is the insurance company's penalty schedule. The penalty period could last for 10 or more years and the penalty itself could be as high as 10 percent for the entire 10-year period. Fortunately, most companies have a penalty period that lasts for five to eight years. And the penalty itself will usually decline each year. As previously mentioned, some companies have no such penalty.

As an example, the LMN annuity may state that its penalty lasts for six years and is structured as "6-5-4-3-2-1-0 thereafter." This means that excess withdrawals made during the first six years are subject to a penalty. Specifically, a withdrawal made during the first year would be subject to a 6 percent penalty; money taken out during the second year would be penalized 5 percent; and so forth. As long as you do not exceed the free withdrawal privilege, the penalty schedule does not apply. And, if it does apply, remember that the penalty applies to only the excess amount.

Are there ways to avoid this penalty schedule altogether? The answer is yes. The insurance company penalty can be completely avoided in any of the following ways: (1) death, (2) disability, (3) annuitization, (4) withdrawals limited to those allowed under the free withdrawal privilege, and (5) waiting until the penalty period lapses.

As inhibiting as the penalty may appear to you, it is very important to take note of the fact that if an emergency arises you will probably have other sources of capital to tap. And, even if you need to take money out of your annuity, it may not exceed the free withdrawal percentage. Keep in mind that well over 75 percent of all the people who invest in an annuity never take out any money.

MORTALITY AND EXPENSE FEE

The *mortality fee*, which pays for the guaranteed death benefit, is a cost found with almost all variable annuities. It is the insurance industry's major, and perhaps—by some measurements—only, source of profit. The mortality and expense fee helps to cover the insurer's overhead, reimburses it for the commission paid out to the agent that sold you the policy, pays for the setup and issuance of the annuity policy, and acts as a war chest to pay off any death benefit claims.

mortality fee   an annual percentage of the total value of the annuity contract, used to pay for the guaranteed death benefit.

The death benefit charge ranges from 0.15 percent to 1.80 percent annually, depending on the insurer and terms of the variable annuity contract. The most common mortality charge is 1.25 percent. Whatever the percentage charged by your particular insurer, it can never be increased; the fact that the percentage is frozen is clearly spelled out in every variable annuity contract. It is a hidden fee in that it is not shown on any of your quarterly or annual statements. It is described in the *prospectus*.

prospectus   outlines the different subaccounts, their performance, and any charges.

A prospectus is something you must be given at, or prior to, the time of purchasing a variable annuity. The prospectus spells out the different types of subaccounts (investment choices) within the variable annuity, charts the previous performance of these investments, and lists any and all charges that will be deducted from your variable annuity portfolio(s).

The mortality fee is a small percentage figure based on the total value of your variable annuity. The greater your account grows, the more the insurance company will end up collecting. Thus, if the annual mortality charge is 1.3 percent, a $10,000 account will be charged $130 per year; when the investment grows to $15,000 the yearly charge will increase to $195 (1.3 percent times $15,000). And, even though the fee is described as an annual charge, it is actually calculated and subtracted each day from the contract's value.

There are three good things that you can say about the mortality charge. First, it does help to pay for commission and overhead costs that you would normally pay in the form of either an upfront or an ongoing sales charge. Second, it gives the insurance company an incentive to hire the best possible money managers for each portfolio. Since the insurer makes more money if your account grows, the company wants to make sure you do well. Conversely, if the account shrinks in value, you both lose. Third, the mortality charge ensures the integrity of the guaranteed death benefit.

You cannot find this type of guaranteed benefit with any other type of investment in the world with two recent exceptions. As of the middle of 1998, American Skandia and Sun America now offer mutual funds with a guaranteed death benefit. It provides an individual or couple with great peace of mind. Some companies do not offer a guaranteed death benefit and therefore do not impose a mortality and expense fee.

ANNUAL CONTRACT MAINTENANCE CHARGE

The only other remaining negative of a variable annuity is the contract maintenance charge, a fee that is small in comparison to the mortality fee. The annual contract maintenance charge ranges from zero to $50, depending on the variable annuity company. The most common charge is $35 per year. Several companies do not impose this charge if the value of the account is above a certain level.

The maintenance charge shows up on your fourth-quarter statement issued by the insurer. It is simply deducted from the then-current value of your variable annuity. The fee is the same for a $5000 investment and a $1 million contract; it is a flat charge. It is the only charge that shows up on a quarterly or annual statement.

A good thing about this fee is that it can never increase. The wording in every variable annuity states that the annual contract maintenance fee can never go up during the life of the contract. Fixed-rate annuities do not impose any contract maintenance fee.

SUMMARY OF ALL COSTS

All annuities, fixed-rate and variable, have potential IRS *and* insurance company penalties; both of these penalties disappear in time or through death or disability. Two other charges, mortality and contract mainte-nance, are unique to variable annuities. A small number of variable annu-ity contracts do not have a mortality and/or maintenance charge.

In deciding which annuity to purchase, it is not enough to look at only the contract fees and charges. Contracts with low expenses and charges may not be cost-effective over the long term if they have inferior investment performance.

Chapter

Features of
Fixed-Rate Annuities

T his chapter will include all of the features found in a fixed-rate
account. The next two chapters, which detail the different aspects of variable annuities, are much longer because variable accounts are more complex and provide more options than their fixed-rate
counterparts.

The features that all fixed-rate annuities possess are: (1) a guaranteed amount at the end of a specific period, (2) free bail-out provision, (3)
the ability to add new contracts, and (4) a secured future. Many companies also offer what is known as a CD/annuity; this is a special type of annuity for short-term investing.

THE GUARANTEES

We already are familiar with the fact that principal in a fixed annuity is
guaranteed each and every day. In addition, you can also ensure that at the
end of a specified period of time you will have an exact amount you can
count on.

When you invest in a fixed-rate annuity you decide which of the one
or more rates of return you wish to lock in. Typically, the longer you are
willing to commit, the higher the rate you will get. The annuity contract
you are looking at may provide the following choices: one year at 5.5 per-

cent, three years at 5.75 percent, or five years at 6.10 percent. What this means is that you must choose one of the options. It also means that whatever option is chosen, the rate of return is guaranteed to be what is stated. Thus, if you wanted the three-year option at 5.75 percent, you would get 5.75 percent compounded annually for exactly three years, regardless of whether interest rates went up, the stock market declined, or the economy went into a recession during those three years.

The rates mentioned are for illustration purposes. The different rate options and periods of time in which such rates are locked in depend on the company you are looking at and the general level of interest rates. You will usually find that the range of rates offered coincides with those rates offered by CDs at banks, savings and loan associations, or money market accounts.

The question arises as to how long you should tie up your money at the offered rate. The answer depends on what you think will happen to interest rates in the future. If you think that interest rates will go up during the next several years, choose a one-year contract. At the end of the year, you can roll over your annuity into a higher rate, with either the same or a different company. If you think rates will be falling, choose the longest term offered, usually five to ten years. If interest rates do end up falling, you will be thankful that you are getting a yield on your investment that none of your friends can touch.

If you are uncertain as to the direction of interest rates, opt for something in the middle, about two to four years. This middle-of-the-road approach means that you are not committed for any unbearable period of time. If rates end up falling, you will still be getting a higher rate than those around you for at least a few years. If rates go up, your lower rate of return can be moved into a higher-yielding contract at the end of a couple of years.

In addition to the guaranteed rates and periods described above, fixed-rate annuities provide for an absolute minimum guarantee, no matter what other interest rates are or the state of the economy. This rate can range from 3 to 6 percent, but it is almost always 4 percent. Thus, if bank CDs, the prime interest rate, or other generally followed interest rates ever fell to 2 or 3 percent, you are always guaranteed at least 4 percent.

As impossible as this scenario might sound, there is a chance that this feature will turn out to be of value. In the world of investments we often lose sight of history. A few decades ago, many traditional investments had returns of well under 3 percent. And, although it is hard to envision such a situation in the foreseeable future, think back to the 1980s. During

1981, the prime interest rate peaked briefly at 21.5 percent. When it hit this rate, many investment advisers and financial gurus felt that the prime would not stop until it hit 25 or 30 percent. Few, if any, predicted that prime would actually fall by over two-thirds. Yet, during the final year of the Reagan presidency, the prime rate dropped to 7.75 percent. So, you can see that what we currently think of as amazing can turn out to be humdrum and ordinary.

The length of time you choose is your decision; you cannot alter the rate specified by the insurer. If at any time you end up not being satisfied with the contract, you can always cancel it and invest in another annuity. Whether your old company will levy a penalty depends on the specific provisions of the contract. If your old company hits you with a penalty, there is a small chance that the new insurer will absorb part or all of it.

FREE BAIL-OUT

This section is closely tied into the guaranteed interest rate provision of a fixed-rate annuity. It is a feature that can later prove to be highly beneficial to the contract owner.

The *bail-out* provision is quite straightforward: After the guaranteed interest rate period is over, if the renewal rate is ever lower than 1 percent less than previously offered, the owner can liquidate part or all of the annuity, principal *and* interest, without an insurance company cost, fee, or penalty. This provision gives the investor the security of knowing that he or she will always be getting a competitive rate.

bail-out   owner can liquidate the annuity without fees or penalties if the interest renewal rate is lower than the original rate by 1 percent.

To illustrate this point, let us assume that you went into a fixed-rate annuity and decided on the three-year guarantee of 6 percent. At the end of the three-year period, the insurer offers you a new rate of 4.99 percent for the next three years. You decide that there are other annuities or alternative investments that are more appealing. As long as you contact the insurance company within 30 days after receiving notice of the renewal rate, the annuity will be terminated and all of your principal, plus 6 percent compounded annually for three years, will be sent to you or whoever you direct the company to send the check to. You get this free bail-out since the renewal rate being offered was more than 1 percent lower than your previous locked-in rate.

Let us slightly change the facts in the previous example. Let us now suppose that at the end of three years your annuity company offers you a renewal rate of 5.01 percent or higher. You always have the choice of accepting the new rate, whether it is higher or lower than the past yield. But again, let us assume that you decide you need the money or have found a better place to invest. You can still withdraw all of the money, principal and interest, but you may be subject to an insurance company back-end penalty (described earlier).

ADDING MONEY

An investment in a fixed-rate annuity is a contractual relationship. The insurance company guarantees you a rate of return based on a specific investment, no more and no less. If you want to add more money, you must purchase a second or third annuity.

As an example, Jim Ward has recently purchased a fixed-rate annuity with a locked-in rate of 7 percent for five years. A few weeks later he decides to invest another $10,000 and would like to add to his existing annuity. This cannot be done. Jim will have to purchase another annuity at the then-current rates and terms. It may turn out that his best deal is with the insurer that he originally invested with; nevertheless, even if he deals with this company it will be a new and separate contract. The terms may end up being identical, but it must be a separate investment.

A SECURED FUTURE

One of the great features of a fixed-rate annuity is that you always know where you stand. There is an exact amount of money you can count on at the end of each period. A contract owner with $10,000 who signs up for a five-year annuity that guarantees a 7 percent return knows that there will be exactly $14,025.52 in the account at the end of the five years ($10,000 times 1.07 times 1.07 times 1.07 times 1.07 times 1.07 equals $14,025.52).

In a world that is sometimes filled with uncertainty, this is something we can count on. The annuity contract will tell you what you can expect in the way of growth of principal as well as detail the exact amount of any penalties or fees that may exist and when such costs completely disappear.

THE CD/ANNUITY

During the late 1980s, a new type of fixed-rate annuity emerged. It was created to satisfy the comfort level of people who were attracted to certificates of deposit (CDs). It also fulfilled the needs of short-term investors. This relatively new type of fixed-rate annuity is known as a *CD/annuity*. It is given this name largely for marketing purposes.

CD/annuity a contract with a one-year life.

The CD/annuity is a contract that has a one-year life. At the end of a year, the investor is free to take all of the money out, both principal and interest, without any insurance company penalty, cost, or fee. The partial or complete liquidation can be sent directly to the contract owner or to another insurer. By using a 1035 tax-free exchange, the investor will not trigger a tax event.

As you may recall from Chapter 3, if the proceeds are not sent to another annuity, a tax event will be triggered on the amount that is considered interest. A 10 percent IRS penalty will also occur if the contract owner is not at least 59½ or if the annuitant is not dead or disabled. The potential 10 percent penalty is also avoided under the provisions of the 1035 exchange.

As with any other type of investment, the prospective purchaser should have his or her adviser seek out a CD/annuity with the highest possible interest rate that is offered by a highly-rated insurer. If at the end of one year the existing insurer offers a rate that is acceptable to you, simply do nothing. Your account will automatically be renewed, just like a CD maturing at a bank. If you do not like the renewal rate, for whatever reason, simply write to the annuity company within 30 days of receiving the renewal notice and instruct the company as to where you wish the proceeds sent.

SURVEY OF SINGLE-PREMIUM IMMEDIATE ANNUITIES

The August 1997 issue of *Best's Review*, a standard within the life insurance and annuity industry, includes an analysis by A.M. Best covering the past 10 years plus a ranking of the highest payouts from 107 different insurance companies.

Over the past 10 years, monthly payouts of single-premium immediate annuities (SPIAs) have decreased, due to the overall drop in interest rates. According to A.M. Best, from 1987 to 1997, the median monthly payout decreased by 13 percent, from $894 to $777. The decline was even more extreme from 1985 to 1995 when the median monthly payout decreased by 23 percent, from $1035 to $798. But, the trend may be starting to change slightly. During the 1996 calendar year, the median monthly payout *increased* by 2 percent, from $762 to $777.

The lifetime-only annuitization option typically provides the highest monthly payment until death because the insurance company keeps any and all money remaining in the contract (it does not pass it on to your heir or beneficiary). Still, the annuitant is guaranteed a steady flow of lifetime income. However, such a guaranteed income stream is subjected to the constant erosion caused by inflation. This is why it is recommended that those who opt for this plan also include additional investments in equities such as common stocks, mutual funds that invest in stocks, and real estate in an overall retirement plan.

Table 5.1 reflects what a 65-year-old person would have received monthly, for life, assuming the person was 65 years of age and deposited $100,000 with the insurer on June 1, 1997. The table is broken down into four categories: male and qualified money (meaning money in a retirement plan such as an IRA or profit-sharing plan), female with a qualified plan (since women have a history of living longer than men), male and nonqualified money, and female and nonqualified money.

TABLE 5.1   Comparison of Monthly Payments

Male, Age 65, Qualified Money		Female, Age 65, Qualified Money	
Name of Insurer	Monthly Check	Name of Insurer	Monthly Check
Life of Georgia	$856	Penn Insurance	$800
Mutual of Omaha	$855	Penn Mutual Life	$800
Security Mutual of New York	$847	Mutual of Omaha	$796
		Presidential Life	$779
Modern Woodmen	$844	AmerUS Life	$773
Presidential Life	$838		

Male, Age 65, Nonqualified Money		Female, Age 65, Nonqualified Money	
Name of Insurer	Monthly Check	Name of Insurer	Monthly Check
Life of Georgia	$856	Mutual of Omaha	$796
Mutual of Omaha	$855	Presidential Life	$779
Equitable Life of Iowa	$845	CUNA Mutual Life	$771
		Life of Georgia	$770
Modern Woodmen	$844	Modern Woodmen	$766
CUNA Mutual Life	$840		

LOW RATES

When interest rates hit historic lows, fixed-rate annuity sales suffer. For 1996, fixed-rate annuity sales dropped to $39 billion, a 21 percent drop from 1995. In 1985, fixed-rate contracts accounted for 82 percent of all annuities sold. In 1996 that figure dropped to 35 percent. Surprisingly, according to LIMRA, a financial services research organization, of the more than 700 companies that offer annuities, more than 600 sell only fixed-rate annuities.

ANNUITIZATION AND LIFE INSURANCE

Combining an annuity program with *seven-pay life insurance* can be a powerful combination. The IRS allows you to borrow money tax-free from the cash value in a life insurance policy if certain tests are met. Basically, the owner of the insurance policy needs to make sure that insurance premiums are paid in over a minimum period of time, a period that can be as little as five years. This may not sound right since the key to tax-free borrowing is known as the seven-pay test. Nevertheless, insurance advisers can show investors how this test can be fulfilled in as little as five years.

seven-pay life insurance a whole-life policy that is structured so that the contract owner can make tax-free withdrawals (policy loans). "Seven-pay" refers to IRS regulations that require premium payments to be paid in over at least seven years so that the life policy maintains its integrity as insurance and not just an investment that can produce tax-free income each year.

As long as the seven-pay test is met, the only other thing the contract owner of the insurance policy must be conscious of is that the vehicle maintain its integrity as a life insurance contract. This simply means that you do not cancel the policy or borrow all of its cash value. If both of these tests are met, money can be freely borrowed from the insurance company every year, indefinitely.

Annuitization can work well in conjunction with seven-pay universal or whole-life policies (see Chapter 3 for a discussion of annuitization). A seven-year period certain immediate annuity that funds a *universal life* contract is a good option for anyone who has a lump sum ready to deposit and wants to take advantage of the seven-pay life insurance test for future tax-free liquidity, and may also need a substantial death benefit right away. The advantages of this combination include: (1) the client makes only one payment; (2) the exclusion ratio on the immediate annuity makes the distributions about 80 to 85 percent tax-free; (3) if the insured dies within the first six years, the beneficiary of the annuitant receives the remaining payments; and (4) death of the insured means that there is a windfall to the beneficiary of the life insurance policy.

universal life a type of whole-life insurance. Whole-life insurance can be described as term insurance with a forced savings plan (what is called the "cash value" of the policy). This means that part of each premium payment goes toward insurance (paying the insurance company to take on the risk of someone dying) and part goes toward the cash value. With traditional whole-life insurance, the cash value grows at a set rate of return. With universal life, the cash value is invested in a money market account, wherein the interest rate is constantly changing, reflecting the then-current level of short-term interest rates. Universal life also allows the contract owner more flexibility in premium payments and loans.

By first making a lump-sum deposit into an annuity and requesting immediate annuitization over at least a five-year period, the investor is assured that the life insurance policy is funded properly during the next several years. The immediate annuitization to the insurance company means that premiums are being paid when they should be. This takes care of the seven-pay test, thereby giving the insurance policy owner the ability to borrow the cash value from the life policy tax-free.

Annuitization certainly offers some great tax benefits, but these benefits are not all considered tax-free. More specifically, you cannot borrow money from an annuity without triggering a taxable event, unless the annuity is part of a 403(b) retirement plan. By using a combination of an annuity that is annuitized and having the payments earmarked to pay for life insurance premiums, the investor can later take advantage of income that is 100 percent free of income taxes and receive some life insurance as an added bonus.

People who seek this type of tax-free income will still have the opportunity to add more money to the life insurance side after seven policy years. With universal life, the client can add some attractive riders to the policy, such as long-term care, catastrophic illness, prime term, child or additional insured, and premium continuation for disability.

WHO BUYS FIXED-RATE ANNUITIES?

Certificate of Deposit Owners

A large number of CD buyers roll over their CDs upon maturity. Sometimes the renewal rate is higher; sometimes it is lower. When you invest in a fixed-rate annuity, you can lock in a return for a specific period of time, ranging from one to 10 years. A fixed-rate annuity is usually able to offer a rate of return that is higher than those offered by banks or savings and loan associations. This is because the insurance industry knows that most people keep money in an annuity indefinitely. They can, therefore, commit funds to longer-maturing, higher-yielding bonds and mortgages.

The other disadvantage the CD investor faces is that an IRS Form 1099 is generated each year. When you invest in an annuity a 1099 is generated for only those years in which withdrawals are made. This minimizes one's taxes and reduces tax preparation expenses.

Table 5.2 shows the advantage of a fixed-rate annuity versus a certificate of deposit. The example assumes a $100,000 original investment, a taxpayer who is in the 28 percent bracket, and a 9 percent interest rate. As you can see from this example, the annuity investor comes out ahead every single year.

Money Market Investors

As of the beginning of 1998, over $1 trillion is invested in money market funds. Investors are attracted to these accounts because of their liquidity

TABLE 5.2 CD versus Fixed-Rate Annuity		
Year	Certificate of Deposit	Fixed-Rate Annuity
1	$106,480.00	$109,000.00
2	111,565.50	118,810.00
3	115,556.60	129,502.90
4	118,688.82	141,158.16
5	121,146.99	153,862.39
		Less tax −$ 15,081.47
	Total $121,146.99	Total $138,780.92
	Difference: $17,633.93	

features, a competitive interest rate, and safety. The fixed-rate annuity provides most of those same features. Historically, fixed-rate annuities have proven to be about as safe as money market accounts; they are safer conceptually since their reserve requirements exceed 100 percent of all investors' contributions.

Fixed-rate annuities are not designed with the liquidity features of a money market fund, but these annuities are accessible. Owners can make partial or full liquidations at any time. Flexible-premium annuities allow the investor to make additional contributions each year in the same contract, similar to adding cash to a money market account. Annuities usually offer a higher rate of return than money market accounts.

Conservative Growth-Oriented People

Millions of people who invest in bank CDs, second trust deeds, government obligations, or money market accounts do so with the intent of reinvesting the interest. In this way, these investments can be considered growth vehicles. However, the growth rate is severely stunted since the interest from these accounts is taxable each year.

An investment that yields 6 percent will double in value every 12 years. Once taxes are subtracted, that same investment may take 18 years to double since it is growing at only 4 percent (6 percent minus 2 percent for taxes). You and I have only so many doubling periods until we retire or die. It will not be the first doubling period that we will miss—when $100,000 grows to $200,000; it will be the second or third doubling period when $200,000 grows to $400,000 or $400,000 grows to $800,000.

The growth-oriented investor can end up with an investment worth $400,000 more ($100,000 growing 6 percent annually tax-deferred for 36 years) by simply choosing an annuity instead of a government bond, bank CD, or money market account. All of these investments offer tremendous safety, but the annuity just grows faster since it is tax-deferred.

Income-Oriented Investors

A lot of us need money every month for living expenses. Just like there are millions of people who invest in bank CDs, second trust deeds, government obligations, or money market accounts for growth, even more people look to these investments for current income. Fixed-rate annuities can provide the income-oriented customer a means of getting monthly income that is higher than what other types of safe investments offer.

Regular income from an annuity can be accomplished in one of two ways: a systematic withdrawal program (SWP) or by annuitization. The SWP way allows the investor ongoing flexibility, but with no special tax benefits. Still, the yield or monthly return is often higher than other alternatives such as CDs, money market accounts, or government obligations. By opting for annuitization, you can have a specific dollar amount sent out regularly and the checks you receive are tax-advantaged. You do not get this tremendous tax break from other investments that are usually used by income-oriented investors.

Safety-Conscious Individuals and Couples

No matter what rate of interest or growth you are promised or project, no investment is worthwhile if you lose sleep over it. Fixed-rate annuities provide a guarantee not found with CDs, money market accounts, or even government bonds or T-bills. When you invest in a fixed-rate annuity, your principal is guaranteed each and every day. This is unlike a CD in which the penalty may eat into your principal or you could lose if the institution goes out of business and your account is underinsured. Annuities are also unlike government bonds or T-bills in that government securities are guaranteed only if you hold them until maturity; fixed-rate annuities guarantee your principal every single day. And finally, money market accounts are extremely safe, but they are generally not guaranteed.

Estate Planners

Other, perhaps better-known investments, do not afford you any type of estate planning opportunities. When you die, income taxes must still be paid by your spouse, children, or other heirs. Furthermore, to make sure that your assets are distributed properly, you will also need a will. A will does not avoid the expense or delay of probate, so you should also probably have a living trust.

None of these hassles, costs, or delays occur with an annuity. Since you name the beneficiary in all types of annuities, the value of the account passes free of probate to the named beneficiary(s). A trust and will are not necessary with this investment.

Another important aspect of annuities is the income tax flexibility they provide. Upon your death, income taxes are normally due. With an annuity, taxes can be delayed for up to five years after the death of the second spouse. If there is no spouse, income taxes can be delayed for five years or the investment can be annuitized for immediate distribution and some tax relief.

Chapter 6

Features of
Variable Annuities

A variable annuity represents an investment company, an entity that makes investments on behalf of individuals and institutions that share common financial goals. Some variable annuities allow initial investments of as little as $250, while others require you begin with at least $10,000. The subaccount, or portfolio (very similar to a fund within a mutual fund family), pools the money of many people, each with a different amount to invest.

Professional money managers then use the pool of money to buy a variety of stocks, bonds, or money market instruments that, in their judgment, will help the subaccount's shareholders achieve their financial objectives. Usually the objective of the manager is easy to discern; if the subaccount is called the "ABC Growth Portfolio," it is safe to assume that most, if not all, of the portfolio is comprised of common stocks. Similarly, if the name of the subaccount is the "ABC High-Yield Portfolio," then it is safe to assume that management is concentrating on high-yield corporate bonds. Whether you invest a hundred dollars or a million, you get the same investment yield or rate of return as everyone else in the subaccount.

Each subaccount has an investment objective, described in the prospectus, which is important to both the manager and the potential investor. The portfolio's manager uses the prospectus as a guide when choosing investments for the subaccount. Prospective investors use it to determine which subaccounts are suitable for their own needs. By law, you must receive a prospectus prior to or at the time of your investment. The prospectus details investment objectives and restrictions as well as all of the costs and expenses associated with the investment. Variable annuity investment objectives cover a wide range. Some follow aggressive investment policies, involving greater risk, in search of higher returns; others seek current income from more conservative investments.

When the subaccount earns money (e.g., dividends, interest, and/or capital gains), the money is automatically reinvested. The automatic reinvestment is reflected in an increase in the price per unit of the variable annuity subaccount (versus a mutual fund wherein the investor can end up with more shares). Mutual fund investors may see an increase in the price per share *or* an increase in the number of shares (which would be caused by having dividends, interest, and/or capital gains reinvested). Variable annuity owners do not have this option; any and all gains, dividends, and/or interest payments, as well as any losses, are reflected in the price per unit; the number of shares increases only if the investor adds more of his or her own money to the contract.

Variable annuities are popular because they are convenient and efficient investment vehicles that give all individuals—even those with small sums to invest—access to a splendid array of opportunities. Variable annuities are uniquely democratic institutions. They can take a portfolio of giant blue-chip companies like IBM, General Electric, and General Motors, and slice it into small enough pieces that almost anyone can buy.

A large number of variable annuities allow you to participate in foreign stock and bond markets you could not normally invest in, due to either time, expertise, or expense required. International subaccounts make investing across sovereign borders no more difficult than investing across state lines.

What is heavily marketed is not necessarily what is appropriate for you to invest in. A global biotech subaccount may be a great investment, but it may not be the right portfolio for you. Buying what is hot rather than what is appropriate is one of the most common mistakes made by investors and an issue that is addressed throughout this book.

PRICING

Investing in a variable annuity means buying units (shares) of one or more subaccounts. An investor becomes an owner of a set number of units in a subaccount, just as he or she might be an owner of shares of stock in a large corporation. The difference is that a variable annuity's only business is investing in securities; the price of the units in any given subaccount is directly related to the value of the securities held by that specific subaccount.

Variable annuity subaccounts, just like mutual funds, continually issue new shares for purchase by the public. Existing investors' price per unit does not decrease due to the ongoing issuance of new units (shares), since each unit created is offset by the amount of new money coming in. A subaccount's unit price can change from day to day, depending on the daily value of the securities held in the portfolio. The unit price is calculated as follows: The total value of the subaccount's investments at the end of the day, after expenses, is divided by the number of units outstanding.

Unlike mutual funds, variable annuity subaccounts are not reported by newspapers on a regular basis. In fact, the only publication that reports the values of subaccounts on a weekly basis is *Barron's*. Variable annuity information in *Barron's* is found toward the back of each weekly issue. An example from the January 5, 1998, issue of *Barron's* is shown in Table 6.1.

The first line, "Allianz Life Insurance Co.," indicates the name of the insurance company offering this particular variable annuity product. All variable annuities are formed by insurance companies.

The second line, "Franklin Valuemark II & III," is the name of the variable annuity contract. As is often the case, the title tells us which company is managing the subaccounts. In this case, Franklin, a well-known mutual fund company, is overseeing the various portfolios (subaccounts).

Below the contract name are the four different column headings:

1. Under "Fund Name" are the names of the subaccounts—in our example, Franklin Valuemark II and Valuemark III subaccounts.

2. "Unit Price" is the price per unit (share) as of a specific date; notice that the price per unit is taken out to three decimal points.

3. "Four-Week Percent Total Return" is a percentage figure that indicates how much the portfolio has gone up or down over the previous four weeks. As an example, Zero Coupon 2010 was up 0.92 percent for the four weeks ending December 31, 1997.

Fund Name	Unit Price	Four-Week Total Return	52-Week Total Return
		TABLE 6.1 Sample Report from *Barron's* on a Variable Annuity	
		Allianz Life Insurance Co.	
		Franklin Valuemark II & III	
Asset Allocation	13.786	−0.83%	10.17%
Capital Growth	13.081	−0.85	16.24
Developing Markets	10.320	−2.20	−10.16
Global Growth	15.157	−0.75	11.78
Global Income	16.944	0.05	0.98
Growth and Income	24.528	1.00	25.85
High Income	21.298	0.38	9.93
Income Securities	25.025	2.41	15.28
International Equity	17.723	−1.09	10.21
International Small Company	10.826	−1.88	−2.87
Money Market	13.863	0.29	3.77
Mutual Discovery	11.925	−0.43	17.13
Mutual Share	11.934	0.48	15.53
Natural Resources	11.327	−3.05	−21.71
Pacific Growth	9.350	−7.26	−37.38
Real Estate	28.115	1.24	18.79
Rising Dividends	20.095	−0.41	31.32
Small Cap	14.784	−2.53	14.49
U.S. Government	19.922	0.48	7.64
Utility Equity	25.807	7.12	24.95
Zero Coupon 2000	19.474	0.36	5.41
Zero Coupon 2005	22.467	0.73	9.51
Zero Coupon 2010	24.630	0.92	14.44

4. "52-Week Percent Total Return" is a percentage figure that indicates how much the portfolio has gone up or down over the previous 52 weeks. Zero Coupon 2010 was up 14.44 percent for the 52 weeks ending December 31, 1997.

OPERATIONS

A variable annuity subaccount is owned by all of its contract owners, the people who purchased units of the subaccount, just like in a mutual fund. The day-to-day operation of a subaccount is delegated to a management company. The management company, often an outside mutual fund group, but sometimes the organization that created the variable annuity, may offer other financial products and services as well as different kinds of insurance.

The investment adviser manages the subaccount's portfolio of securities. The adviser is paid for his or her services in the form of a fee that is based on the total value of the fund's assets; annual fees average 0.82 percent (versus 1.34 percent for the typical mutual fund). The adviser employs professional portfolio managers who invest the subaccount's money by purchasing a number of stocks, bonds, and/or money market instruments, depending on the portfolio's investment objective (as described in the prospectus).

These professionals decide where to invest the subaccount's assets. The money managers make their investment decisions based on extensive, ongoing research into the financial performance of individual companies, taking into account general economic and market trends. In addition, they are backed up by economic and statistical resources. On the basis of their research, money managers decide what and when to buy, sell, or hold for the portfolio, in light of the subaccount's specific investment objective.

In addition to the investment adviser, the variable annuity company may also contract with an underwriter who arranges for the distribution of the subaccount's units to the investing public. The underwriter may act as a wholesaler, selling units to securities dealers, or it may retail directly to the public. This is very similar to how a mutual fund group operates.

No Junk Bond or Real Estate Worries

With fixed-rate annuities, the monies you invest are commingled with the insurance company's general portfolio. This general portfolio includes the good and the bad; in theory, *your* account could be compromised either temporarily or permanently. A few insurers, such as American Skandia and Hartford, maintain separate accounts for their fixed-rate accounts.

Such separation means that investors do not need to worry about whether the insurer might fall into financial trouble.

One of the advantages of a variable annuity is that if the insurance company runs into financial problems, the subaccounts are beyond the reach of the company's creditors. Variable annuities are also subject to regulation by the Securities and Exchange Commission (SEC) and the National Association of Securities Dealers (NASD), as well as state regulatory bodies. Fixed-rate annuities are regulated by each state's insurance commissioner. New York and California have two of the more stringent regulatory bodies. Thus, if an insurance product is approved for sale in New York, there is a very strong likelihood that not only is the company financially strong but also that the products it offers are considered to be fair to the public.

STANDARD CONTRACT FEATURES

Ease of Purchase

Mutual subaccount shares are easy to buy. For those who prefer to make investment decisions themselves, subaccounts are as close as the telephone or the mailbox. Those who would like help in choosing a subaccount can draw upon a wide variety of sources.

Many variable annuities sell their products through stockbrokers, financial planners, or insurance agents. These representatives can help you analyze your financial needs and objectives and recommend appropriate subaccounts. In the case of over 98 percent of the variable annuities out there, the investor pays no fee or commission; 100 percent of his or her money is invested in one or more subaccounts. Ongoing fees charged by a subaccount are described in the prospectus.

Access to Your Money

Variable annuity companies stand ready on any business day to redeem any or all of your shares at the current unit value. The value may be greater or less than the price you originally paid, depending on the market and the type of subaccount.

To sell shares back to the subaccount all you need to do is give the subaccount proper notification, as explained in the prospectus. The subaccount will then send your check promptly. You receive the price your shares are worth on the day the subaccount gets proper notice of redemption. This is the same process used by mutual funds.

Exchange Privileges

As the economy or your own personal circumstances change, the types of subaccounts you hold may no longer be the ones you need or want. Many subaccounts are part of a family of funds and offer a feature called an *exchange privilege*.

exchange privilege   the ability to move assets among subaccounts.

Within a variable annuity family, there may be several choices, each with a different investment objective, varying from very conservative subaccounts to those which are aggressive and carry a much higher degree of risk. An exchange privilege allows you to transfer from one of these subaccounts to another. Exchange policies vary from company to company. Most variable annuities allow you to make several changes per calendar year without any type of charge. These exchanges can usually be done by making a toll-free telephone call; some variable annuities require the exchange request to be in writing. For the specifics about a subaccount's exchange privilege, check the prospectus.

Automatic Reinvestment

Interest, dividends, and capital gains are automatically reinvested; such reinvestment is reflected in the unit price. The number of units owned never changes unless you make a partial or complete liquidation or make an additional investment in the subaccount.

Automatic Withdrawal

You can make arrangements with the variable annuity company to automatically send you, or anyone you designate, checks from the subaccount. The checks can be for a specific dollar amount or for a certain period of time (e.g., five years, during the lifetime of a person or couple, etc.). Money can be sent to you on a monthly, quarterly, semiannual, or annual basis. This system works well for retirees, families who want to arrange for payments to their children at college, or anyone needing income checks.

Guaranteed Death Benefit

Virtually all variable annuities have a guaranteed death benefit. This means that, upon the annuitant's death, the beneficiary (you and/or your spouse, children, living trust, etc.) receives what was originally invested (plus any additional contributions made along the way) minus any withdrawals or the value of the investment contract on the date of the annuitant's death, *whichever is greater*. An example may prove useful.

Let us suppose that you invested $500,000 in a variable annuity and a couple of years later you added another $100,000. During the next several years, the value of your account went up to $2,300,000, dropped to $350,000, and then ended at $1,750,000 on the date of the annuitant's death. The death benefit would be computed since the annuitant is now deceased. The guaranteed benefit would be calculated as follows:

Original investment plus addition	$ 600,000
Value on date of death	$1,750,000
Minus withdrawals	$ 900,000
Death benefit	$ 875,000

One of the nice features of this guaranteed benefit, unlike life insurance, is that you or your spouse do *not* have to die in order for the benefit to kick in. You can pretty much name anyone you want as the annuitant. The annuitant could be a child, parent, friend, neighbor, or relative. As you may recall from a previous chapter, the only requirements are that the annuitant must: (1) be alive when you begin the investment, (2) be under a certain age (usually 75, 80, or 85), and be a person (not a trust or corporation, partnership, or couple). No medical exams or medical questions are asked.

The guaranteed death benefit does not last forever. When the named annuitant reaches the age of annuitization, which ranges from

age 75 to 90, depending on the company you are with, the death benefit ceases. To eliminate this problem, the contract owner can often substitute annuitants. Thus, as the named annuitant comes close to
reaching that magic age, whether it is 75, 80, 85, or 90, simply write to
the insurer and request that a different annuitant be substituted for the
existing one.

Step-Up in Principal

A number of variable annuities now offer the investor a *step-up in principal* provision. This option increases the minimum guaranteed death benefit. Anytime after the penalty period completely lapses, usually in the
sixth or seventh year, the contract owner can renew the contract. By accepting another penalty period, one can have the floor of the death benefit
increased to the value of the contract at the date of renewal. Another example will best explain how this benefit works.

step-up in principal   a death benefit feature found in
many variable annuities. The original contract is
"renewed" after the penalty period lapses, thereby
increasing the minimum death benefit to the contract
value on the date of renewal (which is presumably a
higher figure).

Imagine that you invested $80,000 in a variable annuity in 1980 and
the contract had a six-year contingent deferred sales charge. Sometime after the six-year anniversary, let us say in 1987, the value of your contract
was $220,000. At that point you decided to increase your minimum guar-
anteed death benefit by renewing the investment contract. The annuitant
dies in 1998. On the date of the annuitant's death the contract is worth
$93,000. As the beneficiary, you would receive a check for $220,000, the
new "original investment."

The guaranteed death benefit, regardless of whether you later opt
for any step-up in principal provision, is a very unique feature. Virtually
no investment offered outside the insurance industry provides the investor the option of investing in a wide array of securities, from aggres-

sive growth stocks to money market accounts, with such an assurance. The guaranteed death benefit makes variable annuities the ideal choice for an individual who wants the opportunity to do well in the stock or bond market, for purposes of growth or income or to offset the effects of inflation, while still providing a loved one with a guarantee that takes effect at death.

Enhanced Death Benefit

Some variable annuities have beefed up the death benefit by increasing the minimum (or guarantee) to equal what was invested compounded by 5 percent per year (for a maximum of 200 percent of the value of the principal contributions) or value on the date of the annuitant's death, whichever is greater. Companies that offer this *enhanced death benefit* usually limit the amount of 5 percent compounding and also place an age restriction as to when the benefit stops. The annuity prospectus provides details about the death benefit.

> **enhanced death benefit** minimum benefit equals original invested compounded by 5 percent or value on date of death.

Risk Reduction: Importance of Diversification

If there is one ingredient to successful investing that is universally agreed upon, it is the benefit of diversification. It is also a concept that is backed by a great deal of research and market experience.

The benefit that diversification provides is risk reduction. Risk to investors is frequently defined as volatility of return (also known as *standard deviation*)—in other words, how much an investment's return might vary. Investors prefer returns that are relatively predictable, and thus less volatile. On the other hand, they want returns that are high. Diversification eliminates most of the risk without reducing long-term returns.

standard deviation volatility of return.

A variable annuity's portfolio managers will normally invest the subaccount's pool of money in 50 to 200 different securities to spread the subaccount's holdings over a number of investments. This diversification is an important factor in lessening the subaccount's overall risk. Such diversification is typically beyond the financial capacity of most individual investors. Table 6.2 shows the relationship between diversification and investment risk, as defined by the variability of annual returns of a stock portfolio.

Note that the variability of return, or risk, associated with holding just one stock is more than six times as great as the risk of a 100-stock portfolio. Surprisingly, the increased potential return found in a portfolio comprised of a small number of stocks is minimal at best.

Monitoring Performance

One of the nice features of annuities is that you can always find out how you are doing. Most annuity companies have toll-free telephone numbers, and several companies have an automated service that can give you information—including account balances—24 hours a day, seven days a week.

TABLE 6.2 Relationship between Diversification and Investment Risk	
Number of Stocks	Risk Ratio
1	6.6
2	3.8
4	2.4
10	1.6
50	1.1
100	1.0

In addition to contacting the insurance company, you can also monitor performance by subscribing to one of several periodicals. *Barron's*, a weekly publication, lists unit values of several hundred variable annuities each issue. The *Wall Street Journal* and *Money* magazine have both increased their coverage of annuities and periodically run performance figures on some of the best and worst performing variable annuities. There are also three well-known publications that cover variable annuities extensively: VARDS, Lipper, and Morningstar.

VARDS

The Variable Annuity Research and Data Service (VARDS) Report is a monthly publication; an annual subscription costs $698. It is published by Financial Planning Resources, Inc., 4343 Shallowford Road, #B6, Marietta, GA 30062. Write for a sample copy, or telephone 770-998-5186.

Lipper

Another source you may wish to consider is published by Lipper Analytical Securities Corporation. The *Lipper Variable Insurance Products Performance Analysis Service* contains performance figures on variable life insurance as well as variable annuities. For a sample copy write to Lipper Analytical Services, Inc., 47 Maple Street, Summit, NJ 07901, or telephone 212-393-1300. An annual subscription costs $9000.

Morningstar

One of the best-known variable annuity sources is Morningstar (800-735-0700). Morningstar's *Variable Annuity and Life Performance Report* ($95 for a single issue and $295 quarterly), a 400-page publication, covers approximately 5400 different subaccounts. *Principia for Variable Annuities* (computer software) covers 7500 subaccounts and includes a wide range of tailored reports and statistical comparisons ($95 for a onetime subscription, $195 for quarterly updates. Morningstar's address is 225 West Wacker Drive, Chicago, IL 60640.

Dollar-Cost Averaging

Investors often feel that they have "the kiss of death" when it comes to investing. They strongly believe that the market will go down as soon as they get in. For these people, and anyone concerned with reducing risk, the solution is *dollar-cost averaging*.

> **dollar-cost averaging** investing a fixed amount of money in a given subaccount at specific intervals to average out high and low unit prices.

Dollar-cost averaging (DCA) is a simple, yet effective, way to reduce risk, whether you are investing in stocks or in bonds. The premise behind dollar-cost averaging is that if several purchases of a subaccount are made over an extended period of time, the unpredictable highs and lows will average out. The investor buys some units at a comparatively low price, others at perhaps a much higher price.

DCA assumes that investors are willing to sacrifice the possibility of having bought all of their units at the lowest price in return for being confident that they did not buy every unit at the highest price. In short, we are willing to accept a compromise; a sort of risk-adjusted decision. Another advantage of DCA is that it increases the likelihood that you will follow an investment program. As with other aspects of our life, it is important to have goals and objectives.

DCA is based on investing a fixed amount of money in a given subaccount at specific intervals. Typically, an investor will add a few hundred dollars at the beginning of each month to the XYZ subaccount. DCA works best if you invest and continue to invest on a preestablished schedule, *regardless of price fluctuations*. You will be buying more units when the price is down than when it is up. Most investors do not mind buying units when prices are increasing since this means that their existing units are also going up. When the market is falling and unit prices are decreasing, the investor feels a little better knowing that he or she is now buying more shares with the same amount of money. When this program is followed, losses during market declines are limited, while the ability to participate in good markets is maintained.

Table 6.3 shows what would have happened if DCA had been used just after the October 19, 1987, stock market crash using the growth subaccount from American Legacy II, a variable annuity that uses several of the same portfolio managers who oversee funds within the American Funds mutual fund family.

		TABLE 6.3 The Effect of Dollar-Cost Averaging		
		American Legacy II		
		Growth Portfolio		
Date	Investment	Units Purchased	Price per Unit	Total Value
10/31/87	$ 8,333	12,437	$0.67	$ 8,333
11/30/87	8,333	13,440	0.62	16,044
12/31/87	8,333	12,077	0.69	26,176
1/31/88	8,333	12,077	0.69	34,681
2/29/88	8,333	11,261	0.74	45,312
3/31/88	8,333	11,111	0.75	53,942
4/30/88	8,333	10,964	0.76	63,477
5/31/88	8,333	10,964	0.76	71,341
6/30/88	8,333	10,416	0.80	84,269
7/31/88	8,333	10,548	0.79	91,220
8/31/88	8,333	11,111	0.75	94,995
9/30/88	10,839	14,077	0.77	108,247

All the illustrations assume the following: (1) $100,000 in a 4.5 percent fixed-rate income account is evenly liquidated over a 12-month period; (2) each partial redemption automatically goes into the variable annuity growth subaccount; (3) money not yet transferred into the variable annuity is earning 4.5 percent; and (4) DCA begins on October 31, 1987 (which was less than two weeks after the crash), and ends September 30, 1988.

Contrast this to the investor who placed $100,000 in the same growth portfolio on the highest day of the market in 1987 (several weeks before the October 19, 1987, crash). The lump-sum investment would have bought units for 92 cents each; by September 30, 1988, the lump-sum investment would be worth only $70,634 (versus $108,247 for the investor who dollar-cost averaged over 12 months).

Systematic Withdrawal Plan

This method of getting monthly checks is ideal for the income-oriented investor. A systematic withdrawal plan (SWP) is also a risk reduction technique, a type of dollar-cost averaging in reverse since money is being withdrawn from your account instead of being added. A set amount is automatically sent to you on a monthly, quarterly, semiannual, or annual basis. There is no charge for this service.

In order for a check for a set amount to be sent to you, units of one or more of your subaccount(s) must be sold. During periods when the market is low, a greater number of units must be liquidated than during the times when the market is high and so is your subaccount's price per unit. If you need $500 a month and the subaccount's price is $25 per unit, 20 units must be liquidated; if the price per unit is $20, 25 units must be sold.

Shown in Table 6.4 is an example of a SWP from American Legacy

TABLE 6.4 A Systematic Withdrawal Plan in Action		
American Legacy III		
Growth Portfolio		
Initial investment: $100,000		
Annual withdrawals of: $10,000 (10%)		
First check distributed: 12/31/84		
Date	*Amount Withdrawn*	*Value of Remaining Units*
12/31/84	$10,000	$101,000
12/31/85	10,000	107,000
12/31/86	10,000	125,000
12/31/87	10,000	124,000
12/31/88	10,000	128,000
12/31/89	10,000	152,000
12/31/90	10,000	137,000
12/31/91	10,000	162,000
12/31/92	10,000	166,000
12/31/93	10,000	178,000
12/31/94	10,000	167,000
12/31/95	10,000	205,000
12/31/96	10,000	217,000
12/31/97	10,000	266,000

III's growth subaccount, a conservative growth portfolio. The example assumes an initial investment of $100,000 in the subaccount at its inception, February 8, 1984. A greater or smaller amount could be used. The example shows what happens to the investor's principal over a 14-year period of time. It assumes that $10,000 is withdrawn from the subaccount each year. As you can see, by the end of 1997 the investor would have received (and spent) all $100,000 of the original investment (plus an additional $40,000 of distributions)—while still having an ending balance of $266,000.

Compare this example to what would have happened if the money had been placed in an average fixed-income account at a bank. The $100,000 depositor who took out $10,000 each year from a bank account would be in a far different situation: The original $100,000 would be fully depleted by the end of 1994—the interest earned could not keep up with an annual withdrawal of $10,000. The difference between using the growth subaccount and the savings account is close to $300,000.

Next time a broker or banker tells you that you should be buying bonds or CDs for current income, suggest a systematic withdrawal plan. It's a program designed to really maximize your income and offset something the CD, T-bill, and bond sellers seldom mention: inflation.

REGULATION

Variable annuities must comply with some of the toughest laws and rules in the financial services industry. All subaccounts are regulated by the U.S. Securities and Exchange Commission (SEC) and state insurance commissioners. With its extensive rule making and enforcement authority, the SEC oversees variable annuity compliance by chiefly relying on four major federal securities statutes.

Subaccount assets must generally be held by an independent custodian. There are strict requirements for fidelity bonding to ensure against the misappropriation of shareholder monies. In addition to federal statutes, every state has its own set of regulations governing variable annuities.

While federal and state laws cannot guarantee that a subaccount will be profitable, they are designed to ensure that all variable annuities are operated and managed in the interests of their contract owners. Here are some specific investor protections that every subaccount must follow:

✔ Regulations concerning what may be claimed or promised about a subaccount and its potential.

✔ Requirements that a subaccount operate in the interests of its investors, rather than any special interests of its management.

✔ Rules dictating diversification of the subaccount's portfolio over a wide range of investments to avoid too much concentration in a particular security.

THE PROSPECTUS

By law, you must receive a prospectus prior to or at the time you sign a variable annuity contract. The prospectus summarizes all of the contract's features, benefits, costs, potential penalties, and investment options. The purpose of the prospectus is to provide the reader with full and complete disclosure. The prospectus covers the following key points:

✔ The subaccount's investment objectives (what the managers are trying to achieve).

✔ The investment methods used in trying to achieve these goals.

✔ The name and address of the investment adviser and a brief description of the adviser's experience.

✔ The level of investment risk the subaccount is willing to assume in pursuit of its investment objectives; this will range from maximum to minimum risk, depending on the type of subaccount.

✔ Any investments the subaccount will *not* make (for example, real estate or options).

✔ Tax consequences of the investment for the shareholder.

✔ How to purchase units of the subaccount, including the cost of investing.

✔ How to redeem units (shares).

✔ Services provided, such as IRAs, dollar-cost averaging, withdrawal plans, and any other features.

✔ A statement of fees charged by the subaccount and their effect on earnings.

PRODUCT EXAMPLE

To give you a better feel as to the mechanics of investing in a variable annuity, an example may be helpful. The example used in this section is the Putnam Hartford Capital Manager (1-800-521-0963), a flexible-premium tax-deferred variable annuity. The descriptions below are edited excerpts from the company's 1998 literature (reprinted with permission).

- ✔ Putnam, a 60-year-old money management company, has 220 analysts that oversee well over $170 billion in assets, $34 billion of which is invested in international securities. Putnam is best-known as a Boston-based mutual fund company and manages the different funds (called subaccounts) within the variable annuity family.

- ✔ This particular annuity allows investors to choose one or more portfolios that are modeled after existing Putnam mutual funds. These investment options are: Asia Pacific Growth, Global Growth, Health Sciences Investors, International Growth, International New Opportunities, New Opportunities, Vista, Voyager, Global Asset Allocation, Growth and Income, OTC & Emerging Growth, Utilities, International Growth and Income, The George Putnam Fund, Diversified Income, High-Yield, U.S. Government and High-Quality Bond, Money Market, and a fixed-rate account.

- ✔ The variable annuity is offered in conjunction with ITT Hartford Life Insurance, one of the largest insurance companies in the country (all annuities are designed and set up by insurance companies).

- ✔ Minimum initial investment is $1000; additional investments of at least $500 may be made at any time (for group retirement plans the minimum initial and subsequent investment is $50).

- ✔ Systematic contributions can be automatically made from your checking account into the annuity on a monthly or quarterly basis.

- ✔ The maximum purchase age for owners and annuitants is 85.

- ✔ There is no initial sales charge; 100 percent of your money goes to work for you immediately.

✔ The declining contingent deferred sales charge is as follows: years 1 and 2—6 percent, years 3 and 4—5 percent, years 5—4 percent, year 6—3 percent, year 7—2 percent, year 8—0 percent.

✔ Free partial surrenders (withdrawals) are available: Up to 10 percent of the purchase payments (dollars invested) may be taken out without penalty (no contingent sales charge).

✔ The systematic withdrawal plan provides that the free partial surrenders may be structured as a fixed dollar amount or as a percentage of purchase payments, to be distributed each year on a monthly, quarterly, semiannual, or annual basis without incurring a contingent deferred sales charge; a 10 percent IRS penalty *may* apply to surrenders made prior to the contract owner reaching age 59½.

✔ Annual charges and/or ongoing costs (deducted from the investor's account) are: mortality and expense risk—1.25 percent, administrative fee—0.15 percent, maintenance fee—$30 (waived if the value on the anniversary date is $50,000 or more).

✔ Premium tax (charged by some states when, and if, a contract is annuitized) is up to 3.5 percent of the value of the contract; some states access the tax at the time purchase payments are made, other states wait until annuitization begins.

✔ If the contract owner elects to annuitize the contract, there are four different options: (1) lifetime (for your lifetime or the lifetime of someone else such as a spouse or child); (2) lifetime with 120, 180, or 240 monthly payments certain (in case the owner dies within the first 10 to 20 years, income will still go to an heir); (3) joint and last survivor (payment lasts until the second person dies; the option can be structured so that the payment to the survivor is the same as or lower than what it was while both parties were alive); and (4) monthly income for a designated period, which may be from five to 30 years; if the contract is surrendered during the selected period, the termination value of the contract will be sent to the owner.

✔ The guaranteed death benefit is as follows: If the contract owner, joint owner, *or* annuitant die (any one of these three) prior to annuitization and before age 90, the beneficiary will receive the greatest of: (1) total contributions less any prior withdrawals; (2) the maximum anniversary (yearly) value established up to age 80, plus contributions after age 80 and less any withdrawals; or (3) the current value of the contract (the investment).

INSIDE A RETIREMENT PLAN

During 1996 and 1997, approximately 40 percent of variable annuity sales were done inside an IRA or other qualified retirement plan. Since IRA and retirement accounts grow and compound tax-deferred, just like annuities, an annuity inside a retirement plan provides no additional tax benefit. As a general rule, the expenses associated with an annuity are about 1 percent higher per year than they are in a similar-type mutual fund. The question then becomes whether there is any benefit from investing in an annuity within a retirement plan.

The only special advantage an annuity provides in this situation is the guaranteed death benefit. It has been estimated that less than one-half of 1 percent of variable annuity contracts are surrendered each year due to death or disability. This small figure, coupled with the chance that the annuity experiences an overall loss, means that the odds of someone benefiting from the guaranteed death benefit offered by most companies is extremely unlikely. In fact, the chances of someone benefiting from such a death benefit may be one-tenth of 1 percent, or even lower. Most variable annuities provide a guaranteed death benefit. Each investor in such contracts pays for the death benefit, a charge that generally ranges from 0.75 percent to 1.25 percent annually.

Some of the most generous death benefits come from CIGNA, Hartford Life, and Putnam. With some of their products, the death benefit is reset every year on the anniversary date of the contract. This means that the benefit can be either the current contract value or the highest-ever value of the contract on any anniversary of its purchase date—whichever is greater.

There are a couple of things to keep in mind about a death benefit: (1) It ends if and when the contract is annuitized; and (2) many of the enhanced death benefits are capped at 200 percent of the amount(s) invested and end once the annuitant, or sometimes owner, reaches age 80 (age 75 with a few contracts).

LOW-FEE ALTERNATIVES

With all the expenses associated with the typical variable annuity (sur-render fees, administrative expenses, and mortality charges), one would think that people would be flocking to no-load or low-load choices for this investment vehicle. But this is not the case. Only about 6 percent of the money going into variable annuities is in such low- or no-load products (versus about half of all mutual fund sales). Some sources estimate the sales figure to be more likely in the 2 percent to 3 percent range.

Setting aside any potential surrender charge, the two main charges associated with a variable annuity are the *fund expense* and the mortality and expense fee (the guaranteed death benefit). Any administrative fee is usually in the 0.1 percent to 0.2 percent range. Table 6.5 shows the most popular investment categories within a variable annuity (column 1), the average management fee (column 2), and the average total expense (column 3), which includes the management fee. The figures are as of the middle of 1997.

fund expense   the fee paid to the mutual fund or management company overseeing the investment portfolios.

For investors seeking no-load or low-load variable annuities, con-sider the following companies: Vanguard Group (no surrender fee, and 0.48 percent total expenses), Jack White (no surrender fee, and a 0.45 percent mortality and expense fee), Janus, Scudder, and Charles Schwab.

LOSS CAN INCREASE DEATH BENEFIT

Usually, if the current value of the annuity is less than the original invest-ment, a withdrawal of most of the money can, in a way, convert the annu-ity contract into a form of cheap life insurance. The key to this special situation is based on a loophole in the wording of the death benefit provi-sion used by most insurers.

TABLE 6.5 Variable Annuity Costs		
Type of Portfolio (Subaccount)	Average Management Expense	Average Total Expense
Aggressive growth	0.95%	2.21%
Balanced	0.84	2.12
Corporate bond	0.69	1.94
Government bond	0.64	1.90
Growth	0.86	2.12
Growth and income	0.67	1.94
High-yield bond	0.80	2.09
International bond	1.12	2.42
International stock	1.15	2.42
Money market	0.52	1.79
Specialty (sector)	1.05	2.34
Average equity subaccount	**0.82**	**2.09**
Average fixed-income subaccount	**0.74**	**2.00**

As you may recall, the typical death benefit states that if you (meaning the contract owner with some contracts and the annuitant with most policies) die with a loss, your heirs will receive at least the initial investment(s). Thus, if someone invested $100,000 in a variable annuity, suffered a $20,000 loss and then died, his or her heirs would receive at least $100,000. Let us now modify this example and see how the amount of "insurance" is magnified.

Suppose the $100,000 in the variable annuity fell by $20,000 and then the owner withdrew $79,000 of the remaining $80,000, leaving just $1000 left in the annuity. The annuity contract remains in force since it still has money in it, so the death benefit would still be honored. And, since the death benefit is at least "principal minus any and all withdrawals," the amount paid to the heirs would be $21,000 (the $100,000 principal minus the $79,000 withdrawal). Thus, in this example, until the remaining $1000 grew to $21,000, the heirs would receive any difference between these two figures from the insurance company.

A nice feature of the aforementioned example is that the $79,000 withdrawn would not be subject to income taxes or any IRS penalty since the investor, regardless of age, was only receiving principal. The $79,000 taken out could then be invested to take advantage of any subsequent bull market.

Such a strategy may even make sense if part or all of the money withdrawn were subject to a surrender charge imposed by the annuity. Keep in mind this is not the best way to buy "life insurance": (1) You must suffer a moderate or large loss in order for the leveraging to make sense, and (2) the death benefit (or "life insurance") is subject to income taxes to the extent it plus prior withdrawals exceed the original principal. Real life insurance benefits are not subject to income taxes.

Existing annuity contracts that contain the traditional death benefit guarantee (which could also be an enhanced death benefit) cannot be changed by the issuer; however, you will still want to check the contract. Some companies have a guaranteed death benefit that is proportionately reduced to take into account any withdrawals. Such proportionate reduction would wipe out any chance of a windfall "life insurance" benefit. A few contracts state that if more than 90 percent of the cash value is taken out, such an event would be treated as a complete surrender (full withdrawal) and the policy would no longer be in force.

IMMEDIATE VARIABLE ANNUITIES

Currently, only about a dozen companies offer immediate annuities. The major players in this arena are: Fidelity Investments, Hartford Life Insurance, American Skandia Life Assurance, and Equitable. Immediate variable annuities do something most variable annuities do not do: They give the contract owner an immediate income stream. An income stream may now be more important than it was in the past because people are living longer. One mortality study estimates that 60 percent of today's 65-year-olds will live to age 85, another 21 percent will reach 95, and 8 percent will live to at least 100.

With a variable annuity, the investor can choose among one or more subaccounts (similar to a mutual fund family) and can take out part of all of the account value at any time or move to another company prior to annuitization. With *immediate* variable annuities, investors can usually still make switches among the different funds offered but cannot switch to another annuity provider once annuitization has begun.

COMPARED TO SINGLE-PREMIUM VARIABLE LIFE

Variable annuities have become a popular substitute for mutual fund investors seeking tax deferral. However, since taxes are only deferred, any tax liability due at death can add to the cost of settling an estate. A *single-premium variable life* contract may be better than an annuity since the death benefit is not subject to income taxes, and withdrawals during the lifetime of the owner can be structured as loans and therefore are not usually subject to taxation.

single-premium variable life a type of whole-life insurance wherein the policy owner can select how the cash value of the policy is to be invested. Investment choices are similar to those found in a mutual fund family and range from conservative (money market) to aggressive (small-company growth stocks). "Single-premium" means that a lump sum is invested, a single investment.

Table 6.6 shows the income tax consequences of an annuity and life insurance. The following assumptions were made:

1. The amount of $50,000 is deposited into the annuity and also into the single-premium variable life policy.

2. Both vehicles have an assumed growth rate of 12 percent (before any expenses or deductions).

3. The annuity has annual charges that equal 2.22 percent (1.25 percent mortality, 0.82 percent management fee, and 0.15 percent administration fee) and a $36 contract maintenance fee.

4. The variable life insurance product includes all relevant charges, such as the cost of insurance, management fees, and mortality and expense charges.

5. The investor is in a 31 percent federal income tax bracket.

TABLE 6.6   Taxes Due on an Annuity versus Life Insurance

	Variable Annuity			Variable Life Insurance	
Age	Death Benefit	Taxes on Gain	Net Death Benefit	After-Tax Death Benefit	Advantage over Annuity
61	$ 54,815	$ 1,493	$ 53,322	$ 110,500	$ 57,178
62	60,097	3,130	56,967	110,500	53,533
63	65,891	4,926	60,965	110,500	49,535
64	72,248	6,897	65,351	110,500	45,149
65	79,221	9,059	70,163	110,500	40,337
66	86,871	11,430	75,441	110,500	35,059
67	95,263	14,032	81,232	110,500	29,268
68	104,469	16,885	87,584	118,830	31,246
69	114,569	20,016	94,552	129,265	34,713
70	125,648	23,451	102,197	140,602	38,405
75	199,410	46,317	153,093	206,844	53,751
80	316,603	82,647	233,956	326,422	92,466
85	502,798	140,367	362,431	524,711	162,280
90	798,624	232,073	566,550	842,800	276,250
95	1,268,630	377,775	890,855	1,325,442	434,587

WHO BUYS VARIABLE ANNUITIES?

Mutual Fund Owners

Over 72 percent of all mutual fund owners reinvest their dividends and capital gains. Even though distributions are not being made directly to the investor, a tax event is triggered every time such reinvestments occur. Variable annuities avoid the tax event triggered by reinvestment of gains, dividends, and interest payments. Insurance companies do not send out Form 1099s to contract owners at the end of the year if the account is set up for automatic reinvestment.

The majority of mutual funds charge a commission. These charges usually occur at the time of the initial investment, plus whenever the investor adds more money, but sometimes are seen when there is a partial liquidation or complete liquidation. Variable annuity owners do not pay a commission. One hundred percent of their investment goes to work immediately. Depending on the insurer, 10 percent to 15 percent of the account can be withdrawn each year without penalty. Once the penalty period is over, the entire account can be terminated without any cost, fee, or penalty from the annuity company.

People Who Switch Investments

Transfers, also known as switches or exchanges, within a mutual fund family, or from one fund company to another, result in a taxable event. The mutual fund group also charges a $5 fee for each switch that is made. When you own a variable annuity, there is no tax event when you switch among the subaccounts (moving from one fund to another). There is also no taxation when money is transferred from one company to another. The typical variable annuity allows up to 12 free switches per year.

People Who Worry about Market Volatility

A variable annuity offers a guaranteed death benefit, which states that when the annuitant dies the beneficiary receives the greater of principal (all purchase payments) or account balance at death. There is no investment outside the insurance industry that provides such protection.

Several annuities offer an enhanced death benefit. This means that the minimum death benefit is now stepped-up to the value of the contract at the end of the penalty period, which may be as little as five years. Therefore, when death of the annuitant later occurs, the beneficiary, who is often the investor and contract owner, gets the greater of the account balance at death or the stepped-up value. Some companies have beefed up their death benefit so that the minimum guaranteed death benefit is original principal, plus any future contributions, *plus* 5 percent of the contract value, compounded annually.

Investors Who Want to Add Money

With some investments, such as bank CDs, government securities, and fixed-rate annuities, you cannot add to your original investment. If you wish to purchase more, you must make a new contract or invest-ment, often at a different rate or with different provisions. A variable annuity is a flexible-premium product that allows you to keep adding to your original investment without filling out a new agreement or contract.

When you invest in a variable contract, you can make additional contributions anytime, in virtually any amount. Many insurers also offer automatic check withdrawal plans or salary reduction programs. Under these two provisions, your account is added to automatically at a specific time each month. These ongoing contributions assure you of a disciplined investment plan. In a sense, these two plans force you to adhere to a very important risk reduction tool: dollar-cost averaging.

Companies That Want a Retirement Plan

Variable annuities offer the employer a convenient method of establishing and contributing to employees' retirement plans. The annuity companies offer corporations, sole proprietors, and partnerships a wide range of plans, including IRAs, Keoghs, pension plans, profit-sharing programs, TSAs, SEP-IRAs, and 401(k) plans.

By eliminating the need to set up cash reserves for monthly redemp-tion plans, variable annuities offer the employer and the employee the opportunity for enhanced returns. In a world of corporate takeovers and bankruptcies, families like the idea that these plans offer guaranteed death benefits and other forms of security not found with other retire-ment plans.

Those Who Want an IRA Alternative

IRAs can be an excellent retirement vehicle, but not everyone qualifies for such an account. Furthermore, those who do must limit their con-tributions to no more than $2000 per year. On top of that, withdrawals must be made after the worker reaches age 70½ (unless you have a Roth IRA).

Variable annuities do not face any of these restrictions. Anyone, even a child, can contribute to an annuity. There are no annual contribution limits; you can make a single investment and never contribute again or make an investment every day of the year. It is always your choice. Furthermore, withdrawals do not need to be made when you reach 70½. In fact, the account can pass to your spouse, children, living trust, friend, or other without triggering an immediate tax event.

Tax-Free Exchanges

Also known as a 1035 exchange (named after the Internal Revenue Code section that covers this subject), this feature allows the investor (contract owner) to have his or her investment transferred from one variable annuity company to another without triggering an IRS penalty or tax. Whether you change companies or not, investors can always make transfers or exchanges within a variable annuity family without triggering a taxable event.

Ease of Tax Preparation

Since money in all annuities grows and compounds tax-deferred, tax preparation becomes easier. Your tax preparer does not have to list any annuity activity on your tax return (unless a partial or full redemption has been made).

Privacy from the IRS

There is nowhere to indicate the amount of growth or interest earned from your annuity anywhere on your tax return. Unlike most forms of income or realized growth, including interest earned from tax-free bonds, the IRS does not need to know the value of your annuity or any resulting growth.

Detailed Recordkeeping

The variable annuity will handle all the paperwork and recordkeeping necessary to keep track of your investment transactions. A typical statement will note such items as your most recent investment or withdrawal. Statements are sent automatically each quarter.

Retirement Plans

Financial experts have long viewed variable annuities as appropriate vehicles for retirement investing (particularly in light of the guaranteed death benefit, which can protect the surviving spouse or family members). They are quite commonly used for retirement investing. They can be used in Keoghs, IRAs, 401(k) plans, and other employer-sponsored retirement plans. Most annuities offer prototype retirement plans and standard IRA agreements.

Chapter 7

Variable Annuity Investment Choices

T here is a wide range of investment choices available to variable annuity investors. The number of choices and their respective risk levels depend on the insurer and the type of management selected to oversee a particular portfolio. These options, known as subaccounts, provide the potential for rewards and risk. As you will see, these categories are identical to the types of categories or investment options found within a mutual fund family. Some insurers offer only a couple of these categories; others offer most, if not all, of the portfolios described in this chapter.

TERMS YOU SHOULD KNOW

The descriptions include facts and figures that should be of interest to the novice as well as the sophisticated investor. Some of the statistical information presented includes terms, abbreviations, and phrases you may not be familiar with; these items are explained in the next several paragraphs.

Standard Deviation

Standard deviation has to do with an investment's predictability of returns, sometimes referred to as volatility. The higher the standard deviation (SD), the less likely yield or return expectations will be met in any 12-month period. The lower the SD, the more predictable the rates of return will be.

117

Volatility is not necessarily bad; upward or positive volatility results in a type of unpredictability that we all look forward to. Standard deviation (SD) is the dispersion of actual returns around the average annual compound return.

Since the standard deviation measures how much an asset's return fluctuates, it is often used as a measure of risk. Given a choice between two assets or portfolios providing virtually identical returns and all other factors being equal, the asset with less risk (a smaller standard deviation) would obviously be preferred. Table 7.1 is completely hypothetical and is designed to show you how the *expected* ranges of returns for a portfolio change depending on the standard deviation.

As you can see, the more certain you wish to be of being within a particular range, the wider that range of returns must be. The "expected range of returns" columns are calculated by taking the standard deviation (for a particular row) and subtracting it from the expected annual return (for the same row) and then adding the standard deviation to the same expected annual return—once for 67 percent (2 out of 3 years) certainty and twice for 90 percent (9 out of 10 years). For example, using the first row, a 12 percent return with a standard deviation of 4.0 equals a range of returns of +8 percent (12 percent minus 4 percent) to +16 percent (12 percent plus 4 percent).

Beta

Beta, like standard deviation, is a type of benchmark or general guide as to the portfolio's level of risk. It has nothing to do with the safety of the un-

TABLE 7.1 The SD Effect on a Sample Portfolio's Returns		Expected Range of Returns	
Portfolio's Standard Deviation	Expected Annual Return	Two out of Every Three Years (67 Percent)	Nine out of Every Ten Years (90 Percent)
4.0%	12%	+8% to +16%	+4% to +20%
7.0%	12%	+5% to +19%	−2% to +26%
10.0%	12%	+2% to +22%	−8% to +32%
4.0%	15%	+11% to +19%	+7% to +23%
7.0%	15%	+8% to +22%	+1% to +29%
10.0%	15%	+5% to +25%	−5% to +35%

derlying insurance company. Beta measures a mutual fund's or variable annuity subaccount's market-related risk. This has to do with how much of the portfolio's movement is attributable to the U.S. stock market, as measured by the S&P 500 (which has a beta that always stays at 1.0). A subaccount that has a beta of less than 1.0 is not as affected by market conditions as a portfolio that has a higher number. What is misleading about beta is the perception that a low beta—any figure less than 1.0 (e.g., 0.3)—means that the investment is also low-risk. Sometimes this is true, but often it is not (i.e., metals funds and foreign emerging stock funds both have low betas but both are very risky).

> **beta** a measurement of a mutual fund's or variable annuity subaccount's market-related risk.

The beta coefficient is a measure of an individual stock or equity portfolio relative to the S&P 500 index. If a subaccount's beta is 1.0, it is approximately as volatile as the market. If the portfolio's beta is 1.5, the asset is one and a half times as volatile; if the security's beta is .75, the investment is three-fourths as volatile. Beta reflects only the market-related portion of risk. Accordingly, it is a narrower measure than standard deviation. (See Table 7.2.)

The portfolio's (subaccount's) returns become more magnified the greater the change in the stock market (the S&P 500) and the higher the beta. Do not lose sight of the fact that beta measures only market-related risk.

Price/Earnings Ratio

Price/earnings (P/E) ratio is a means of measuring the selling price of a stock in relation to the company's earnings for the year. As an example, let's say the XYZ Corporation has a P/E ratio of 12. If you bought the entire company (100 percent of its outstanding stock), you would recoup your entire investment in 12 years, assuming current earnings levels. Price/earnings ratios are best utilized when compared to other companies' P/E ratios in the same industry or compared to the market as a whole (the S&P 500).

price/earnings (P/E) ratio a measurement of the selling price of a stock in relation to the company's earnings for the year.

According to the *Wall Street Journal*, "The P/E ratio is determined by dividing the closing market price by the company's . . . per-share earnings for the most recent four quarters." The P/E ratio is a rough estimate of how speculative a security might be. As a broad generalization, the higher the P/E ratio, the riskier a stock or portfolio of stocks becomes.

Indexes and Averages

Throughout this book, and particularly in this chapter, there are quite a few comparisons of category performance versus selected indexes and averages. There are five indexes used in this book: (1) the S&P 500, (2) EAFE (Europe, Australia, Far East), (3) Lehman Brothers Corporate Bond Index, (4) Lehman Brothers Government Bond Index, and (5) the consumer price index (CPI), as well as various variable annuity subaccount category averages.

TABLE 7.2 How a U.S. Equity Subaccount's Expected Returns Change Depending on Beta and Market Conditions		
Portfolio Beta	Change in Stock Market	Change in Portfolio's Expected Return
+1.5	+10%	+15.0%
+1.5	+2%	+3.0%
+1.3	+10%	+13.0%
+1.3	+2%	+2.6%
+1.0	+10%	+10.0%
+1.0	+2%	+2.0%
+0.9	−10%	−9.0%
+0.9	−2%	−1.8%
+0.5	−10%	−5.0%
+0.5	−2%	−1.0%

S&P 500

The S&P 500 represents the performance of 500 of some of the largest domestic (U.S.) and foreign stocks traded in the United States. This, like the EAFE index discussed next, is market-weighted, meaning that bigger companies affect the index more heavily than those of smaller companies. The S&P 500 is a more accurate measurement of the U.S. stock market than the Dow Jones Industrial Average (DJIA). The DJIA contains only 30 stocks and is not updated or changed nearly as often. Thus, even though you hear that the Dow (referring to the DJIA) was up or down X number of points on a given day, the figures are not quite as representative of the market as an index comprised of 500 equities.

EAFE

EAFE (Europe, Australia, Far East) is the most commonly used index to show how markets outside the United States are doing. Even though the index's name represents only three regions, it includes the stock markets of 15 different countries. Japan represents the largest percentage of the entire index.

Lehman Brothers Bond Indexes

The Lehman Brothers Corporate Bond Index, as the name implies, is an index of all high-quality corporate bonds. The Lehman Brothers Government Bond Index is also an index of bonds, but one comprised solely of U.S. government obligations (excluding mortgage-backed instruments such as GNMAs and FNMAs).

The shortcoming of these, and all other indexes, is that they do not fully represent what goes on in the real world. That is, they do not take into account transaction costs and management fees (or an offsetting amount that places some monetary value on the time spent by individuals and couples who select and oversee their own portfolios). Obviously, there is always a cost of buying and selling securities, one not reflected in any of the indexes and averages described. Additionally, there is some value in having a portfolio, be it mutual funds or variable annuities, that is professionally managed and provides for conveniences such as performance updates, withdrawal programs, dollar-cost averaging, and a toll-free phone number to access management company representatives to answer questions.

Consumer Price Index

The consumer price index (CPI) is the most widely used measurement for inflation in the United States. Out of all of the indexes used in this book, it is the one that has the highest *first-auto correlation*, which means that there is at least a rough relationship between last year's (or period's) numbers and what can be expected to happen this year (or period).

> **first-auto correlation**   the relationship, correlation, or predictability of an investment's return from one year to the next. A high first-auto correlation means that the investment's return for the next period, which could be a day, week, month, quarter, year, or multiple years, will most likely be very similar to its return for the most recent past period (e.g., a money market account or bank CD). A low correlation means that there is little, if any, relationship or likelihood that the past return will be similar to the future return (e.g., common stocks and real estate).

Category Averages

Finally, a number of category averages (e.g., "growth and income," "balanced," etc.) are used for comparison purposes. These descriptions refer to variable annuity subaccount averages. These averages are a fair measurement of how a subaccount you might be interested in has fared, since the averages represent the real world—how all of the subaccounts in a particular category have fared after all expenses, fees, and costs have been deducted.

Now that you have a better understanding of what several of the terms in this chapter mean, let us dive right into category descriptions, statistics, and figures. (See Appendix B for corresponding bar graphs for many of these categories.)

AGGRESSIVE GROWTH

The investment objective of aggressive growth subaccounts is maximum capital gains, with little or no concern for dividends or income of any kind. What makes this category of variable annuity subaccounts unique is that portfolio managers often have the ability to use borrowed money (leverage) to increase positions. Sometimes they deal in stock options and futures contracts (commodities). These trading techniques sound, and can be, scary, but such activities represent only a minor portion of the subaccounts' holdings.

Due to management's bullish beliefs, these subaccounts will usually stay fully invested in the stock market. For investors, this means better than expected results during good (bull) markets and worse than average losses during bad (bear) market periods. Fortunately, the average bull market is almost four times as long as the typical bear market.

Do not be confused by economic conditions and stock market performance. There have been eight recessions since World War II. During seven of those eight recessions, U.S. stocks went up. During all eight recessions, stocks posted impressive gains in the second half of every recession. By the same token, do not underestimate the impact of a loss. A 20 percent decline means that you must make 25 percent to break even. A loss of even 15 percent does not happen very often to aggressive growth subaccounts, particularly on a calendar year basis, but you should be aware that such extreme downward moves are possible. Brokers often like to focus on the +45 percent and +56 percent years, such as 1980 and 1991, while glossing over a bad year, such as 1984, when aggressive growth subaccounts were down almost 13 percent on average.

Because of this potential for loss, aggressive growth subaccounts should be owned by only two types of investors: (1) the person or couple who can live with high levels of daily, monthly, quarterly, and/or annual price-per-unit fluctuations, or (2) people who realize the importance of a diversified portfolio that cuts across several investment categories—investors who look at how the entire package is performing, not just one segment.

The typical price/earnings (P/E) ratio for stocks in this category is 32, a figure approximately 20 percent greater than that found with S&P 500 stocks (which has a 26.0 P/E ratio). This group of subaccounts has an average beta of 1.0, making its market-related risk the same as the S&P 500 (which always has a beta of 1.0, no matter what market conditions or levels are).

TABLE 7.3 Average Annual Rates of Return— Aggressive Growth Subaccounts				
Category	*One Year*	*Three Years*	*Five Years*	*Ten Years*
Aggressive growth	16.4%	21.2%	17.8%	16.7%
S&P 500	33.4	31.1	20.3	18.0
EAFE Index (foreign stock)	1.8	6.3	11.4	6.3
Lehman Brothers Government Bond Index	9.6	10.0	7.3	8.9
Rate of inflation (CPI)	1.8	2.6	2.6	3.4

Historical returns over the past one, three, five, and ten years (through 12/31/97) for aggressive growth subaccounts in comparison with commonly used indexes are shown in Table 7.3. All of the numbers given in the table are average annual rates of return.

The average standard deviation for aggressive growth subaccounts is 20 percent. The aggressive growth category is dominated by technology stocks, with this single group representing over 25 percent of the typical aggressive growth subaccount's portfolio. The next three top sectors are: service, retail, and health care stocks.

BALANCED

This type of subaccount invests in common stocks and corporate bonds. The weighting given to stocks depends on the subaccount manager's perception or belief in the market. The more bullish the manager is, the more likely the portfolio will be loaded up with equities. Yet, no matter how strongly management feels about the stock market, it would be very rare to see stocks equal more than 75 percent of the portfolio. Similarly, no matter how bearish one becomes, it would be unlikely for a balanced subaccount to have more than 70 percent of its holdings represented by bonds. Often, a subaccount's prospectus will outline the weighting ranges; the subaccount's managers must stay within these wide boundaries at all times. A small portion of these subaccounts is comprised of cash equivalents (T-bills, CDs, commercial paper, etc.), with a very small amount sometimes dedicated to preferred stocks and convertible securities.

The typical price/earnings (P/E) ratio for stocks in this category is 27, a figure approximately 4 percent greater than that found with S&P 500 stocks. This group of subaccounts has an average beta of 0.7, making its market-related risk 30 percent less than the S&P 500. Beta refers to a portfolio's stock market–related risk—it is not a meaningful way to measure bond risk.

Three other categories—income, convertible, and asset allocation—have been combined with balanced subaccounts for purposes of this book. Income subaccounts typically emphasize bonds more than stocks or cash equivalents. It is not uncommon to see an income subaccount that has 60 to 90 percent of its holdings in bonds and 10 to 40 percent in stocks.

Convertible subaccounts, as the name implies, are comprised mostly of convertible preferred stocks and convertible bonds. The conversion feature allows the owner, the subaccount in this case, to convert or exchange securities for corporations' common stocks. Conversion and price appreciation take place during bull market periods. Uncertain or down markets make conversion much less likely; management instead falls back on the comparatively high dividend or interest payments that convertibles enjoy.

convertible subaccount   allows owner to convert or exchange securities for corporations' common stocks.

Asset allocation subaccounts, like other categories that fall under the broad definition of "balanced," are hybrid in nature—part equity and part debt. These subaccounts have a tendency to emphasize stocks over bonds. A subaccount manager who wants to take a defensive posture may stay on the sidelines by converting moderate or large parts of the portfolio into cash equivalents.

asset allocation subaccount   part equity and part debt, has a tendency to emphasize stocks over bonds.

TABLE 7.4 Average Annual Rates of Return— Balanced Subaccounts				
Category	One Year	Three Years	Five Years	Ten Years
Balanced	17.4%	17.7%	12.0%	11.1%
S&P 500	33.4	31.1	20.3	18.0
High-yield corporate bond	12.8	13.8	10.8	10.3
Lehman Brothers Corporate Bond Index	10.2	11.7	8.4	9.9
Growth and income	26.9	26.2	18.8	15.0

Historical returns over the past one, three, five, and ten years (through 12/31/97) for balanced subaccounts in comparison with commonly used indexes and other category averages are shown in Table 7.4. All of the numbers given in the table are average annual rates of return.

The average standard deviation for balanced subaccounts is 8.0 percent, well under half the level of aggressive growth subaccounts. The equity portion of balanced subaccounts is dominated by finance stocks. The next three top sectors for this category are technology, industrial cyclicals, and service stocks.

CORPORATE BOND

Corporate bond subaccounts invest in debt instruments (IOUs) issued by corporations. These subaccounts have a wide range of maturities. The name of the subaccount will often indicate whether it is comprised of short-term or medium-term obligations. If the name of the subaccount does not include the words "short-term" or "intermediate," then the subaccount most likely invests in bonds that have average maturities of over 15 years. The greater the maturity, the more the subaccount's unit value can change.

There is an inverse relationship between interest rates and the value of a bond; when one moves up, the other goes down. The greater the bond's remaining maturity, the more its value will be altered when interest rates change. The weighted maturity date of the bonds within this group averages just under 11 years, with a typical *coupon rate* of 7 percent (coupon rate represents what the corporation pays out annually on a per-bond basis).

> **coupon rate** part of the description of a corporate, municipal, or government bond (the name of the issuer and the bond's maturity date are the other ways in which one bond is distinguished from another). The coupon rate represents how much the issuer—the corporation, municipality, or government—is paying in interest each year, based on the bond's $1000 face value (what the bond will be worth at maturity). Thus, a 5 percent bond pays 5 percent of $1000 each year ($50), a 6.5 percent bond pays $65 in interest each year, and so on.

All bonds have a maturity date—a date when the issuer (the government or corporation) pays back the face value of the bond (which is almost always $1000 per bond) and stops paying interest. There are dozens, sometimes hundreds, of different securities in any given bond subaccount. Each one of these securities (bonds in this case) has a maturity date; these maturity dates can range anywhere from a few days to up to 30 years. "Weighted maturity" refers to the time left until the average bond in the portfolio comes due (matures).

Historical returns over the past one, three, five, and ten years (through 12/31/97) for corporate bond subaccounts in comparison with commonly used indexes and other category averages are shown in Table 7.5. All of the numbers given in the table are average annual rates of return.

The average standard deviation for corporate bond subaccounts is 4.0 percent, a figure close to half the level of balanced subaccounts. This means that one's expected return for any given month, quarter, or year will be more predictable than almost any other category of variable annuity subaccounts.

TABLE 7.5 Average Annual Rates of Return— Corporate Bond Subaccounts				
Category	One Year	Three Years	Five Years	Ten Years
Corporate bond	7.8%	8.2%	5.5%	7.1%
Government bond	7.5	7.2	5.1	7.2
Global bond	1.0	7.2	4.9	6.6
Lehman Brothers Corporate Bond Index	10.2	11.7	8.4	9.9
Rate of inflation (CPI)	1.8	2.6	2.6	3.4

FIXED RATE

This is the only investment category wherein the risk is assumed by the insurer and not the contract owner. The variable annuity investor who selects this category is guaranteed a specific rate of return for a known number of years, as with a fixed-rate annuity. And, just like a fixed-rate annuity contract, the rate of return and its guaranteed duration depend on the competitiveness of the insurer, the general level of interest rates, and how long the investor is willing to tie up his or her money.

Historically, the rates of return provided by fixed-rate annuities and fixed-rate subaccounts are somewhere between what is offered by a money market fund (or U.S. Treasury bill) and long-term corporate bonds. The longer the lock-in period, the closer the rate will be to what 10- to 15-year bonds are yielding. One-, two-, and three-year periods will offer a rate that is similar to or somewhat higher than the return from a short-to-intermediate-term CD.

GLOBAL AND INTERNATIONAL STOCK

Also known as world stock subaccounts, global stock subaccounts have the ability to invest in any country, including the United States. International subaccounts, also known as foreign subaccounts, do not invest in U.S. securities (some foreign subaccounts are broadly diversified, including stocks from European as well as Pacific Basin economies, while other international subaccounts specialize in a particular region or country).

The more countries a subaccount is able to invest in, the lower its overall risk level will be; often return potential will also increase. Frequently, global (or world) funds have more than half of their assets invested in U.S. securities.

The typical price/earnings (P/E) ratio for stocks in the global category is 26, identical to that of the S&P 500. This group of subaccounts has an average beta of 0.7, meaning that its U.S. market–related risk is about 30 percent less than that of the general market, as measured by the S&P 500. Beta is not a proper measurement of market-related risk for a foreign or international variable annuity subaccount since beta does not include foreign market risk.

Historical returns over the past one, three, five, and ten years (through 12/31/97) for global and international equity subaccounts in comparison with commonly used indexes and other category averages are shown in Table 7.6. All of the numbers given in the table are average annual rates of return.

The standard deviation for global stock subaccounts is 11.0 percent, a figure that is only slightly lower than that found with the average growth subaccount. Finance stocks dominate this category of variable annuities. The next three top industry groups are industrial cyclicals, service stocks, and utility stocks.

GLOBAL BOND

International, also known as foreign, bond subaccounts invest in fixed-income securities outside of the United States. Global, or world, bond

TABLE 7.6 Average Annual Rates of Return— Global and International Stock Subaccounts				
Category	One Year	Three Years	Five Years	Ten Years
Global and international stock	4.9%	15.5%	13.6%	9.8%
Growth and income	26.9	26.2	18.8	15.0
Growth	22.1	25.4	17.3	14.8
Aggressive growth	16.4	21.2	17.8	16.7
EAFE (foreign stock)	1.8	6.3	11.4	6.3

subaccounts can invest everywhere, including the United States. Foreign bond subaccounts normally offer higher yields than their U.S. counterparts but also provide additional risk. Global bonds, on the other hand, often provide less risk than a pure U.S. bond portfolio but may also enjoy greater rates of return.

Global diversification reduces risk because the major economies around the world do not move up and down at the same time. As we climb out of a recession, Japan may be just entering one and/or Germany may still be in the middle of one. Similarly, when Italy is trying to stimulate its economy by lowering interest rates, Canada may be raising its rates in order to curtail inflation. By investing in different world bond markets, you are not at the mercy of any one country's political environment or fiscal policy.

The weighted maturity date of the bonds within this group is seven years, versus an average of 11 years for domestic corporate and government bond subaccounts. This means that this bond category has much less interest rate risk than its domestic counterparts. Global bond subaccounts have an average coupon rate of 7 percent.

Historical returns over the past one, three, five, and ten years (through 12/31/97) for global bond subaccounts in comparison with commonly used indexes and other category averages are shown in Table 7.7. All of the numbers given in the table are average annual rates of return.

The standard deviation for global bond subaccounts is 8.0 percent—a moderate figure, but one that is still about 50 percent higher than that of the typical U.S. government bond subaccount.

TABLE 7.7 Average Annual Rates of Return—Global Bond Subaccounts				
Category	One Year	Three Years	Five Years	Ten Years
Global bond	1.0%	7.2%	4.9%	6.6%
Government bond	7.5	7.2	5.1	7.2
Corporate bond	7.8	8.2	5.5	7.1
High-yield bond	12.8	13.8	10.8	10.3
Rate of inflation (CPI)	1.8	2.6	2.6	3.4

GOVERNMENT BOND

These subaccounts invest in securities issued by the U.S. government or one of its agencies (or former affiliates), such as GNMA or FNMA. Investors are attracted to bond subaccounts of all kinds because effective management can control interest rate risk by varying the average maturity of the subaccount's portfolio. If management believes that interest rates are moving downward, the subaccount will load up heavily on long-term obligations. If rates do decline, long-term bonds will appreciate more than their short- and medium-term counterparts. Such appreciation would be reflected as an increase in the subaccount's price per unit. Conversely, if the manager anticipates rate hikes, average portfolio maturity can be pared down so that there will be only modest principal deterioration if rates do go up.

Government bond subaccounts have portfolios with a wide range of maturities. Many subaccounts use their names to characterize their maturity structure. Generally, "short-term" means that the portfolio has a weighted average maturity of less than five years. "Intermediate" implies an average maturity of 5 to 15 years, and "long-term" is over 15 years. The longer the maturity, the greater the change in the subaccount's price per unit (your principal) when interest rates change. Longer-term bond subaccounts are riskier than short-term subaccounts, but tend to offer higher yields.

The weighted maturity date of the bonds within this group averages just over 11 years, with a typical coupon rate of 7 percent (representing what the government pays out annually on a per-bond basis)—figures that are virtually identical to the corporate bond category.

Historical returns over the past one, three, five, and ten years (through 12/31/97) for government bond subaccounts in comparison with commonly used indexes and another category average are shown in Table 7.8. All of the numbers given in the table are average annual rates of return.

Government bond subaccounts have an average standard deviation of 4.0 percent, a number that is the same as that of corporate bonds. This means that corporate and government bonds have similar volatilities.

GROWTH

These subaccounts seek capital appreciation with dividend income as a distant secondary concern. Indeed, the average annual income stream

TABLE 7.8 Average Annual Rates of Return—Government Bond Subaccounts

Category	One Year	Three Years	Five Years	Ten Years
Government bond	7.5%	7.2%	5.1%	7.2%
S&P 500	33.4	31.1	20.3	18.0
Global bond	1.0	7.2	4.9	6.6
Lehman Brothers Government Bond Index	9.6	10.0	7.3	8.9
Rate of inflation (CPI)	1.8	2.6	2.6	3.4

from growth subaccounts is just over 1 percent. Investors who are attracted to growth subaccounts are aiming to sell stock at a profit; they are not normally income-oriented. Growth subaccounts focus on equities from large, well-established corporations.

Unlike aggressive growth subaccounts, growth subaccounts may end up holding moderate cash positions during market declines or when investors are nervous about recent economic or market activities. The typical price/earnings (P/E) ratio for stocks in this category is 27, versus 26 for the S&P 500. This group of subaccounts has an average beta of 1.0, a figure that is the same as that of the S&P 500.

Historical returns over the past one, three, five, and ten years (through 12/31/97) for growth subaccounts in comparison with commonly used indexes and other category averages are shown in Table 7.9. All of the numbers given in the table are average annual rates of return.

The average standard deviation for growth subaccounts is 14.0 per-

TABLE 7.9 Average Annual Rates of Return—Growth Subaccounts

Category	One Year	Three Years	Five Years	Ten Years
Growth	22.1%	25.4%	17.3%	14.8%
S&P 500	33.4	31.1	20.3	18.0
EAFE (foreign stock)	1.8	6.3	11.4	6.3
Aggressive growth	16.4	21.2	17.8	16.7
Rate of inflation (CPI)	1.8	2.6	2.6	3.4

cent. Technology stocks dominate this category of variable annuities. The next three top industry groups are finance, service, and industrial cyclical stocks.

GROWTH AND INCOME

With a name like this, one would think that this category of variable annuity subaccounts is almost equally as concerned with income as it is with growth. The fact is, growth and income subaccounts have an average dividend yield that is only 0.5 percent higher than growth subaccounts (1.0 percent for growth and income versus 0.5 percent for growth subaccounts).

The typical price/earnings (P/E) ratio for stocks in this category is 24, a figure that is about 10 percent lower than that of growth subaccounts. This group of subaccounts has an average beta of just under 0.9, meaning that its market-related risk is about 10 percent less than that of the general market, as measured by the S&P 500.

Historical returns over the past one, three, five, and ten years (through 12/31/97) for growth subaccounts in comparison with commonly used indexes and other category averages are shown in Table 7.10. All of the numbers given in the table are average annual rates of return.

The average standard deviation for growth and income subaccounts is 12.0 percent, a figure that is 15 percent less than that found with the average growth subaccount. This means that, as a group, growth and income subaccounts have returns that are more predictable than growth subaccounts. Finance stocks dominate this category of variable annuities.

TABLE 7.10 Average Annual Rates of Return— Growth and Income Subaccounts				
Category	*One Year*	*Three Years*	*Five Years*	*Ten Years*
Growth and income	26.9%	26.2%	18.8%	15.0%
Growth	22.1	25.4	17.3	14.8
Aggressive growth	16.4	21.2	17.8	16.7
EAFE (foreign stock)	1.8	6.3	11.4	6.3
Rate of inflation (CPI)	1.8	2.6	2.6	3.4

The next three top industry groups are utilities, industrial cyclicals, and energy stocks.

HIGH-YIELD BOND

These subaccounts generally invest in lower-rated debt instruments. Bonds are characterized as either bank quality (also known as investment grade) bonds or junk bonds. Investment grade bonds are those bonds that are rated AAA, AA, A, or BAA. Junk bonds are those instruments rated less than BAA—ratings such as BBB, BB, B, CCC, CC, C, and D. High-yield bonds, also referred to as junk bonds, offer investors higher yields but have additional risk of default (although defaults in recent years have been running only about 1 percent annually). High-yield bonds are subject to less interest rate risk than regular corporate or government bonds. However, when the economy slows or people panic, these bonds can drop in value.

The weighted maturity date of the bonds within this group is just under nine years, less than that of high-quality corporate and government bond subaccounts. When it comes to high-yield bonds, investors are generally better off sticking with a portfolio that has an overall rating of BBB, BB, or B.

Historical returns over the past one, three, five, and ten years (through 12/31/97) for high-yield bond subaccounts in comparison with commonly used indexes and other category averages are shown in Table 7.11. All of the numbers given in the table are average annual rates of return.

TABLE 7.11 Average Annual Rates of Return—High-Yield Bond Subaccounts				
Category	One Year	Three Years	Five Years	Ten Years
High-yield bond	12.8%	13.8%	10.8%	10.3%
Government bond	7.5	7.2	5.1	7.2
Corporate bond	7.8	8.2	5.5	7.1
Balanced	17.4	17.7	12.0	11.1
Rate of inflation (CPI)	1.8	2.6	2.6	3.4

The average standard deviation for high-yield bond subaccounts is 4.0 percent, a figure that is the same as corporate and government bond subaccounts as a whole, but less than balanced subaccounts (8.0 percent).

METALS

These subaccounts invest in precious metals and mining stocks from around the world. The majority of these stocks are located in North America, South Africa, and Australia. Most of these companies specialize in the mining of gold. Some subaccounts own gold and silver bullion outright. Direct ownership of the metal is considered to be a more conservative posture than owning stocks of mining companies; these stocks are more volatile than the metal itself.

Metals subaccounts, also known as gold subaccounts, are the most speculative group represented in this book. They are considered to be sector or specialty subaccounts, types of subaccounts that are able to invest in only a single industry or country. Metals subaccounts enjoy international diversification but are still narrowly focused. It is this limitation of the subaccount that makes it so unpredictable. Usually, management can invest in only three things: mining stocks, direct metal ownership (bullion or coins), and cash equivalents.

Despite their volatile nature, gold subaccounts are included in the book because they can actually reduce portfolio risk. This happens because gold and other investments often move in opposite directions. As an example, when government bonds are moving down in value, gold subaccounts often increase in value. This is a situation wherein a wild investment becomes somewhat tame when included as part of a team effort.

The typical price/earnings (P/E) ratio for stocks in this category is 32, a figure that is about 25 percent higher than that of the S&P 500. This group of subaccounts has an average beta which is extremely low and often slightly negative (e.g., −0.3 percent), meaning that its stock market–related risk is nil—but do not let this fool you. We are talking about only *stock market* risk. Metals subaccounts, as shown by their wild track record, are anything but conservative. A negative beta indicates that this category of subaccounts often moves in a somewhat opposite direction to the S&P 500.

TABLE 7.12 Average Annual Rates of Return—Metals Subaccounts				
Category	One Year	Three Years	Five Years	Ten Years
Metals (natural resources)	–7.1%	6.5%	11.7%	–2.3%
Aggressive growth	16.4	21.2	17.8	16.7
Global stock	4.9	15.5	13.6	9.8
High-yield bond	12.8	13.8	10.8	10.3
Utilities	26.1	20.4	14.2	NA

Historical returns over the past one, three, five, and ten years (through 12/31/97) for metals subaccounts in comparison with commonly used indexes and other category averages are shown in Table 7.12. All of the numbers given in the table are average annual rates of return.

The average standard deviation for metals (gold) subaccounts is 27 percent, versus 17 percent for natural resources and 20 percent for aggressive growth.

MONEY MARKET

These subaccounts invest in short-term money market instruments, often referred to as cash equivalents. By maintaining a short average maturity, usually less than 60 days, and investing in high-quality instruments, money market subaccounts are able to maintain tremendous stability. No one has ever lost a dime in a money market subaccount. These subaccounts are designed as a place to park your money for a relatively short period of time, until conditions appear more favorable for stocks, bonds, or a fixed-rate subaccount.

This type of variable annuity subaccount is not covered further in this book because the performance record for this category is so poor. As a point of comparison, consider bank certificates of deposit (CDs)—often a major component in money market accounts and fixed-rate annuities, two popular investments. Yet, bank CDs (as well as money market subaccounts and money market mutual funds) have lost money in 15 of the past 18 years once inflation and income taxes are factored in (money in an annuity grows and compounds tax-deferred, not tax-free; eventually, income taxes must be paid by either you or your heirs).

Historical returns over the past one, three, five, and ten years (through 12/31/97) for money market subaccounts in comparison with commonly used indexes and other category averages are shown in Table 7.13. All of the numbers given in the table are average annual rates of return.

The average standard deviation for money market subaccounts is lower than any other category of subaccounts (approximately 1.0 percent).

If this type of subaccount appeals to you, a fixed-rate annuity would be a better choice under most circumstances. Information on money market subaccounts has been included here only because there are several hundred such subaccounts and it is important that you know how this category has performed. Do not make the same mistake that millions of other variable annuity investors have made by looking at money market (and CD-type investments) as something other than a temporary position.

SPECIALTY (SECTOR)

These subaccounts represent a sort of hodgepodge category that is generally regarded as quite risky or aggressive. However, when some of these subaccounts are combined with other categories shown in this chapter,

TABLE 7.13 Average Annual Rates of Return—Money Market Subaccounts				
Category	One Year	Three Years	Five Years	Ten Years
Money market	4.5%	4.5%	3.7%	4.7%
Rate of inflation (CPI)	1.8	2.6	2.6	3.4
Corporate bond	7.8	8.2	5.5	7.1
Government bond	7.5	7.2	5.1	7.2
Growth and income	26.9	26.2	18.8	15.0

one's overall risk level can be reduced (since investments like these can move in opposite directions to other, more traditional categories). The most common types of specialty subaccounts are natural resources (minerals, timber, farmland, etc.), real estate (outright ownership or investments in real estate investment trusts or real estate stocks), metals, and utilities. This broad category also includes subaccounts that invest in a single industry (i.e., banking, entertainment), region (i.e., Pacific Basin or Latin America), or country (i.e., Thailand, Mexico).

Historical returns over the past one, three, five, and ten years (through 12/31/97) for specialty subaccounts in comparison with commonly used indexes and other category averages are shown in Table 7.14. All of the numbers given in the table are average annual rates of return.

The average P/E ratio for stocks owned by specialty subaccounts is 28, a figure that is close to 10 percent higher than the P/E ratio of the S&P 500.

UTILITIES

These subaccounts invest in common stocks of utility companies. A small percentage of the subaccounts' assets are invested in bonds. Investors opposed to or in favor of nuclear power can seek out subaccounts that avoid or own such utility companies by reviewing the subaccount's annual report or by telephoning the variable annuity, using its toll-free phone number.

If you like the usual stability of a bond subaccount but want more appreciation potential, then utilities subaccounts are for you. Since these

TABLE 7.14 Average Annual Rates of Return— Specialty Subaccounts				
Category	One Year	Three Years	Five Years	Ten Years
Specialty	13.8%	15.9%	10.6%	7.6%
High-yield bond	12.8	13.8	10.8	10.3
Utilities	26.1	20.4	14.2	NA
Aggressive growth	16.4	21.2	17.8	16.7
Metals (natural resources)	−7.1	6.5	11.7	−2.3

subaccounts are interest-rate–sensitive, their performance somewhat parallels that of bonds; but it is also influenced by the stock market. The large dividend stream provided by utilities subaccounts makes them less risky than other categories of stock subaccounts. Recession-resistant demand for electricity, gas, and other utilities translates into a comparatively steady stream of returns.

Historical returns over the past one, three, five, and ten years (through 12/31/97) for utility subaccounts in comparison with commonly used indexes and other category averages are shown in Table 7.15. All of the numbers given in the table are average annual rates of return.

The average standard deviation for utilities subaccounts is 9.0 percent, a figure lower than any other equity subaccount category—30 percent lower than growth and income subaccounts, and only slightly higher than balanced subaccounts.

These outstanding results have been partially due to the general decrease in energy prices over the past several years (the largest cost incurred by a utility company) and a downward decline in interest rates (the second largest cost a utility company faces). The future direction of fuel costs and interest rates certainly cannot be predicted, but it is fairly safe to assume that one or both will increase sometime during the next few years.

ALL CATEGORIES

As you can see from these different tables, patience pays off. (See Table 7.16.) The only poor performers over the past 10 years have been metals and money market subaccounts. Metals are suited for aggressive and/or

TABLE 7.15 Average Annual Rates of Return—Utilities Subaccounts				
Category	One Year	Three Years	Five Years	Ten Years
Utilities	26.1%	20.4%	14.2%	NA
High-yield bond	12.8	13.8	10.8	10.3%
Government bond	7.5	7.2	5.1	7.2
Balanced	17.4	17.7	12.0	11.1
Rate of inflation (CPI)	1.8	2.6	2.6	3.4

TABLE 7.16 Average Annual Returns for the 10-Year Period Ending 12/31/97	
Category	10 Years
Aggressive growth	16.7%
Balanced	11.1
Corporate bond	8.6
Global and international stock	9.8
Global bond	6.6
Government bond	7.2
Growth	14.8
Growth and income	15.0
High-yield bond	10.3
Metals (natural resources)	−2.3
Money market	4.7
Specialty	NA
Utilities	NA
Average (all categories)	9.3

hard asset investors. Money market subaccounts, T-bills, and CDs should be viewed as places to temporarily park your money until market conditions change. These types of accounts are best suited to earning interest when rates are continually increasing.

STANDARD DEVIATION REVIEWED

Another important consideration is the range of returns a subaccount category has experienced. As previously mentioned, volatility, or range of returns, is represented by a subaccount or category's standard deviation. Volatility is a two-way street: It can be positive or negative. Thus, when standard deviation figures are used, a category may not be as risky as it appears if recent months' volatility has been upward.

The formula used to compute standard deviation weighs upward as well as downward volatility equally. In some cases, a subaccount or its category average may experience greater upward volatility than downward losses. I have yet to meet a client who gets upset over *upward* volatility. Still, standard deviation is at least a fair (and sometimes excellent) measure of risk. The numbers in Table 7.17 are computed from data over 36 months, ending December 31, 1997.

Notice that in every bond category except world bond, variable annuity debt subaccounts have experienced ⅓ to ⅕ the volatility of equity subaccounts (which translates into less risk according to most financial publications). At the very least, this means that when it comes to performance, debt instruments have been much more predictable than stocks.

A common theme throughout this book is that, given time, equity (the different stock categories) always outperforms debt (the different bond categories). This does not mean that all of your money should be only in different equity categories. Not everyone has the same level of patience or time horizon. It does mean that the great majority of investors need to review their portfolios and perhaps begin to emphasize domestic and foreign stocks more.

TABLE 7.17 Standard Deviations for the Three-Year Period Ending 12/31/97

Category	Standard Deviation
Aggressive growth	20%
Balanced	8
Corporate bond	4
Global and international stock	11
Government bond	4
Growth	14
Growth and income	12
High-yield bond	4
Metals	27
Utilities	9
World bond	8

PERFORMANCE STUDIES

Newspapers and periodicals that cover variable annuities focus on how a subaccount or variable annuity family has performed in the past. Studies clearly point out that a subaccount whose performance is in the top half one year has a 50–50 chance of being in the bottom half the next year, or the year after that. Since there is little correlation between the past and the future when it comes to market returns, this book concentrates on the amount of risk being taken, something that is fairly predictable from one period to the next.

According to *Barron's*, "Academics and other researchers have scoured their databanks repeatedly, searching for even a hint of evidence to support the notion that choosing funds based on historic results makes sense. And almost every time, they reach the same conclusion: Past performance helps not a whit in predicting future returns." These studies have not been done with variable annuities, but since both of these products share a great number of similarities, often including the same portfolio managers or management team, there is not a single reason to think that any such studies would result in a different conclusion.

At the beginning of 1994, Dalbar, a mutual fund consulting firm, conducted a study that sought to determine the value of buying funds with the best 10-year performance records. According to the Dalbar study, people who at the beginning of 1993 invested in the 100 best-performing stock funds (over the preceding 10 years) would have underperformed a portfolio of the 100 funds with the *worst* prior 10-year performance. The 10-year leaders returned an average 15.8 percent in 1993; the worst performers, a 22.2 percent average.

Dalbar has repeated its study for each of the past six years, again using 10-year time frames. The results have been similar, but much narrower. The "buy the best 100 funds" strategy ended up producing an average annual return of 14.2 percent; the "buy the worst" averaged 14.5 percent annually. Other studies bear out similar conclusions.

SEI, a well-known research firm, published the results of its findings in the January/February 1994 issue of *Personal Financial Planning*. SEI sought to determine whether investors were better off buying funds that had five-year track records among the top quartile of the fund universe or those which ranked in the bottom quartile. SEI's findings matched Dalbar's: "It's clear that historical performance rankings should not be the primary criterion for selecting mutual funds." If this is the case, how should one select a mutual fund or variable annuity subaccount?

First, keep in mind that performance with many categories of investments is dependent on management's investment style and experience. You want someone who has a clearly defined investment style, a seasoned person or team who has weathered bad times. Second, you should seek out portfolio managers who do not attempt to time the market. According to SEI, "Switching strategies to time the market is a major reason for underperformance." Third, and most importantly, you want to stick with investment categories (e.g., growth, high-yield bonds, international stocks, etc.) that have performed well over the long haul, not just the most recent 1- to 10-year period.

Chapter

Variable Annuities versus Mutual Funds

A s of the beginning of 1998, it was estimated that somewhere between $4 trillion and $5 trillion was invested in mutual funds, versus an estimated $300 to $600 billion for variable annuity assets. There are approximately ten thousand different mutual funds and roughly five thousand different variable annuity subaccounts. Something like 95 percent of all the money that goes into variable annuities is placed with the 100 biggest policies (contracts).

Before we begin to compare annuities and mutual funds, let's look at the traits common to both investment vehicles. Both investments are easy to invest in and monitor. Both annuities and mutual funds offer professional management. Each of these vehicles also offers an outstanding track record and several different investment options. Money can be added to or taken out of either investment at any time; both types of investment vehicles offer dollar-cost averaging and systematic withdrawal programs. Annuities and mutual funds can be started with as little as a few hundred dollars. Part or all of the investment can be moved within the family of investment options offered by the mutual fund group or variable annuity contract.

Even though there are several common traits shared by annuities and mutual funds, there are also a number of differences. These differences include: (1) commissions, (2) taxation, (3) performance, (4) withdrawal options, (5) investment choices, and (6) safety. Each of these points is discussed in the following sections.

COMMISSIONS

Most mutual funds charge some type of commission ("load") and/or an ongoing "sales and distribution charge," also known as a 12b-1 fee. The commission charged ranges anywhere from a fraction of 1 percent to 8.5 percent, most commonly 4 percent. Whatever the upfront commission, this fee is subtracted from your contribution as the investment is being made. Thus, a $5000 investment in a mutual fund may mean that only $4575 is going to work for you ($5000 minus 8.5 percent equals $4575), so you may have to make close to a 10 percent return on your money before you break even. The ongoing 12b-1 fee ranges anywhere from zero to 1.25 percent annually.

Unlike *A shares*, which charge an upfront commission, *B shares* levy a back-end sales charge, also referred to as a contingent deferred sales load (CDSL), if more than a certain amount is taken out during the first several years. Typically, the CDSL lasts for four to six years and only withdrawals in excess of 10 percent are subject to the back-end penalty. There are also a large number of mutual fund families that include what are referred to as *C shares*. With C shares there is no upfront commission and there is no back-end load or sales charge, but the account is debited 1 percent per year. Many funds are what is known as "low-load," charging an upfront commission that ranges from 1 percent to 3 percent. Approximately 40

A shares   charge an upfront commission.

B shares   charge a back-end sales fee.

C shares   no upfront or back-end commission; 1 percent is debited annually.

percent of all mutual funds do not charge a commission (referred to as "no-load" funds).

Finally, a large percentage of mutual funds that normally charge a small or regular load are offered on a noncommission (no-load) basis through brokerage firms. Such an arrangement is generically referred to as a *wrap fee account* (each firm has its own name for such a program). Under a wrap fee account, the investor never pays a commission on any mutual fund or individual securities trades but instead pays an annual fee (billed quarterly) that ranges from a fraction of 1 percent to 3 percent per year. The average yearly fee charged by the brokerage industry for wrap accounts is in the 1.5 percent range. It is quite possible that your favorite fund group offers A, B, C, *and* wrap fee shares.

wrap fee account   instead of commissions, an annual fee is billed quarterly.

The great majority of variable annuities do not charge a commission to the investor. Whenever you invest in any annuity, 100 percent of your investment goes to work for you immediately; the same is true for any additional contributions made. As an example, if you start off with $10,000 and the account grows by 20 percent during the year, your account is now worth $12,000.

By having *all* of one's money earning interest or growing, the investor can reap a higher rate of return. The 1 percent to 8.5 percent commission you might have paid to invest in a mutual fund could have been earning interest or growing in an annuity. In time, this modest amount can really make a difference.

TAXATION

When you own mutual fund shares, there are three potential sources of income tax: (1) the dividends or interest earned by the securities in the portfolio, (2) the capital gains realized whenever the fund manager sells stocks or bonds, and (3) the capital gains when *you* sell shares of your mutual fund or make an exchange within the mutual fund family. Points one and two cannot be controlled by the investor; you are at the mercy of the fund. It would be ridiculous to think that you could tell a fund not to accept a stock's dividend or the interest payment from a bond. It would be equally absurd to think that you could tell management not to sell so many stocks or bonds because you were in a high tax bracket and wanted to minimize your tax bill for the year.

The only tax aspect of a mutual fund that you can control is your purchase and sale of the fund's shares. You decide when part or all of the account should be liquidated. It is also you alone who decides whether money should be switched from the XYZ bond fund to the XYZ stock or money market fund. Unfortunately, all of these events trigger a taxable event. Some people are under the illusion that if they switch their money among funds within the same family this does not result in any taxation. This is incorrect; the IRS considers this to be a sale and subsequent purchase.

Fortunately for equity mutual fund investors, dividends and the sale of securities by the fund's management usually result in a small or modest tax consequence for two reasons. First, only 31 percent of U.S. stocks pay a dividend and the typical dividend is less than 2 percent a year. Second, the sale of appreciated securities is at least partially offset by the sale of losing stocks. Oftentimes, the winners are not sold and are kept in the portfolio. The fund's higher price per share reflects the winning stocks that are still held. The typical stock (equity) mutual fund is much more tax-efficient than the vast majority of investors suspect. Moreover, despite what you have read, there is virtually no relationship between a fund's turnover rate and its tax liability for the year.

Unfortunately for debt (bond) investors, over the long term almost all of the fund's return is due to interest payments, something that is taxable each year to the mutual fund investor. True, there have been individual years and even blocks of years when a small or even large part of the fund's total return was due to bonds being sold for a profit (or loss). And, in such cases, the investor (shareholder) would be taxed on that portion of the gain. However, it is also true that studies show that the long-term results of a bond fund are extremely similar to the yield of the bonds in the portfolio. The yield is fully taxable for the mutual fund and individual bond investor (unless municipal bonds are used).

When you invest in an annuity, money grows and compounds tax-deferred indefinitely. The only time you pay income taxes is when a withdrawal is made, and you only pay taxes on those withdrawals that are considered accumulated growth or interest, not on monies received that are considered a return of principal. Phrased another way, do you want to pay taxes on what you earn (the growth or interest) or only on what you spend (what is withdrawn)?

As economic conditions change, opportunities arise, or personal temperament changes, you may wish to become more conservative or aggressive in your investment program. In an annuity, assets can be repositioned to accommodate such changes without triggering a tax event. You do not have the dilemma of wanting to sell a security that has a low cost basis but whose future performance no longer looks good (e.g., a stock or mutual fund you bought for $10 a share that went up to $40 a share and is now sliding downward). With an annuity you can freeze your gains or limit your losses at any time without having to pay taxes.

This is where there is a real difference when comparing the tax consequences of mutual funds versus annuities. Being able to make a change from one category to another would trigger a large tax liability if there was a big gain in the price per share, even if the change was in the same fund family. Whether a potential exchange, which is actually a sale in the eyes of the IRS, triggers a small or a large taxable gain, such a consequence is unimportant to the annuity investor.

To give you an idea as to how distressing such a decision can be, let us look at an actual example. An international stock fund offered by the American Funds Group, EuroPacific Growth, began operations during 1984. Since its inception on April 16, 1984, through May 31, 1998, the fund had an average annual growth rate of 15.9 percent (after-tax rate of 14.0 percent). Using dollar figures, an initial investment of $10,000 grew to $80,600. During this 14-year period, the investor received $7942 in dividends and $16,099 in taxable capital gains (both of these figures are low for a mutual fund that invests in stocks).

Continuing the example, $3442 was paid in taxes on dividends (50 percent state and federal tax rate), plus $3923 was paid in taxes on capital gains (the old maximum bracket of 28 percent). Assuming that no shares of the fund were sold by the investor, total tax liability comes to $7365.

During this same period, the principal appreciated from $10,000 to $40,577 (a $30,577 gain). Finally, additional shares that were obtained by the reinvestment of dividends and capital gains appreciated $16,982 along the way. If the investor decided to move money out of the fund at the end of this period, either into another fund family or within the same fund group, the 28 percent capital gains tax incurred would result in a tax liability of $13,332 [(30,577 + 16,982) × 28% = $13,332]. The tough question is this: Would you, as an investor in this fund, switch your money at a cost of $13,332? This is quite a bill to pay or hurdle to jump for someone who needs money or thinks another investment looks better. The variable annuity investor would not have such a dilemma

PERFORMANCE

The track record of the best-performing variable annuities often exceeds those of the top mutual funds. (See Appendix C for a visual comparison of performance by category.) This happens because the portfolio managers of a variable annuity are overseeing a smaller pool of assets than their mutual fund counterparts, although in fact, the majority of variable annuities are managed by the same individuals and groups who oversee mutual funds. These "clone funds" have an enormous advantage over their larger brethren since being smaller they can react to market conditions more quickly. More importantly, a smaller portfolio can be more selective in the securities it buys and sells.

Most mutual funds, due to their tremendous size, are forced to buy stocks and bonds that may not be their first or even hundredth choice. This is because a diversified mutual fund is required by the SEC to follow certain rules of diversification. A variable annuity, on the other hand, can load up more heavily on those stocks and/or bonds it really wants. This is particularly true in the case of hot new issues.

A *hot new issue* is a stock offered by a company that is going public for the first time. It is considered "hot" because a number of institutional buyers have been lining up, trying to buy as much of the offering as possible. Unfortunately, there is only so much of the stock to go around. A billion-dollar mutual fund that is able to get $4 million worth of a hot new issue would be considered lucky; the same is true of an $80-million variable annuity account. If this $4 million worth of stock doubles in value, it will have very little effect on a billion-dollar mutual fund. However, it will have a very positive and dramatic effect in an $80-million portfolio.

hot new issue   stock offered by a company going public for the first time for which there is great demand.

All mutual funds keep a certain amount of their assets in cash. These reserves are partially kept on hand to satisfy investors' demands for liquidations; management does not particularly want to sell off securities in order to pay off shareholder requests. Annuities do not face this same problem since withdrawals are much less frequent. Virtually the entire portfolio can be invested in stocks and/or bonds, making the accounts operate more efficiently and thereby enhancing long-term results.

Several years ago, the *Variable Annuity Research and Data Service (VARDS) Report* calculated the performance of 85 percent of the existing variable contracts based on price appreciation and dividends minus all contract expenses. *VARDS* found that equity accounts within variable annuities generally outperformed their mutual fund counterparts by about 1 percent to 3 percent annually.

With the sometime exception of high-yield bonds, it is a rare event when bond subaccounts' performance equals or exceeds that of bond funds. This is true with domestic as well as foreign debt, short-term, intermediate-term, and long-term. Money market mutual funds always outperform variable annuity money market subaccounts. The added drag of insurance company fees makes it exceedingly difficult for subaccounts that invest in debt instruments to equal or outperform their mutual fund counterparts.

WITHDRAWAL OPTIONS

Mutual funds allow you to make withdrawals or complete liquidations at any time. The same thing is true with annuities. But only annuities offer "lifetime options" in which the investor cannot outlive the income stream. The income options that you cannot outlive were detailed in Chapter 3.

INVESTMENT CHOICES

When you invest in a mutual fund family, you are limited as to investment options and management style. Several variable annuities offer you a choice of management styles within the same contract. If you like the types of money managers found in American Century, American Funds,

Dreyfus, Fidelity, Morgan Stanley, Nationwide, Neuberger&Berman, Oppenheimer, Van Eck, and Warburg Pincus, you would have to invest your money with 10 different mutual fund families. Yet there is a single variable annuity company, Nationwide Life Insurance, that offers you the same managers. Exchanges within this variable annuity "family" can be made with one toll-free telephone call or a letter, even though you are going from Oppenheimer to Fidelity.

There are a number of variable annuities that have assembled money managers from different mutual fund companies. As the investor, you get the benefit (and talent) of several favored mutual fund managers, all under a single variable annuity.

SAFETY

Mutual funds are prohibited from offering you any type of guarantee as to the rate of return or safety of your principal. This is not true with annuities. In a fixed-rate annuity or fixed-rate subaccount within a variable annuity, you know exactly what your rate of return will be for each period, ranging from three months to 10 years. The guaranteed period depends on the option you lock into. These same annuities also guarantee that your principal is secure each and every day. Variable annuities offer the guaranteed death benefit or enhanced death benefit previously described.

No one has ever lost any principal in a variable annuity upon the death of the annuitant (and/or contract owner, depending on the wording of the contract). Fixed-rate annuities have an almost perfect track record (some people lost money in the late 1980s and early 1990s). These same statements cannot be made about mutual funds. Millions of people have lost billions of dollars in mutual funds.

MORNINGSTAR STUDIES

During the beginning months of 1992, Morningstar, a service that tracks the performance of mutual funds and variable annuities in a wide range of publications, conducted a series of studies based on performance and operating expense differences between mutual funds and variable annuities. Morningstar, considered the premier source for fund analysis, wanted to see if variable annuities were better than mutual funds given certain levels of performance and cost.

The Morningstar report began with the following observation: "Variable annuities were originally created as an aggressive alternative to fixed-rate annuities. Logically, it doesn't make much sense to switch from a fixed account to a variable annuity money market account—where yields are likely to be roughly the same, and expenses are likely to be higher. Likewise, as pension investments, variable annuities logically require an aggressive mien if they are to meet the potentially very hefty future retirement liability that they are intended to fund (it is estimated that the average 65-year-old retiree can expect to live to age 85—requiring a substantial nest egg to maintain his or her preretirement standard of living)." Using these comments as a backdrop to the Morningstar studies, let us now see what happened when certain assumptions were used.

Morningstar looked at the operating expenses of variable annuities versus mutual funds. According to Morningstar, the typical mutual fund charged 1.25 percent annually for operating expenses while a similar variable annuity charged 0.77 percent, meaning that variable annuities were 38 percent more efficient in this area. On the other hand, variable annuities charged an average 1.25 percent for mortality (the guaranteed death benefit), something not found with mutual funds. Factoring in this extra expense, variable annuities are, on average, 0.77 percent more expensive to run each year than mutual funds for the period covered by the study.

The Morningstar studies assumed the following set of circumstances: (1) a variable annuity and mutual fund averaged a 15 percent annual return; (2) the investor was in a 37.4 percent tax bracket (state and federal tax combined); (3) there were no surrender charges for the annuity or mutual fund owner; (4) there was no penalty tax for the annuity owner; and (5) money was distributed from the annuity by annuitization or when the contract owner was in a 21.4 percent tax bracket. (*Note:* Morningstar assumed that the investor was in a lower tax bracket once income was needed.) Given these circumstances, the variable annuity became a better investment after only two to three years. In fact, it took only two years for a subaccount to begin to outpace a comparable mutual fund; the time horizon stretched out to five years if 5 percent rates of return were used.

Surprisingly, the Morningstar studies show that, based on actual performance of U.S. stock subaccounts (aggressive growth, growth, and growth and income) and their mutual fund counterparts, variable annuities still came out ahead after just five years, even assuming a 37.4 percent tax rate during accumulation (for the mutual fund owner) and 37.4 percent during the distribution period (for the annuity owner). In fact, even under the worst-case situation—high distribution taxes and a 10 percent IRS penalty—aggressive growth portfolios still beat aggressive growth mutual funds after nine years (the 10 percent penalty applies to only investors who are younger than $59\frac{1}{2}$ or are not disabled).

Looking at other categories, we see that annuities maintained their winning streak (again assuming a 15 percent annual return, a 37.4 percent accumulation tax rate for the mutual fund owner, a distribution tax rate of 21.4 percent for the annuity owner, and no surrender charges or IRS penalty). High-yield bond subaccounts and international stock subaccounts outperformed their mutual fund brethren in less than four years (less than two years if annual returns were 10 percent). Keeping the same assumptions except with 12 percent returns all around, growth, growth and income, and balanced portfolios also came out ahead after just two years. Even using just a 5 percent return, variable annuities became the winners within four years. Using actual performance figures of government and corporate bond subaccounts, again, versus mutual funds with similar objectives, variable annuities took the lead in just two years.

The figures described in the previous paragraphs will come as a surprise to the majority of investment advisers due to the hurdle of the insurance expense incurred by the different variable annuity subaccounts. The reason why variable annuities fared so well across the board is that such mortality costs are often only modest once you factor in the cheaper management and administrative expenses experienced by variable annuities versus similar mutual funds, plus the Morningstar studies assumed the complete sale and liquidation of all mutual fund shares.

TAX RELIEF 1997

A reduction in capital gains rates, and with it new multiple tax rates, brought a debate over whether it makes more sense to invest in a variable annuity or in a mutual fund. An analysis by a major international actuarial firm as to the accuracies of projections used plus a determination as to the reasonableness of such assumptions by an investment law firm provided some interesting conclusions. Before going into the findings of this analysis, let us quickly review capital gains rates as they stand as of the beginning of 1998.

For Assets Held . . .	*The Maximum Federal Tax Rate Is . . .*
Under one year	39.6 percent
12 months or more	20 percent
Five years or more (beginning in the year 2001)	18 percent

The analysis considered three different investment blends: (1) growth, (2) balanced, and (3) income; considered both systematic withdrawals of various sizes and annuitization with the variable annuity; and used real-world assumptions as to different tax brackets, ages, and investor behaviors. Three major questions were considered:

1. How does the account grow? (What percentage is short-term and what percentage is long-term?)
2. How are the distributions taxed?
3. What is the net (after-tax) payout?

According to the analysis:

✔ If death occurred during the growth period (before withdrawals), the variable annuity had a net payout higher than the income-oriented mutual fund but lower than the growth or balanced mutual fund.

✔ After-tax lump-sum withdrawals from the annuity were usually greater than those of the income or balanced mutual fund, but less than those from the growth-oriented fund (largely due to the benefit received by the growth fund from lower long-term capital gains taxes).

✔ The vehicle for systematic withdrawals depended entirely on the size of the withdrawal and the type of withdrawal.

✔ Dying, after substantial years of systematic withdrawals from either a variable annuity or a mutual fund, brought more benefit to the estate with a mutual fund for smaller withdrawal amounts; the variable annuity was better for the estate if large amounts were taken out prior to death.

✔ When using annuitization, the variable annuity outperformed the growth, balanced, and income-oriented mutual funds.

Chapter

Equity-Indexed
Annuities

An equity-indexed annuity (EIA) provides the investor (contract owner) with participation in the stock market without any downside market risk. This means that there is no such thing as a losing or negative period.

Equity-indexed annuities have been offered in Europe for a number of years but have been available in the United States only since the mid-1990s. For U.S. investors, stock market participation is usually linked to the S&P 500. One would therefore think that such an equity instrument would be classified as a *variable* annuity; yet, most equity-indexed annuities are fixed-rate contracts.

In a fixed-rate annuity, the insurer (the company offering the investment product): (1) guarantees a rate of return for a specified period of time (the rate is usually similar to what a bank CD pays); (2) guarantees a minimum rate of return for any period(s) after the specified period of time has elapsed (the minimum rate is typically 4 percent); and (3) guarantees the investor's principal at all times. In short, the insurer bears any and all investment risk.

In a variable annuity: (1) all investment risk is assumed by the investor; (2) money is invested in one or more subaccounts, similar to the choices found in a mutual fund family; and (3) investment choices range from very conservative (e.g., a guaranteed rate of return for one or more years or a short-term U.S. government bond portfolio) to aggressive (e.g., a small-cap growth portfolio or a subaccount that invests in only Pacific Basin stocks). The investor bears any and all market reward and risk (except if a fixed-rate subaccount is selected).

Equity-indexed annuities have all of the features of most fixed-rate annuity contracts except the interest credited to the investor's account is linked to a well-known market index, usually the S&P 500. And, unlike a variable annuity held for the contracted period of time, an EIA held for its contracted period of time cannot decrease in value. Besides having a fixed minimum guarantee (somewhat similar to a fixed-rate contract), the value of the investor's account can only increase due to stock market appreciation. It can never decline in value due to a flat or declining market.

All deferred annuities, including EIAs, have the following 15 features:

1. The annuity has a contract.

2. There are four parties to every contract—the contract owner, the beneficiary, the annuitant, and the issuer (the insurance company).

3. Growth is tax-deferred.

4. Free partial withdrawals can be made at any time.

5. Withdrawals in excess of the free withdrawal privilege are usually subject to an insurance company penalty.

6. The insurance company penalty typically ranges from zero to eight years.

7. Withdrawals are considered to be ordinary income and do not qualify for the more favorable capital gains tax rates.

8. Only withdrawals of growth and/or interest are subject to taxation.

9. Withdrawal(s) of principal are not taxable.

10. All income and/or growth must be withdrawn first.

11. Income and/or growth withdrawn prior to the contract owner reaching age $59\frac{1}{2}$ is subject to a 10 percent IRS penalty unless the contract owner has died, become disabled, or annuitized the contract.

12. Tax-favored income is possible if the contract is annuitized.

13. Annuitization means that part of each check received is considered principal (not taxed) and the remainder is considered to be interest or growth (taxed).

14. There is a guarantee of principal at all times (for a fixed-rate annuity) or a guaranteed death benefit (for variable annuities).

15. There is a probate-free death benefit (unless the contract owner names his or her estate as the beneficiary).

Figuring out the terminology, how returns are calculated, and what type of EIA, if any, is best for you makes the EIA a rather complex investment product. We will begin with the different phrases used exclusively with an equity-indexed annuity contract.

TERMS TO KNOW

In addition to the standard language found in a fixed-rate annuity, there are seven words or phrases that are important for the prospective EIA investor to understand: (1) term, (2) participation rate, (3) index credit period, (4) administrative fee, (5) cap rate, (6) floor, and (7) reference or contract value.

Term

The term of the contract refers to how long the insurance company's penalty lasts or when the investor has the option to renew the contract. The most common term for an EIA is between three and seven years. Some contracts are for as little as one year; a few last as long as 10 years.

Participation Rate

The *participation rate* is one of the most important as well as distinguishing features of the EIA contract. Sometimes called the index rate, the participation rate refers to the percentage increase in the S&P 500 that the investment will grow by (e.g., "80 percent of the S&P 500's increase for any given calendar year"). Used by itself, the participation rate means that the investor is most likely going to receive some figure less than what the S&P 500 increases for the contract period (also see "cap rate" below).

> **participation rate** also known as the index rate; refers to the percentage increase in the S&P 500 that the investment (equity-indexed annuity) will grow by.

The impact of the participation rate increases as the S&P 500 Index goes up. As an example, if the index goes up 10 percent and there is an 85 percent participation rate, there is a 1.5 percent difference between what the index did and what is initially credited to the investor's account (10 percent minus 8.5 percent equals 1.5 percent). Yet, if the index increases by 20 percent, the reduction in the amount credited jumps from 1.5 percent to 3 percent (85 percent of 20 percent is 17 percent; 20 percent minus 17 percent equals 3 percent).

Index Credit Period

The index credit period is perhaps the biggest difference between traditional fixed-rate annuities and EIAs. *The amount that is credited to the investor is done at specific points in time.* This amount, or credit, is based on the increase to the index that takes place between defined points in time (e.g., the difference in the S&P 500 from January 1, 1998, to January 1, 2002). The defined point in time is also known as the "current crediting rate" (this concept is discussed in detail in a later section titled, "Different Index Credit Periods and Methods").

Administrative Fee

The administrative fee, sometimes known as the annual fee, spread yield, or expense load, is a reduction from the increase in the S&P 500. This reduction is a fixed rate that is subtracted by the insurer (e.g., "The contract owner will receive 100 percent of the increase in the S&P 500 for the period measured after first deducting 1 percent from the increase in the Index").

There is usually an administrative fee on contracts that have a 100 percent participation rate. This means that if the participation rate is less than 100 percent, there is a strong likelihood that there is no administrative (or expense) fee. If there is such a fee, it ranges from 1 percent to 2.25 percent annually. Table 9.1 illustrates this point.

Cap Rate

The *cap rate* is the annual maximum percentage increase allowed. The cap rate, along with the participation rate, are ways in which the insurer is able to reduce the costs of offering this product with its fixed minimum guarantee—that is, making sure that the investor does not have a losing period when the S&P 500 Index goes down. Not every EIA has a cap rate.

 cap rate the annual maximum percentage increase allowed for an equity-indexed annuity.

Floor

The *floor* refers to the minimum amount that will be credited to the investor, irrespective of the index's performance. The floor is frequently 3 percent per year, but may be as low as zero during periods of low interest rates (a concept more fully explained later).

TABLE 9.1 Administrative Fees and Participation Rates			
Percent of Index Credited	Index Increase	Administrative Fee	Effective Annual Yield
90%	12%	0.00%	10.80%
100	12	1.00	11.00
100	12	2.25	9.75

floor the minimum amount credited to the investor, regardless of the index's performance.

Reference or Contract Value

When all is said and done, the bottom line is the reference or contract value. The investor is always entitled to the greater of the current account value (minus any surrender charges that may still remain) or the investor's principal. What is frequently found in an EIA is a contract value that equals 90 percent of all dollars invested plus 3 percent compounded annually. Some contract value equations include a figure higher or lower than 90 percent. The purpose of the reference or contract value is to provide the investor with an additional guarantee: No matter how much the stock market may go down or remain flat each and every year, the value of the contract will increase if the investment is held for the agreed-upon period.

THE TRADE-OFF

In order the reduce the cost of this product, the insurer must make certain compromises. This means that the higher the participation rate, the lower the cap (the maximum that the account will grow during the period, regardless of how well the stock market performs). Some examples of this compromise are:

- ✔ "90 percent participation rate in the S&P 500 with a 13 percent cap."

- ✔ "80 percent participation rate in the S&P 500 with a 14 percent cap."

- ✔ "75 percent participation rate in the S&P 500 with no cap."

DIFFERENT INDEX CREDIT PERIODS AND METHODS

Even though the objective of all EIAs may be the same (stock market participation with downside protection), this insurance product is offered in many different forms (contracts). How the EIA is structured by the in-surer impacts the amount and timing of the investor's gains. Every EIA product limits the amount of gain, through either its participation rate, cap rate, the administrative fee, *liquidity* (when the investor has access to the money, how much money he or she has access to, and whether there is a penalty involved), or how the index credit period is calculated.

liquidity   the ability to get back all, or almost all of your investment at any time. Money market funds, certificates of deposit, passbook savings accounts, and U.S. Treasury bills have a great deal of liquidity. Whereas long-term bonds, real estate, collectibles, and stocks may be quite marketable, their liquidity can range from excellent to poor (since value can fluctuate quite a bit in a relatively short period of time).

Comparing EIA products is difficult because few, if any, of these in-surance products are exactly alike. Fortunately for comparison purposes, all of the differences in the index credit periods and methods fall into one of three broad categories: annual reset, point-to-point, and annual high-water mark with look-back.

Annual Reset

Appreciation in the S&P 500 is based on the anniversary date (when your investment begins). This means that the *annual reset* is calculated by tak-ing the ending value of the index 365 days after the investment began, and subtracting from it the value of the index at the end of the first day (the anniversary date). The difference between these two points, as mea-sured in percentage terms, is how much the investor's account is credited (minus any administrative fees, multiplied by the participation rate, and subject to any upward cap rate).

Volatility during the year is unimportant; the annual reset method, also known as the annual ratchet method, is concerned only with two index figures, one at the beginning of the year and one at the very end of the year. This also means that any compounding is done on an an-nual basis. A few examples may prove useful. Table 9.2 assumes that

TABLE 9.2 Using the Annual Reset Method to Calculate Gains		
Calendar Year	*Change in S&P 500*	*Increase in Account**
1998	$(660 - 550) \div 550 = 20\%$	20%
1999	$(660 - 627) \div 660 = -5\%$	0 (no change)
2000	$(690 - 627) \div 627 = 10\%$	10

*Before any deductions for expenses, participation rate, or cap rate adjustments.

the S&P 500 was at 550 on January 1, 1998, the contract's anniversary date.

annual reset used to determine annually how much is credited to the equity-indexed annuity investor's account, based on beginning and ending values of the S&P 500.

For 1998, the example assumes S&P 500 increased 20 percent and had an ending value of 660. For 1999, any gains or losses are based on a new starting point, what the S&P 500 Index was at the very beginning of the year (660 in this example). In the example, the S&P 500 declines from 660 to 627 during the year. Even though this represents a 5 percent loss, the value of the account does not decline and maintains any gains from previous calendar years. The beginning of the year 2000 has a new starting point (627 in this example), so any percentage change, just like any other year, is based on the value of the index on January 1. For the year 2000, the index rose 10 percent (from 627 to 690).

In dollar terms, an initial investment of $100,000 grew to $120,000 at the end of year one, stayed at $120,000 at the end of year two, and then went to $132,000 by the end of the third year ($120,000 plus a 10 percent increase).

To get a better idea as to how a participation and cap rate work, let us continue with this example and assume that this particular EIA contract has a 90 percent participation rate and a 15 percent cap rate (see Table 9.3).

This means that if the EIA had a beginning balance of $100,000 on

| | | Change Due to | Amount |
| Increase | Multiplied by | 15 Percent | Earned by |
in Account	Participation Rate	Cap Rate	Investor
1998: 20%	90% of 20% = 18%	–3%	15%
1999: 0%	90% of 0% = 0%	0	0
2000: 10%	90% of 10% = 9%	0	9

TABLE 9.3　Using Participation and Cap Rates

January 1, 1998, the contract value would be $115,000 at the end of the year (a 15 percent increase), $115,000 at the end of 1999 (no increase), and $125,350 ($115,000 plus 9 percent) at the end of the year 2000 (a 9 percent increase).

As you can see from this example, the annual reset method allows investors to profit after a bad year. In fact, investors who are in contracts using this method of calculating gains may even hope for a negative year (since next year's starting point, the S&P 500 Index, would be even lower, making it more likely for there to be a recovery). As you will see, using the other common methods of calculation (point-to-point and annual high-water mark with look-back), no new gains can be made until the S&P 500 Index exceeds whatever the previous high was since the inception of the contract.

Despite some amazingly good years for U.S. stocks over the past 15 years, a higher participation rate should be viewed more favorably than a high cap rate. U.S. stocks have averaged 12 percent over the past 50 years. Looking at the historical distribution of returns over the past half century, the vast majority of annual returns have been below 15 percent. Thus, more often than not, it would seem to make sense to keep more (a higher participation rate) of what is earned most years than to accept less during those years with the hope that the market will experience 15 percent to 30 percent returns (which would be reduced by quite a bit due to the lower participation rate).

Financial writers who describe EIAs sometimes use a chart that shows the performance of the S&P 500 over a period of time divided into three zones: (1) zone one represents the beginning of the investment and shows the S&P 500 moving up; (2) zone two starts where zone one leaves off, but then the index falls to a point below the starting point; and (3) zone three includes a period of time when the S&P 500 surpasses the high point reached in zone one. The purpose of the zone illustration is to provide the reader (or prospective investor) with a visual depiction of possible stock market activity to see whether the method used to compute gains results in a gain in zone one, zone two, and/or zone three.

One of the advantages of the annual reset method is that there is a profit possibility in all three zones (when the market is going up, when it drops below its original starting value, and when it then climbs past the previous high point).

Point-to-Point

The *point-to-point* measurement is very straightforward: Volatility from day to day or even from year to year is unimportant; any and all crediting is based on only the beginning value of the index and its ending value at the end of the term (which is typically five years, but may be more or less). Like the annual reset method, the beginning of the term is referred to as the anniversary date.

point-to-point   used to determine the account's credit by subtracting the value of the S&P at the end of the term from the beginning value.

Using the same example (and therefore assuming a term of exactly three years and an anniversary date of January 1, 1998), notice in Table 9.4 the modest difference in returns for the same period of time.

The point-to-point method of calculating gains results in a 23 percent increase (remember: only the beginning and ending value of the index is used) versus a 25 percent increase for the contract using the annual reset method ($100,000 growing to $125,350). At this point, it appears that the annual reset method is better, but this is not necessarily the case.

Contracts that employ the point-to-point method of calculating gains usually have a higher participation rate than annual reset contracts. Secondly, what is true for one period of time in the market may not be true during a different type of market.

TABLE 9.4 Using the Point-to-Point Method		
Calendar Year	Change in S&P 500	Increase in Account*
1998	Increase from 550 to 660	0%
1999	Decrease from 660 to 627	0
2000	Increase from 627 to 690	0
	(690 – 550) ÷ 600	23

*Before any deductions for expenses, participation rate, or cap rate adjustments.

Point-to-point is appropriate for the investor looking at a specific future point in time. This investor (contract owner) does not care about interim values, only the value of the index at the end of a specific number of years (the contract period).

Annual High-Water Mark with Look-Back

This method is somewhat similar to point-to-point except with the *annual high-water mark with look-back* method the highest anniversary value is used to calculate the gain. Thus, over a five-year term, if the S&P 500 peaks at the end of year two and never surpasses that peak at the end of years three, four, or five, the value at the end of year two is used. Let us look at an example to see what kind of increase there is using the annual high-water mark with look-back method. We will assume that the contract (investment) began on January 1, 1998 (this also means that the starting point or anniversary date for calculation is the 1997 year-end value of 550).

annual high-water mark with look-back   credit on an equity-indexed annuity is calculated by using the highest anniversary value.

As you can see from Table 9.5, the client's account is credited with any new year-end high in the S&P 500; a new high only occurred at the

Calendar Year	Year-End Value of S&P 500	Cumulative Account Increase
1997	550	
1998	660	20%
1999	690	20
2000	610	20
2001	635	20
2002	623	20

TABLE 9.5   Using the Annual High-Water Mark with Look-Back Method

end of 1998. Such crediting allows the investor access to at least part of the account's annual increase, subject to the contract's vesting schedule (vesting is described later in this chapter).

Generally the annual high-water mark with look-back method is more liquid than the point-to-point method and less liquid than the annual reset method. One nice feature of the annual high-water mark with look-back is that it does not have a cap rate (meaning that during extremely good years, when the S&P 500 might increase 20 percent to 35 percent, the investor is credited the full gain, subject to any participation rate and minus any administrative fee).

Using the highest point of the S&P 500 for each policy year may sound quite appealing, but some policies using this method of calculation credit the account only on the very last day of the term, which may be several years. This means that if the owner dies, cashes in, or annuitizes the contract prior to that last day, the value of the contract being distributed may be based on only the minimum guaranteed value (usually 3 percent as described later in this chapter). Remember, such a harsh result occurs with a few EIA contracts that use the annual high-water mark with look-back method of calculation.

The investment's return is determined at the end of the contract period. If such a period was six years, the highest values for each of those six years (which would be based on an anniversary date and not a calendar year) would be compared. The value of the index at the end of the very first day of the contract (the original anniversary date) would then be subtracted from the highest single value of the index. The resulting figure is then divided by the beginning value of the index to determine the overall percentage gain. Thus, if the beginning value of the S&P 500 were 800 and the highest value during the six-year term were 1200, the overall gain would be 50 percent (1200 minus 800 equals 400; 400 divided by 800 equals 50 percent).

The high-water mark method, like point-to-point, is concerned with only two dates: the first day of the contract and a particular anniversary value. The only difference between the two methods is that the high-water mark method is looking at several anniversary values and then selecting the one that is the greatest. Unlike the point-to-point client, the high-water mark client has many chances to hit a high point, just like the annual reset investor. However, the point-to-point contract usually has a higher participation rate than the other two methods.

POINTS TO REMEMBER

How much an investor actually earns (known as the *index benefit*) depends on four things:

1. The index used, which is usually the S&P 500, and how much it increases.
2. The participation rate (what percentage of the gain you are entitled to).
3. What index credit period and method is used.
4. If there is a cap, the cap rate (which is relevant only during a very good period).

   index benefit how much an investor actually earns.

An EIA contract that results in comparatively lower index increases often has a higher participation rate; some participation rates are higher than 100 percent and have no cap. Keep in mind that like any other investment, a specific EIA must give up some things in order to provide other benefits. You cannot tell which EIA contract is better than another simply by looking at one component of the equation. The index benefit depends on the four things just mentioned plus the kind of stock market that is experienced during the contract period.

DIFFERENT TYPES OF STOCK MARKET EXPERIENCES

As for what index credit method is best (annual reset, point-to-point, or annual high-water mark with look-back), one must also consider what kind of stock market experience is to be expected for the next several years. The following are generalities and should not be considered absolutes or used without considering other aspects of the EIA contract.

✔ *Annual reset is best during a typical or average stock market.* The 10-year period from late 1955 until the end of 1964 is about as close as you can get to an "average" market. Annual reset also turns in the best results if there is a single year during the period when the market drops quite a bit (as it did in 1973 and 1974).

✔ *Point-to-point is best when the market has a very high number of good years.* Such a period could also be described as a very strong bull market. Pretty much any 10-year period starting in late 1982 through 1988 (meaning an ending period of 1991 through 1997) could be described as a strong bull market. *Point-to-point is also best if there is a dramatic single-year upswing in the index.* If you began with a low point, say the end of 1980 or 1981, and your contract used a typical three- to seven-year period, you would have ended up with a very nice gain.

✔ *Annual high-water mark with look-back is often best when there is quite a bit of volatility in the market—a period when the market has lots of up and down years.* The years from 1957 through 1966 are an excellent example of such volatility. During such periods, the annual reset and point-to-point methods can produce somewhat similar returns.

CAN YOU BEAT THE MARKET?

Because of the participation rate and cap rate, the question is often raised as to whether the investor can approximate, equal, or even exceed the stock market's performance. The answer is yes.

During a strong bull market, the returns from the S&P 500 and the index benefit (what the investor ends up with) can be extremely close—using the annual reset method.

During a contract period when the market has an extremely strong year, the index benefit can be slightly higher than the S&P 500—using the point-to-point method.

When the market goes through a very bad year, the index benefit can be substantially higher than the S&P 500—using the annual reset or annual high-water mark with look-back method.

Finally, during a period that includes quite a bit of volatility (several up and down years), the index benefit can result in better returns than the S&P 500—using the annual high-water mark with look-back method (annual reset and point-to-point are fairly close).

AVERAGING

Regardless of what index credit method is used, quite a few EIA contracts will determine any increase based on the index's average value over a specified period of time. Thus, you could have a product that used the annual reset method but did not use the year-end value of the index. Instead, such a product might use the monthly changes in the S&P 500 and then average such changes (e.g., add up all 12 month-end figures, divide by 12, and then subtract the starting point from this figure. As an example, suppose the S&P 500 had the following month-end values for the year:

January	800
February	820
March	815
April	830
May	820
June	810
July	825
August	835
September	840
October	855
November	855
December	880

Adding up all of these numbers equals 9985; 9985 divided by 12 equals 832; 832 minus 790 (we will assume that the S&P 500 Index was 790 on December 31 of the previous year) equals 42; and 42 divided by 790 (the starting point) equals 5.3 percent. Using the annual reset method *without averaging* would result in a gain of 11.4 percent for the same year (880 minus 790 equals 90; 90 divided by 790 equals 11.4 percent).

As one might suspect, averaging smooths out the ups and downs of the stock market, and may be beneficial during years that include several downward months. However, if the market is moving upward overall, results are dampened and the investor's gains can be reduced by quite a bit. During a year when the market starts moving upward and then trends downward there could be some gains with averaging, whereas there might not be registered gains using other calculation methods. Keep in mind that over the past 100 years, about one in every four years has been a down year.

In order to make the playing field more level, EIA contracts that use some form of averaging often have no cap rate and may have a participation rate that is close to or even exceeds 100 percent. Thus, in the example just given, the annual reset contract using averaging might have its results bumped up from 5.3 percent to, say, 6.4 percent (if a 120 percent participation rate were used) and the annual reset contract without averaging could have its index credit reduced from 11.4 percent to 8.6 percent (if a 75 percent participation rate were used).

As previously mentioned, some EIA contracts limit the annual S&P 500 increase to a maximum percentage (the cap rate), such as 14 percent. This limit is on a per annum basis, meaning that if the index goes up 4 percent in year one, 12 percent in year two, and 20 percent in year three, the maximum increase credited in year three would be 14 percent, even though the average annual return for these three years was 12 percent (4 percent plus 12 percent plus 20 percent equals 36 percent; 36 percent divided by 3 equals 12 percent).

DON'T FORGET THE ADMINISTRATIVE FEE

Another way the investor's return from the S&P 500 is reduced is by the insurer deducting a flat or fixed percentage just before crediting the account. Also known as an annual fee, spread yield, or expense load, the administrative fee may or may not be fixed (guaranteed) for the contract period. An administrative fee may be used with any type of EIA.

WHEN INVESTMENTS CAN BE MADE

Most EIA contracts, like most traditional fixed-rate annuities, allow only a onetime investment, referred to as a single premium. This means that if you want to add more money, you will have to enter into another contract with the same or a different insurer. Obviously, the terms of such a contract may be different from the original, even if the second policy is issued by the same insurance company. The minimum single premium allowed generally ranges from $5000 to $10,000 for nonqualified money and is $2000 for qualified accounts such as IRAs, Keoghs, and 401(k) plans.

Some companies have what is referred to as a flexible premium. This means that additions can be made to the same (original) contract. These companies may even let you set up a systematic payment plan wherein as little as $100 per deposit is allowed.

LIQUIDITY

For a number of investors accessibility to one's principal and/or gain(s) is important. Some EIA contracts limit withdrawals by having a *vesting schedule* (e.g., "you can take out up to 20 percent of the contract's value each year without penalty") or a surrender charge. Eventually such limitations end, but it is important for the investor to know when, and how much, of the contract can by freely liquidated.

vesting schedule   outlines the amount that can be withdrawn yearly without penalty.

Oftentimes, EIAs that use averaging or point-to-point methods of calculating gains have very limited liquidity during the contract period since any gains are not calculated until the end of the period. This means that the investor may have to wait four to eight years before he or she realizes the fruits of the stock market. On the other hand, a contract that computes gains using the annual reset method can calculate and credit gains at the end of each year and therefore often provide the greatest liquidity.

Even though gains (crediting) may be calculated comparatively frequently, this still does not mean that the investor has access to such gains until the very end of contract (its term). Such illiquidity of gains is accomplished by having a surrender penalty that equals any and all index gains or by having a vesting schedule that stays at zero percent until the end of the term.

Monies are normally available without any type of insurance company penalty (no surrender charge) or any other kind of adjustment at the end of the contract period. A number of EIA contracts also permit free withdrawals if the contract owner becomes terminally ill or confined to a nursing home. Upon the death of the annuitant (and/or contract owner, depending on how the contract is worded), there are no surrender charges; the beneficiary receives the then-current value of the contract and probate is avoided.

WHAT DOES "FREE WITHDRAWAL" MEAN?

A common phrase in an annuity contract reads, "The investor may take out up to 10 percent per year without penalty. After the penalty period expires, any amount may be withdrawn without penalty." The typical penalty period lasts approximately seven years. The question then becomes, what is the 10 percent based on? Is it 10 percent of the original principal, or is it 10 percent of the principal plus any amount credited to the contract, or is it 10 percent of the minimum guaranteed value (which is usually 90 percent of the original principal, increased by 3 percent each year)?

WITHDRAWALS AND INCREASES

Any withdrawal made by the investor during the contract period (when gains are computed) can greatly affect overall returns, particularly when compared to a contract that experiences no withdrawals during its contract period. To better illustrate this point, let us look at the three most commonly used methods for calculating gains.

With the annual reset design (credit to the account is based on the year-end value of the S&P 500, from which is subtracted the previous year's ending value), any withdrawal made during the year would not be available or credited with that year's gains. Since the sum was withdrawn even as late as the second-to-the-last day of the year, it is no longer part of the investment. Fortunately, any gains already credited to the contract from previous years are not subtracted or prorated against any subsequent withdrawals.

Since the point-to-point method of calculation can be determined only at the end of the contract period (since a new high in the index may be reached on the last day of the period), any and all gains that would normally be applied to the withdrawn amount are lost.

Using the annual high-water mark with look-back method, the investor is entitled to any gains credited to the account, but any withdrawals are not entitled to any subsequent high-water mark (new high in the market).

THE MINIMUM GUARANTEE SURRENDER VALUE

In order to fulfill requirements of the National Association of Insurance Commissioners (NAIC), a certain level of protection must be afforded to all EIA investors. These state insurance commissioners regulate insurance companies that do business in their respective states; such regulation oversees life insurance as well as annuity products.

The most commonly used method states that regardless of when a contract is liquidated (i.e., whether the contract is one day old or several years old), the investor must be able to get at least 90 percent of what was invested plus 3 percent per year. This means that under the worst-case situation, the investment is made whole by the end of the fourth year; however, any remaining surrender charges may be subtracted from the contract's value (or from the dollar figures shown in Table 9.6), depending on the contract's provisions.

Table 9.6 shows how the minimum guarantee works. The illustration assumes a onetime investment of $100,000 and a minimum guarantee of 90 percent of that plus 3 percent per year.

SURRENDER CHARGES

Monies taken out in excess of any free withdrawal provisions are normally subject to a surrender charge. This charge lasts for the term of the con-

End of Year . . .	Guaranteed Account Value	Percent of Deposit	Effective Annual Yield
1	$ 92,700	92.7%	−7.30%
2	95,481	95.5	−2.29
3	98,345	98.3	−0.55
4	101,296	101.3	0.32
5	104,335	104.3	0.85
6	107,465	107.5	1.21
7	110,689	110.7	1.46
8	114,009	114.0	1.65
9	117,430	117.4	1.80
10	120,952	121.0	1.92

TABLE 9.6 How the Minimum Guarantee Works

tract and usually remains level, unlike most other fixed-rate or variable annuity contracts that frequently have a declining surrender charge. The surrender charge for an EIA is typically higher than similar charges for a variable annuity or traditional fixed-rate annuity.

If the EIA contract (policy) has no stated surrender charges, it is extremely likely that any credited index increases are subject to a vesting schedule that might even be greater than a surrender charge. Vesting schedules and surrender charges are necessary in order to make sure money stays with the insurer during bear markets. Surrender charges and/or vesting schedules (if any) normally last for the duration of the term (contract period).

THE CONTRACT PERIOD

The term of the investment, referred to as the contract period, lasts from one to 10 years. At the end of the term, the contract owner usually has up to 30 days to access part or all of the contract value without charge or fee. There is a strong likelihood that any monies not withdrawn or transferred to another annuity (what is known as a 1035 or tax-free exchange since no taxable event is triggered) would automatically be rolled over into a similar annuity with the same company. There is no guarantee that the new contract would have the same provisions or be better or worse than the one that had just ended.

GUARANTEES

The participation rate, the cap rate, and stated expenses of the policy may be guaranteed only for the first year and then be subject to possible change. When comparing prospective policies, check to see how long the guarantees last. There is obviously a strong preference to having any and all important guarantees last for the duration of the contract period. One policy reviewed has an 85 percent participation rate for the first year that can drop to as low as 30 percent in later years.

VESTING

Any increases in the contract's value that are based on the performance of the S&P 500 may not be completely available to the investor when such crediting takes place. A vesting schedule may be structured so that if the investor wishes to make a partial or full withdrawal prior to the end of the contract period, he or she is entitled to only a percentage of those increases. For example, a vesting schedule could allow withdrawals of up to 20 percent the first year, 40 percent the second year, 60 percent the third year, 80 percent the fourth year, and 100 percent the fifth year.

Some EIA contracts have zero vesting (none of the index gains can be taken out early) until the end of the contract, which may be up to seven years from the date of the premium deposit (the original anniversary date). If the owner makes a withdrawal before such a date, the entire increase in the S&P 500 might be lost for the amount that represents the withdrawal.

THE DEATH BENEFIT

When the contract owner dies (or annuitant with certain contracts) there is a death benefit. There can be a huge difference in how the death benefit is determined from one EIA to another. Some contracts may have a death benefit that is quite small: The beneficiary gets an amount equal to the guaranteed minimum (which would be less than the initial investment if death occurred during the first three and a half years). Other contracts are much more equitable (since death is not usually considered a voluntary event): The beneficiary gets an amount equal to the most recently credited period, also referred to as the full index value, without the deduction of any surrender charges or a vesting schedule.

REGULATION

The vast majority of EIAs are regulated by the National Association of Insurance Commissioners (NAIC) and not the Securities and Exchange Commission (SEC). An insurance company can register its EIA product with the SEC and must under certain circumstances. If the EIA is registered with the SEC, only brokers with both a securities license and an insurance license can sell the product. And, like a mutual fund investor, the EIA investor must be given a prospectus at or before any investment is made.

If an insurance company wants to market and sell an EIA without SEC registration, *all* of the following conditions must be met: (1) The insurance company is regulated, (2) the insurer assumes all investment risk, (3) the investor does not have a separate account (assets are commingled, just like they are with most fixed-rate annuities), (4) there is a guarantee of principal and net earnings, (5) there is a guarantee that the account will grow by at least some percentage amount each year, (6) growth in the account will not be changed more than once per year, and (7) the contract cannot be marketed *primarily* as an investment.

COMPARING EIA PRODUCTS

It is usually not difficult to compare traditional fixed-rate annuities by projecting current interest rates into the future. The same can be done with less accuracy when it comes to variable annuities (e.g., it would be highly unlikely if stocks averaged, say, 12 percent and/or bonds averaged 6 percent for the next five years). Projections into the future with EIAs have little meaning or value.

The only somewhat meaningful way to compare one EIA with another is to assume that a specific single premium was invested five to 10 years ago and that the policies being considered were in existence then (the exact same important provisions and guarantees). The typical EIA premium is $35,000. Some sources estimate that within the next few years approximately a third of all fixed-rate annuity sales will be EIAs. In many respects, the EIA bridges the gap between traditional fixed-rate annuities and variable annuities.

COMPARED TO OTHER ANNUITIES

Despite the negative or limiting aspects of the equity-indexed annuity (EIA), the idea of participating in a percentage of the gain in the S&P 500 (which can range from a modest percentage to over 100 percent in certain circumstances) without the chance of suffering a loss (setting aside liquidity considerations), is still very appealing. To see how the EIA stacks up against variable annuities and the more traditional fixed-rate annuity, review the comparison table (Table 9.7).

COMPARED TO MUTUAL FUNDS

EIAs are a new product, something that is not very familiar to most U.S. investors, whereas mutual funds have become so popular that close to half of all U.S. households are invested in at least one fund. All mutual funds fall under one of two broad categories: equities (stocks) and debt instruments (bonds and money market instruments). Table 9.8 provides some comparison between these investment vehicles.

According to Lipper Analytical Services, Inc., equity mutual funds often do not measure up to the performance of the S&P 500 (which is

---

TABLE 9.7   The EIA versus Fixed-Rate and Variable Annuities

	Fixed-Rate	*Variable*	*EIA*
Method of growth	Set rate of return	Investor selects one or more "mutual funds"	Tied to increases in the S&P 500
Guaranteed rate	Yes	No	No
Minimum guarantee	Yes	No	Yes
Potential for loss	No	Yes	No
Potential for gain	Modest	Great	Very good
Access to money	Very good	Very good	Poor to very good

TABLE 9.8 The EIA versus Mutual Funds			
	Stock Funds	*Bond Funds*	*EIA*
Method of growth	Based on the stocks in the portfolio	Based on the bonds in the portfolio	Tied to increases in the S&P 500
Guaranteed rate	No	No	No
Mininimum guarantee	No	No	Yes
Potential for loss	Yes	Yes	No
Potential for gain	Great	Usually modest	Very good
Access to money	Excellent	Excellent	Poor to very good

what an EIA is linked to). The following table shows the percentage of equity (stock) mutual funds that have done *worse* than the S&P 500.

1980	53 percent
1981	37 percent
1982	38 percent
1983	60 percent
1984	78 percent
1985	74 percent
1986	76 percent
1987	76 percent
1988	59 percent
1989	82 percent
1990	64 percent
1991	45 percent
1992	46 percent
1993	40 percent
1994	78 percent
1995	93 percent
1996	54 percent
1997	78 percent

This table makes a convincing case for index investing. Fortunately, there are several mutual funds that basically duplicate the performance of the S&P 500; there are also other index funds whose performance is tied to other indexes. However, no index fund provides the downside protection of an EIA.

THE RISKS OF INVESTING

There is no such thing as the perfect investment. There are positive and negative features to every investment that has or will ever exist. One of the ways to decide which investment vehicle is appropriate for you is to understand the different kinds of risk and decide which ones are important to you. Here are the most common forms of risk and how the EIA deals with each one.

The Risk of Loss (Market Risk)

The stock market can be a great place to be, but it is not an appropriate place for the vast majority of investors whose holding period is less than three to five years. Stocks can be quite rewarding, but their returns are often highly unpredictable over any given week, month, quarter, year, or even couple of years. This is the strongest selling point of the EIA: There is no market risk.

Individual investors typically get nervous with the market's ups and downs. Frequently they buy when the market is high and sell when it is low (the exact opposite of what they should be doing). The downside protection offered by EIAs provides even the most risk-averse investor with comfort and allows that person to stay in the market since there is no downside exposure.

Interest Rate Risk

When interest rates increase, the values of existing bonds decrease, even U.S. government bonds (whose face value is guaranteed only if the bond is held until maturity). The greater the maturity (i.e., 20 to 30 years), the greater the volatility and potential for loss (or gain if interest rates decrease). True, any such losses or increases due to interest rate movements are "only on paper." However, such paper losses become real if the bonds are sold at that point in time. Moreover, one could say that the loss from a stock falling from $80 a share down to $10 a share is only a paper loss (if still held and not sold), but most investors would be highly alarmed by such an event.

Since principal is guaranteed with an EIA, and excluding any discussion of potential penalties, the moderate or aggressive investor is risking only what he or she would have received as an alternative: interest. The conservative investor is risking only the difference between what a CD or money market account would have earned and what the EIA has as a minimum guarantee (typically 3 percent).

Default Risk

When you invest in a fixed-rate annuity, one of your concerns should be the financial strength of the insurer, since an investor's money is not segregated and instead is considered part of a general account. And, even though such a general account can only be used to satisfy the claims of the company's fixed-rate annuity contracts, bad investments could result in (and infrequently in the past have caused) a loss. Such a loss could affect the investor's liquidity, growth rate, and/or principal. Only a few fixed-rate annuities are structured so that each investor's money is considered to be segregated (placed in a separate account). As a side note, variable annuity contracts are always segregated.

Prospective fixed-rate annuity and equity-indexed annuity (EIA) owners can protect themselves by dealing only with an insurance company that has a top rating from at least two of the better-known rating services, such as A.M. Best, Duff & Phelps, Moody's, or Standard & Poor's.

Although there were a handful of companies that defaulted in the late 1980s, the knowledge gained from these financial losses has made insurance regulators and rating services more conscientious; top ratings are now more difficult to get. The aftermath of some highly publicized insurance defaults and near defaults has left the entire industry much stronger. Furthermore, states have reserve requirements (that insurance companies doing business in the state must contribute to if one of their peers runs into financial difficulty) that protect (up to certain limits) EIA and traditional fixed-rate annuity owners.

Inflation Risk

During most periods, bank CDs, money market funds, high-quality corporate bonds, and U.S. government securities have not been very good hedges against inflation. And, for most investors it is the cumulative effects of inflation that should be more worrisome than the ups and downs of the stock market—even if that investor is in his or her sixties. Equities, such as common stocks and certain types of real estate, have been excellent hedges against inflation. EIA investors are able to participate in the stock market's gains, thereby having an excellent opportunity to maintain, and more likely increase, their buying power.

Most investors know that historically, stocks have greatly outperformed bonds. Market historians also know that over the past half century, stocks have outperformed bonds over the vast majority of all one-year (e.g., 1947, 1948, etc.), three-year (e.g., 1947–1949, 1948–1950, etc.), five-year (e.g., 1947–1951, 1948–1952, etc.), and ten-year (e.g., 1947–1956, 1948–1957, etc.) periods. There are no 15- or 20-year periods over the past 50 years when bonds have done better than stocks.

Reinvestment Risk

Suppose you bought some bonds when interest rates were quite high. These bonds provide very high interest payments that remain constant. However, the income you receive, if not spent, must be reinvested. If interest rates fall, you will not be able to reinvest bond interest income at the same rate. Instead, you will be forced to reinvest these monies at a lower—perhaps substantially lower—rate. The same thing is true with a traditional fixed-rate annuity whose guarantee period has expired and whose renewal rate (new interest rate being offered) is less. This is what is referred to as reinvestment risk.

With an EIA you do not have such a risk. Compounding takes place when the period ends (one or more years); the entire account value can then participate during the next period. And, since the stock market has generally had an upward bias for well over 100 years, there is a very strong likelihood that any gains will be greater than most other investments.

THE S&P 500 INDEX

How insurance companies protect you against stock market declines is described in the next section. You will also see why the S&P 500 is the index of choice for the vast majority of EIAs. Four other reasons the S&P 500 is used are:

1. The S&P 500 is more representative of U.S. stocks than the more popularly quoted Dow Jones Industrial Average ("the Dow"). The Dow is made up of just 30 stocks versus 500 stocks in the S&P 500 from a broader array of industry groups such as transportation, utility, financial, and technology.

2. The value of the 500 stocks that comprise the S&P 500 represents close to 75 percent of the value of all U.S. listed stocks.

3. The S&P 500 includes stocks from the New York Stock Exchange, American Stock Exchange, and NASDAQ (the automated over-the-counter market).

4. The U.S. Department of Commerce considers the S&P 500 a leading economic indicator.

HOW THE INSURANCE COMPANY DOES IT

When you "index" an investment or product, your goal is to *match* the performance of the index; you are not trying to outperform the index (if this were the case, the investor would opt for active management and not passive management). Indexed products such as EIAs and certain mutual funds do not necessarily equal the performance of the index they are trying to mimic for one or more of the following reasons: (1) The portfolio does not include all of the securities that are in the index and instead consists of a number of the issues that are believed to be representative of the whole; (2) there are expenses and fees (indexes do not make any allowances or adjustments for buying or selling securities or for the cost of administering, selling, or client services); and (3) the index may not include the reinvestment of dividends but the investment does, or vice versa.

When you purchase an EIA, your investment, also known as "premium dollars," is used by the insurer to buy the kinds of securities found in traditional fixed-rate annuities: government securities, mortgage-backed securities, and corporate bonds. Such investments provide the investor with the guarantees of both principal and a nominal rate of growth (usually 3 percent a year). Part of the interest generated from these instruments is used to buy what are known as *call options* on an equity index,

usually the S&P 500 or the more popular S&P 100 (whose options are referred to as the OEX).

> **call option** there are two types of options: call options
> and put options. Both types of options usually expire
> (meaning they become worthless) within a year. You can
> also buy options that expire in just a few days, weeks, or
> months. When you buy a call, you are betting that a
> certain stock (or stock index such as the S&P 500) is
> going to increase in price within a certain period. There
> is a great deal of leverage going on when an option is
> bought. Purchasers of options can end up making a small
> gain on their money, or they may end up making 100
> percent, 200 percent, or even more. You can also lose
> part or all of your money.

When an option is purchased a form of leverage takes place. In the
case of most options, the leverage is quite high. This simply means that
a modest move in the market can result in a large gain or loss. It is this
leverage that allows the insurance company to give EIA contract owners returns that equal the return of the index (minus certain expenses
and without regard to the cap rate, the participation rate, or how gains
are calculated).

Quite often, a high interest rate environment is not good for the
stock market. After all, why take the risk of investing in stocks if bonds
are offering an attractive return? Yet, high interest rates are good for the
insurer offering an EIA. More income generated by the investments purchased with your premium dollars means that more call options can be
purchased and therefore the chance of an even greater return exists. For
the EIA contract owner this may result in the insurer offering a higher
participation rate and/or cap rate.

A very succinct way to describe the mechanics of the EIA is that the
investor is making a trade-off: a moderate or large portion of what would
have been earned in a fixed-rate annuity (the interest) is used to participate in the stock market instead. The options purchased may fall in value
to zero (they cannot fall below zero), but future interest income for the

conservative debt instruments is used to buy new options, thereby continuing the participation process.

Participation in the stock market using options is not as expensive as it first might appear, because the costs of such participation (also referred to as hedging) are offset by the participation rate and the cap rate.

RISKS AND RETURNS: THEORY AND REALITY

You may have read about stock and bond returns in the past. There are a couple of problems with some of the conclusions that are naturally reached as a result of such information. First, there is a tendency to think that what happened in the past is likely to occur during a similar period in the immediate future (e.g., "If X was up 300 percent over the past eight years, it is reasonable to assume that if I buy X now, I will see a 300 percent gain during the next eight years"). Second, one might conclude that if the stock or bond market was up a certain amount, then investors in these securities experienced similar, if not identical, returns. Let us look at both of these fallacies in greater detail.

The Past versus the Present versus the Future

There is no relationship or correlation between past, present, and future returns in the stock market, even when using a long period of time. As an example, over the past 50 years, U.S. stocks have averaged gains of 12 percent compounded per year. Yet, not once during the past half century have stocks been up *exactly* 12 percent.

Investors are often hesitant or scared to buy into the stock market after the market has experienced a high growth rate. I have been counseling investors for over 15 years and not a month has gone by when a number of financial gurus have not talked about the coming downturn in the stock market. The frequency and magnitude of such impending disasters multiply whenever the market passes a new century mark (i.e., 1100 to 1200 in 1982 or any other 100-point upward move).

The same investors who are afraid to go into a hot market often do not have a plan or point as to when they would enter. Once the market dips, many of these same prospective players now become convinced that the market is headed further south. Surprisingly, it is after a bad month or quarter or even a bad year that the market often experiences some of its best gains. Rarely does the stock market have two negative years in a row.

Although gains in the stock market are limited for EIA contract owners under most, but not all, market scenarios, the EIA eliminates people's greatest fear of investing: loss of principal. Such fear, misunderstanding, and perhaps bewilderment (there are now over ten thousand different mutual funds) is borne out by a study conducted by DALBAR, Inc., a well-known advisory firm that does not buy, sell, or manage any kind of securities.

The study, named "Quantitative Analysis of Investor Behavior," conducted in 1994, shows that there is a huge difference between what the stock market did and what returns equity mutual fund investors actually experienced. The study followed a few hundred equity investors who were in mutual funds from January 1984 through September 1993. During this period of time, the S&P 500 increased 293 percent. Yet, over this same period, these mutual fund investors averaged only 70 percent. Why such a difference?

It is likely that the investors made one or two serious mistakes. First, they tried to time the market (move from a stock fund to a money market fund when it was felt that the market was going to decline and then get back into an equity fund when it appeared that the market was about to or was already beginning to rise again). Secondly, they chased last year's (or last month's, quarter's, or the past three, five, or ten years') winner. It is quite common for someone who is in a fund that is underperforming at the moment (which can be defined as a month, quarter, year, or even couple of years) to swap it for a fund that has just appeared on someone's top 10 list.

With an EIA, the investor is likely to stay the course and thereby participate in the greatest wealth builder in history (yes, stock market returns have been even better than real estate returns even in peak years for real estate such as 1988 or 1989). There are certainly negatives with any EIA contract, but they pale in comparison to the advantage of actually participating in the stock market and getting the market's returns instead of losing out by jumping in and out or switching to the fund of the month (remember 293 percent versus 70 percent!).

AN EIA CONTRACT: EXAMPLE #1

SAFECO Life Insurance (which has a AA rating from Standard & Poor's and an A1 rating from Moody's) offers an EIA called SAFEKEY Index

Annuity (800-952-8389). The main difference between this contract and others is the way interest (growth) is calculated. It is one of the easiest methods to compute and understand. The client's interest rate for any calendar year is simply the percentage gain in the S&P 500 minus the margin (the margin is determined by the insurance company).

As an example, if the S&P 500 were up 14 percent for the year and the margin was 3 percent, the investor's account would be credited an 11 percent interest rate (14 percent minus 3 percent equals 11 percent). This net rate is then multiplied by the account's base value (the initial investment) to determine the current year's interest earnings. Thus, if $10,000 were invested, the base value would be $10,000; 11 percent times $10,000 equals $1100. At the end of the first year, the investment would be worth $11,100 ($10,000 plus $1100).

Continuing the example, if the index was up 15 percent during the second year, the interest rate would be 12 percent (15 percent minus the 3 percent margin). The account would grow by $1200 for the year ($10,000 times 12 percent equals $1200). At the end of the second year the account would be worth $12,300—the base value ($10,000) plus the interest earnings for the first year ($1100) plus the interest earnings for the second year ($1200). As you can see, there is no compounding from year-to-year.

Key provisions in the SAFECO product include:

✔ The base value is increased only every six years.

✔ The new base value every six years reflects all past interest earnings.

✔ Interest (growth) is calculated and locked in each December 31 and upon total surrender.

✔ The interest gain is locked in each year and is never affected by any future S&P 500 decreases.

✔ The margin (3 percent in the example) is guaranteed for the first seven calendar years and can never exceed 5 percent.

✔ S&P 500 gains are based on a full calendar year, but since most purchases and surrenders will not coincide with the start or end of a calendar year, S&P 500 for partial years is calculated somewhat differently:

For the first "year," the interest rate is calculated by using the purchase date and the value at the end of December 31 of that year.

In the year of surrender, the interest rate for that year is determined by using the value of the S&P 500 at the end of the day that the surrender takes place minus the value of the S&P 500 on the previous December 31.

✔ Total or partial withdrawals are subject to withdrawal charges during the first seven calendar years and apply to the entire amount withdrawn according to the following schedule:

Calendar Year of Purchase	Calendar Years Following the Purchase Year						
	1	2	3	4	5	6	7
8%	8%	7%	7%	6%	4%	2%	0%

✔ There are no withdrawal charges if the owner annuitizes, is confined to a nursing home, dies, or takes required minimum distributions (in IRAs).

✔ In most states, the minimum required guarantee is 90 percent of the premium (what you invested) accumulated at 3 percent per year. This exposes the investor to a potential loss during the first four years if the contract is surrendered. SAFEKEY eliminates this risk by guaranteeing 100 percent of the contract owner's principal during that time.

✔ SAFEKEY guarantees a minimum equity value equal to the greater of: (1) 100 percent of the premium (a benefit during the first four years of the contract), or (2) 90 percent of the premium growing at 3 percent a year (which could be a benefit in later years since the minimum would be increasing each year).

✔ Phrased another way, the contract guarantees that 100 percent of your principal is guaranteed at all times; even upon total surrender in the early years, withdrawal charges will never exceed any interest credited or invade your principal.

By looking at the hypothetical growth of $10,000 for selected six-year periods, the following results would have taken place. (*Note:* This illustration assumes that this EIA has been available since 1952, which it hasn't, and that a 3 percent margin rate was deducted every year and never changed.)

✔ The *best* six-year period was also one of the *most recent*—from 1/1/91 to 12/31/96; a $10,000 investment in the S&P 500 grew to $22,432, and to $17,720 with the SAFEKEY Index.

✔ The *worst* six-year period was from 1/1/69 to 12/31/74; a $10,000 investment in the S&P 500 would have declined to $6312 while the SAFEKEY Index would have grown to $12,042.

✔ The *average*, from 1/1/57 to 12/31/62, resulted in a $10,000 investment in the S&P 500 growing to $15,307 over six years, versus $15,437 with the SAFEKEY Index.

AN EIA CONTRACT: EXAMPLE #2

Keyport Life Insurance (which has an A+ rating from A.M. Best) offers an EIA called KeyIndex (800-437-4466). The main difference between this contract and others is that the Keyport product has no cap rate (unless a one-year term is selected). How much the investor will earn largely depends on the performance of the S&P 500 and the participation rate. Contract owners may choose a one-, five-, or seven-year period with or without a cap rate.

As an example, if the S&P 500 were up 14 percent for the year and the participation rate was 70 percent, the investor's account would be credited a 9.8 percent interest rate (14 percent times 70 percent equals 9.8 percent).

Key provisions in the Keyport product include:

✔ Five-year and seven-year rate terms offer interest earnings based on the highest anniversary value of the S&P 500 Index during the term (which would be five or seven years), subject to an overall limit (the cap rate) *if* a cap rate option is selected by the investor.

✔ By locking in the highest S&P 500 Index gain, you are protected against possible S&P 500 declines toward the end of the rate term.

✔ Participation rates are guaranteed for the full rate term (one, five, or seven years) and are reset at the beginning of each rate renewal term.

✔ Suppose:

The original investment was $100,000 and the five-year participation rate was 70 percent and 80 percent for a seven-year contract (and there is no cap rate).

The S&P 500 had year-end anniversary values of 850 (year one), 975 (year two), 950 (year three), 1050 (year four), 1000 (year five), 1075 (year six), and 1025 (year seven).

The starting value (original anniversary date) of the S&P 500 was 850.

Under a five-year term, gains would be computed by taking 1050 (the highest anniversary value during the five years) and subtracting 850 (the beginning value) and then dividing that number (200) by the beginning value (850)—or 23.52 percent.

The 23.52 percent would then be multiplied by 70 percent (the participation rate in this example); 16.46 percent would then be credited to the account (23.52 percent times 70 percent equals 16.46 percent).

A $10,000 original premium would grow to $11,646 by the end of the fifth year ($10,000 times 16.46 percent equals $1646; $10,000 plus $1646 equals $11,646).

If a seven-year term were used, the computations would be similar but there would be a greater gain in this example since the highest anniversary value during the seven years would be 1075 (versus 1050 for the five-year term).

✔ Whether a five- or seven-year term is used, the investor is only entitled to a penalty-free withdrawal equal to a certain percentage (a vesting schedule) of such credited value. Earnings are credited each anniversary (once a year) to the initial premium (or value of the account if the contract is renewed), based on the following vesting schedule:

	Anniversary Year						
	1	*2*	*3*	*4*	*5*	*6*	*7*
Five-year term contract	20%	40%	60%	80%	100%		
Seven-year term contract	14%	28%	42%	57%	71%	85%	100%

✔ There is a 100 percent money-back guarantee at the end of each rate term (even if a one-year period is selected).

✔ Unless otherwise requested, the contract will automatically renew for the same length term.

✔ After age 80, only one-year renewals are available.

✔ you may make a withdrawal free of any penalty during a 45-day period at the end of each rate term (which would be at the end of one, five, or seven years with this product).

✔ Withdrawals during a term will not participate in any future growth.

✔ The starting value for the next term (assuming the investor renews) is the "end-of-term indexed value" (the growth in the S&P 500, using the highest anniversary value, multiplied by the participation rate and possibly reduced by a cap rate—if there is a cap rate).

Chapter

10

Reviewing the Insurance Company

How does the average person ascertain an insurance company's ability to meet its commitments? How can an investor feel confident about an agent or broker from whom he or she is buying an annuity? The quality of the insurance company is critical when selecting a fixed-rate annuity since, in almost all cases, investors' assets are commingled with those of the insurer. If the issuing company's portfolio becomes troubled, so do the contract owners'. Variable annuity monies are not mixed with the issuer's funds; therefore, variable annuity owners need not be concerned with the financial solvency of the parent company.

With only a trip to a reasonably stocked library or a request to a financial adviser for company literature, consumers can do sufficient research to make sure they are dealing with a strong insurance company. Additionally, the investor can make inquiries of the financial planner, broker, or agent to find out whether he or she is dealing with a full-time, professional adviser or someone who is a part-timer or moonlighter. There are four areas the prospective client can look into: (1) company rating, (2) claims-paying ability, (3) annual statements, and (4) the investment portfolio.

COMPANY RATING

Secure a copy of *Best's Agents Guide to Life Insurance Companies*. A.M. Best Company reviews the financial status of thousands of insurers and rates them on their financial strength and operating performance based on the norms of the life and health insurance industry. The Best Company has been in business since 1899. In 1906 it began rating life and health insurers. In 1934, Best stopped its alphabetical ratings (A+, A, etc.) and began a rating system based on general descriptions.

In 1976 Best restarted its alphabetical rating; the same system is still in use today. A.M. Best measures the performance of each company in the areas of: competency of underwriting, control of expenses, adequacy of reserves, soundness of investments, and capital sufficiency. The ratings for A.M. Best are:

Rating	*Description*
A++	Superior
A+	Superior
A	Excellent
A–	Excellent
B++	Very good
B+	Very good
B	Fair
B–	Fair
C++	Marginal
C+	Marginal
C	Weak
C–	Weak
D	Poor
E	Regulatory supervision
F	Liquidation
S	Rating suspended

In the case of fixed-rate contracts, you should deal with only the top four categories. There are no advantages in dealing with a company that has a B++ or lower rating. In the case of variable annuities, the rating of the insurer is unimportant since your assets are not being commingled with those of the company; lack of solvency or bankruptcy does not affect the value or integrity of variable annuity investments.

You might also survey the net yield on invested assets. Be suspicious of a company that is offering you a rate that is the same as or higher than what they are earning on your money. Keep in mind that rapidly changing events can overtake the rating system before the next book is published.

CLAIMS-PAYING ABILITY

There are two very well known rating systems: Moody's Investors Service, Inc., and Standard & Poor's Corporation. Not all of the approximate 2000 life insurance companies have been rated yet by these services.

Moody's rating system consists of Aaa (highest quality) down to C (lowest quality). Claims paying ratings are: Aaa, Aa1, Aa2, Aa3, A1, A2, Baa1, Baa2, Baa3, Ba1, Ba2, Ba3, B1, B2, B3, Caa, Ca, and C. The numerical modifiers indicate whether a company is in the higher, middle, or lower end of the category.

Standard & Poor's ratings are similar, with categories ranging from AAA to BBB and speculative grade ratings from BB down to D. The D rating is for an insurance company placed under a court liquidation order.

ANNUAL STATEMENTS

Annual statements are filed by each insurance company with every state the insurer does business in. In Schedule F of this statement, the amount of claims paid out and claims resisted is listed. The lower the net dollars paid out, the more financially sound the insurer.

INVESTMENT PORTFOLIO

Many fixed-rate annuity companies offer information on their investment portfolio in brochures and other marketing material. If you are interested in a particular company's investment portfolio, a phone call to the marketing department could prove beneficial. Other sources would be the *Wall Street Journal*, *Barron's*, and materials published by A.M. Best, Moody's, and Standard & Poor's, as well as other financial newsletters and periodicals. When all else fails, contact your state's department of insurance.

An insurance company builds a sound business, in part, by diversifying its assets. It does this by holding a prudent mix of risk-free, low-risk, and, to a much lesser degree, high-risk investments in its portfolio. If you are about to buy an annuity, it can be a good idea to ask for a summary of the insurance company's investment portfolio to see how its assets are distributed. After all, the money that you are about to place in the annuity will become part of those assets until you or your heirs fully liquidate the contract.

There is no right or wrong mix of investments, but there are industry norms that have proven sound through good and bad times, and most insurance companies tend to follow them. The American Council of Life Insurance, a nationwide trade association of life insurance companies, reviews the annual financial statements of nearly every U.S. insurance company and reports the industry portfolio averages as follows: 43 percent corporate bonds, 22 percent mortgages, 15 percent government securities, 5 percent policy loans, 5 percent stocks, 3 percent real estate, and 7 percent in other asset categories.

Safest and surest are the securities that are issued or backed by the U.S. government. These are universally considered to be risk-free. Included in the category of corporate bonds are both investment-grade and high-yielding noninvestment-grade bonds. The industry norm for unsecured, noninvestment-grade or so-called junk bonds is less than 6 percent.

Many advisers say consumers can feel pretty confident if they stick to the roughly 25 percent of insurers reviewed by A.M. Best that get the company's A++ or A+ rating—particularly those that have had that rating consistently for years. A second rating from a company such as Standard & Poor's, one of three debt-rating services that have branched out to rate insurer safety in recent years, provides an additional feeling of safety. Moody's Investors Service and Duff & Phelps, the two other debt-rating companies, now rate insurers as well.

Unfortunately, most insurers, while rated by Best, are not rated by the debt-rating agencies. The debt-rating companies, unlike Best, rate only those insurers that pay to be rated; the largest and those most likely to get a high rating have chosen to do so.

PAST INSOLVENCIES

During April 1991, Executive Life Insurance Company was seized by California regulators due to defaults and declining values in its huge portfolio of junk bonds. Close to two-thirds of the company's assets were invested in junk issues; the industry average is less than 6 percent. Executive Life had 170,000 life insurance policies outstanding, with a face value of $38 billion. It had sold 75,000 fixed-rate annuities with a value of $2.5 billion.

Prior to Executive Life's troubles, the best-known issuer of annuities that became insolvent was Baldwin-United, an annuity writer that failed in 1983. No investor lost a dime due to Baldwin's demise, but contract owners learned in 1987 they would get only 7.5 percent on their money, not the 13.6 percent initially promised.

STATE GUARANTY LAWS

If your insurer goes under, the effect on the value of your policy hinges at least partly on where you live, what kind of policy you hold, and what the policy is worth. Guaranty laws established in 46 states are meant to protect policyholders against insolvency. They set a limit of $100,000 on cash values of life insurance policies and up to $300,000 on combined benefits from all life insurance policies. Guaranty funds are backed by assessments against solvent insurers when one of their peers goes under. Annuity investors are protected, with overall coverage limits normally being higher.

Forty-six states have guaranty laws that protect life insurance policyholders if the insurance company goes broke. If you are a resident of one of the 46 states listed in Table 10.1 and conduct insurance or annuity business with a company licensed in your state, you are protected. The five places that do not have the protection of these laws are Alaska, Colorado, the District of Columbia, Louisiana, and New Jersey.

Table 10.1 lists the maximum protections allowed for each insured life. Maximum cash value usually applies to cash value of life insurance policies. Where no figure appears for death benefit, the total cannot exceed the combined maximum protection. Finally, states indicated by a check mark also protect out-of-state residents when insurance companies headquartered within their borders go broke. Details vary and change often.

The protection afforded by these guaranty laws protect annuity investors as well as the beneficiaries of life insurance. Coverage is for up to 80 percent of the annuity contract's value or $100,000, whichever is less; the same formula applies to the cash value in a life insurance policy. If you have multiple policies, you automatically obtain multiple coverages. All annuities are covered by these guaranty laws with the exception of those contracts owned by corporations or partnerships, what are referred to in the industry as "unallocated annuities."

In the case of an insurance company's death benefit, your protection against an insurer's insolvency is covered for up to $250,000 per policy or 80 percent of the death benefit, whichever is less.

TABLE 10.1 Maximum Protections Allowed by State

State	Minimum Cash Value	Maximum Death Benefit	Out-of-State Coverage
Alabama	$100,000		√
Arizona	$100,000		√
Arkansas	$100,000		
California	$100,000	$250,000	
Connecticut	$100,000		
Delaware	$100,000		
Florida	$100,000		
Georgia	$100,000		
Hawaii	$100,000		
Idaho	$100,000		
Illinois	$100,000		
Indiana	$100,000		
Iowa	$100,000		
Kansas	$100,000	$100,000	
Kentucky	$100,000		
Maine	$100,000		√
Maryland			
Massachusetts	$100,000		
Michigan	$100,000		
Minnesota	$100,000		√
Mississippi	$100,000		√
Missouri	$100,000		
Montana		$300,000	
Nebraska		$300,000	
Nevada	$100,000		√
New Hampshire	$100,000		√
New Mexico	$100,000		√
New York			
North Carolina			√
North Dakota	$100,000		
Ohio	$100,000		
Oklahoma	$100,000		

TABLE 10.1 (Continued)			
State	Minimum Cash Value	Maximum Death Benefit	Out-of-State Coverage
Oregon	$100,000		√
Pennsylvania	$100,000		√
Rhode Island	$100,000		
South Carolina			√
South Dakota	$100,000		
Tennessee	$100,000		
Texas	$100,000		
Utah	$100,000		
Vermont		$300,000	√
Virginia	$100,000		√
Washington	$500,000		√
West Virginia		$300,000	√
Wisconsin			√
Wyoming	$100,000		

Chapter 11

Insurance
Company Ratings

The large bankruptcies seen in 1990 and 1991 resulted in a loss of confidence in the rating agencies, particularly the best-known service, A.M. Best. The majority of the insurance companies that suffered severe losses held an A+ rating from A.M. Best until just a short time before their problems became widely known. Although less publicized, Standard & Poor's, as well as Moody's, had also given high ratings to these same companies until the end. What, then, is the source of these misguided ratings?

All insurance rating agencies take their raw data from a company's annual statutory report, as designed by the National Association of Insurance Commissioners (NAIC). Even though rating services knew of Executive Life's large junk bond holdings (the largest insurance company default in history), the agencies should not be given all of the blame. Junk bonds became popular during the 1980s; there was not enough history or experience to forewarn the rating agencies as to what might happen or the possible degree of decline. In fact, studies up to that time were generally quite positive when it came to the issue of bond defaults and the resulting losses. The NAIC changed their policy in 1990 due to some well-publicized insolvencies.

As far as real estate losses are concerned, the majority of these declines were due to unrealistic appraisals and large loan-to-value ratios.

Such mistakes could have been fully detected only if each mortgage had been carefully analyzed and all of the different appraisers carefully questioned. This would be an incredibly difficult and expensive task. Most rating agencies do review large mortgages and closely scrutinize a sampling of the smaller loans.

The losses the real estate industry sustained in the early 1990s were caused by the simultaneous economic downturn and decline in the real estate market too soon after the properties were developed. Quick succession of these events did not give the properties a chance to become profitable and build up some type of safety cushion. Fortunately, such a set of circumstances is very rare. Nevertheless, even these combined problems would not have hurt the insurance industry if there had not been massive policyholder withdrawals, which wiped out cash and marketable security reserves. In the past, rating services had never factored a "run on the bank" into their ratings.

CLASSIFYING RATING SERVICES

Agencies that rate or grade insurance companies are divided into two camps: those that charge the companies a fee to be rated and those that do not. Those that do not, *Weiss Reports* and *Standard & Poor's Insurer Solvency Review*, make their money by selling their reports to investors and brokers.

The companies that charge a fee, Standard & Poor's (in certain instances), Duff & Phelps, Moody's, and A.M. Best, hope that insurers that do not have any kind of rating will look worse to agents and annuity purchasers than companies that have a low rating. These raters hope that the weak insurance companies will try to improve their situation so that they can obtain a quality rating.

A great number of insurers either have decided not to pay a rating fee or do not see the need to obtain a letter grade from more than one service. Those companies that obtain a high rating see these letter grades as a valuable advertising tool. More and more insurance companies with high marks are publicizing their ratings in newspapers, magazines, flyers, and letters to agents. When viewed by an uninformed investor or broker, ratings can be very misleading. Those not knowledgeable cannot tell if a company's financials are being bogged down by excellent, good, or bad investments. Only someone who knows how to look beyond the letter grade would be able to see the true picture.

Rating is a complex task. The *Weiss Reports* and *Standard & Poor's Insurer Solvency Review* are targeted toward the average investor rather than the sophisticated broker or financial adviser. Although both of these publications are easy to understand, neither one of them tells the whole story; the same can be said about A.M. Best. There is also the problem of consistency.

Often, rating services do not agree. As an example, *Weiss Reports* lists a company as being one of the five weakest, while A.M. Best reported it as having "insufficient experience" and both Standard & Poor's and Duff & Phelps gave the same insurer a AA− rating.

To gain a better idea as to what goes into a rating and how the different raters approach this task, let us look at each of the major rating services individually.

A.M. BEST COMPANY

Each company's figures are updated and reviewed by Best every quarter. According to a company officer, Best is in "constant communication" with each of the insurance companies it reviews. The rating process begins by having a financial questionnaire completed by the insurer at the beginning of each year. The evaluation looks at an insurance company's profitability, leverage, and liquidity in comparison with insurance industry norms. Best feels that a company's numbers are the foundation for the evaluation, but that it is the interviews that take place with an insurance company's officers that tell the real story. When it comes to evaluating management, Best looks for competence, experience, and integrity.

In addition to a quantitative evaluation, A.M. Best also makes a qualitative judgment, looking at the quality of a company's investments—how well risk is spread out in addition to the amount and caliber of reinsurance. An insurer's assets are looked at under the assumption that these items might have to be sold unexpectedly. In short, Best is looking for liquidity and quality; the greater the quality and the more marketable a security is, the less uncertainty there is about its future value. Investments reviewed include mortgages, real estate, joint ventures, collateral loans, common stocks, and junk bonds. The Best ratings are based on the long-term prospects, not the short-term.

After all of this is done, the insurer is assigned an analyst, who rates the company on a letter scale ranging from A+ to C–. Before the rating is assigned, several people have already compiled numbers and then passed such information on to support analysts. These analysts then make a recommendation to a senior analyst. This primary analyst, after reviewing the material, either accepts or revises the recommended grade assignment before sending it to the rating committee. After the committee has discussed and reviewed the rating, the chief executive officer of the insurance company is contacted and asked for comment. The insurer then has the option of either accepting the rating or meeting with Best analysts and officers to discuss the letter grade.

Once this process is completed, Best then publishes the ratings in the "Rating Monitor," a special section in its weekly publication, *Best's Insurance Management Reports*, followed by a write-up in the monthly magazine, *Best's Review*, and the annual report, *Best's Insurance Reports*. Many insurance companies are not rated for one or more reasons: First, the insurer may not want to pay the fee. Second, the company may request that its rating not be published; Best will still report on the company but will leave out the letter grade.

STANDARD & POOR'S

Even though Standard & Poor's (S&P) has been in the business of rating the financial strength and credit quality of debt issues (bonds and notes) for over 50 years, it has been rating insurance companies for about 25 years. And even then, its ratings were not made public until 1983. The company's reputation in the financial guarantee area, however, has enabled S&P to assume a number-two position in an already growing field of competitors.

At S&P, the process of evaluating the ability of a life insurer to meet its obligations to policyholders begins with a formal letter from an insurance company. The letter commits the company to providing S&P with the information necessary to achieve a final rating. All claims-paying ability ratings are voluntary, arrived at with the company's complete cooperation. A rating from S&P costs anywhere from $15,000 to $30,000 per year, depending on the company's size.

Once the commitment has been formalized, S&P assigns a lead analyst to work with the company. The information the analyst requests, which covers about six years of the company's performance, is organized into seven main areas for evaluation: management and corporate strategy, industry risk, business review, operational analysis, capitalization, liquidity, and financial flexibility.

In addition to requesting records, financial statements, company press releases, and other documentation, the analyst also sets up a meeting with the company's management team at the home office. The purpose of this meeting is to get a better picture of the quality of the company's management. Discussed are management style and strategy, the top executives' plans for the company's future, and their commitment to success.

Essential parts of the rating methodology are identifying the company's product lines and distribution systems and determining its strengths and weaknesses compared to the insurance industry as a whole. Among the questions asked:

✔ What has been the compound growth rate of revenue over the past five to six years?

✔ How is the revenue distributed by business unit, geography, product, and distribution channel?

✔ What is the company's market share, both overall and for its individual product lines?

Investment performance, which plays an important role in the final rating, covers the following questions:

✔ How are the company's investment assets allocated?

✔ What is the interest rate risk of the company's interest-sensitive portfolios and guaranteed investment contracts?

✔ What is the company's credit quality?

✔ What is the company's asset concentration by industry and issuer?

✔ What is the current portfolio yield?

✔ What is the total return on the portfolio?

✔ What is the average maturity and duration of the entire portfolio?

✔ What are the delinquency ratios for select asset types such as commercial mortgages and below-investment-grade bonds?

The lead analyst takes approximately three weeks to arrive at a preliminary rating of the company, then submits this rating to a committee of peers—plus a couple of vice presidents and managing directors—between seven and 10 in all.

The purpose of the meeting is to subject the preliminary rating to rigorous scrutiny, question its assumptions, verify the material facts, and challenge the analyst's conclusions. The committee has access to all the analyst's data, including confidential material, so the proceedings are considered privileged.

By the end of the meeting, the committee must reach a consensus on what the final rating will be. That rating is then communicated to the company for its approval. If the company approves the rating, S&P deletes the confidential material and publishes the information gathered in three basic formats:

✔ *S&P's Insurance Book* is a loose-leaf collection of full, in-depth reports on each rated insurer, complete with charts and graphs, updated throughout the year as necessary.

✔ *S&P Insurance Digest* is a quarterly publication containing the company's letter rating and a rationale for the rating. It also includes selected statistics.

✔ *S&P's Insurer Ratings List* is a monthly listing of insurers and their letter ratings.

If, however, the company for some reason considers the rating to be incorrect, it can appeal the rating to the committee. If the company can prove that material information influencing the rating decision was inaccurate or misinterpreted, S&P will most likely change the rating accordingly. If not, the rating stands. The company then has the right to deny publication of the rating and choose to remain unrated.

AAA companies are so financially sound that they often have more capital than they need. They get that way because they pay a very conservative rate of return to policyholders. Companies rated AA or A may be willing to take more risks (though not drastic ones) and they usually pay a better rate of return.

MOODY'S

Moody's Investors Service, which started in the bond rating business in 1904, has been evaluating life insurance companies since the 1970s. In 1986, Moody's introduced insurance financial strength ratings to provide guaranteed investment contract (GIC) investors with objective, independent credit opinions. In 1991, the firm revised several elements of its benchmark capital ratio to reflect the changing nature of risk in the life insurance industry, and also to improve the accuracy and usefulness of the ratio.

Carriers pay about $30,000 for the service, but Moody's perceives its real clients as financial intermediaries such as brokers, pension plan sponsors, structured settlement advisers, and agents. Much of its attention has been given to carriers involved in the group pension and individual annuity business. Coverage has significantly expanded from initial focus on companies selling GICs to annuity providers, universal life writers, and providers of other life products. Consequently, Moody's rates a number of small companies as well as the giants.

Moody's Life Insurance Credit Report service includes a quarterly handbook, detailed reports on individual companies, "Special Comments" on industry issues, "Flash Reports" of rating actions, and access to analysts and briefings for investors. For an annual fee of $125, its quarterly *Life Insurance Handbook* gives ratings, explains its rationale, and provides executive summaries for all life insurance companies.

Carriers that contract with Moody's can refuse to have a rating published, but only if they do not become active in the market that Moody's currently covers (group pension and individual annuities). If the carrier enters the market later on, or Moody's expands to cover the carrier's market, Moody's can release the rating.

Moody's ratings are opinions of the relative financial strength or weakness of insurance companies. They are intended to summarize its opinion concerning the likelihood that an insurance company will be able to meet its future obligations to policyholders. Consequently, in Moody's terminology, financial strength actually means "claims-paying ability." In assigning a rating, Moody's uses much the same financial data that other rating companies use and takes into consideration other factors that are not so easily measured. Analysts meet with management at the carrier's home office and a close personal relationship is maintained as an integral part of the evaluation proceedings.

Moody's is generally regarded as highly reliable on the issue of carrier solvency and clearly keeps a sharp eye out for shifts in a company's financial health. Applying its long-established system and expertise developed through the years as a bond and credit rating firm, Moody's takes pride in the objectivity of its analysis. Moody's has broad experience; all of its analysts and senior management have been active in the insurance business or related fields for at least seven years and spend 100 percent of their professional time conducting research and communicating with clients.

DUFF & PHELPS

The Duff & Phelps (D&P) insurance company rating process, which was first used in 1986, is divided into steps. First, a company that has requested and paid $20,000 for a D&P rating receives a letter requesting financial reports. Then, after the reports have been received, D&P representatives travel to the insurance company for an initial on-site interview. During that meeting, the rater meets in groups and individually with key management personnel, including the chief executive officer, chief financial officer, chief investment officer, and product managers.

D&P next invites a group of executives from the insurance company to its Chicago headquarters to confer with members of the rating committee. This meeting gives the insurance company the opportunity to meet its evaluators and to get a better sense of the rating process. Finally, the D&P rating committee, consisting of three to five financial and technical experts appointed by D&P management, convenes to establish a rating. They present the grade and an analysis to the insurance company, which, upon acceptance of the rating, can opt to either publish or discard the results.

The D&P team places weight on how the company answers questions and how it deals with each aspect of the rating process. For example, if in their investigation of a company, they learn it has invested heavily in cable television, D&P asks about the company's knowledge in this area and if it has expert advice. The rating team is looking for a solid philosophy.

The insurance company that is being rated has agreed in its contract with D&P to provide relevant financial information quarterly, which D&P includes in its quarterly ratings updates. There is also an annual review meeting at the start of the new rating year. D&P operates under the principle that D&P should get the rating right the first time, but that company strength can change rapidly. If D&P ever felt that a company had withheld information or knowingly provided misinformation, that company would be dropped. This has never occurred.

WEISS RESEARCH, INC.

Weiss thinks a rating system should "flag potential problems in such a way that the average consumer will be adequately informed in a timely fashion." The company employs about 50 people, including analysts, programmers and technicians, clerks, and customer service counselors. All but a handful of the firm's employees are at its Florida headquarters. Off-site employees, including writers and a consulting actuary, are located around the country and maintain close contact with headquarters through computer hookups.

Weiss Research developed a proprietary computer model that uses some 200 ratios derived from 750 pieces of data to determine an insurer's rating. Data for these calculations come from the statutory reports insurance companies submit to the state insurance commissioners, plus supplemental data from the companies. Weiss Research does not interview managers of the insurance companies. "Good management will produce good results; and bad results cannot be explained away by discussions of management's experience," according to Weiss.

The results of the analysis and the ratings are sent to the companies with a request that the data be examined and verified. Some companies do not respond to these requests. Others object to the rating received. Still others object so strenuously they threaten lawsuits. Weiss Research receives quarterly reports from the insurance companies. New information is added to the analytical process and is reported in quarterly updates.

SOME FINAL THOUGHTS

Insurance companies are getting quite a bang for their buck when it comes to a favorable rating. Many of these issuers tout their grades in advertisements and even issue press releases to announce a stellar rating. Yet, in uneducated hands, ratings can be potentially misleading.

Most sources agree that it is a mistake to rely too heavily on one rating service.

An annuity issuer does not have to have the top rating to be safe. By way of comparison, there are only a few banks that carry the top rating, AAA. One should never lose track of the fact that ratings are still an opinion or interpretation; they are not a guarantee.

Chapter 12

Tax-Sheltered Annuities

eachers, school personnel, doctors, nurses, hospital employees, and members of nonprofit organizations are eligible to participate in a retirement plan referred to as a *tax-sheltered annuity* (TSA). These qualified programs are authorized under Section 403(b) of the Internal Revenue Code. TSAs offer advantages not found in other types of annuities and retirement plans. If you are not a member of one of these groups you may choose to skip the balance of this chapter and move directly to the next chapter.

> **tax-sheltered annuity**   a retirement plan for school, hospital, and nonprofit employees under Section 403(b) of the Internal Revenue Code.

TSAs are annuity contracts purchased from an insurance company; the participant can choose a fixed or a variable account. Contracts are issued on either an individual or a group basis (i.e., the XYZ school district). The insurer receives contributions directly from the employer. The participant's contributions may vary yearly. Contributions are spelled out in a salary reduction agreement; they are made from payroll deductions on a pretax basis. Despite the deductibility, Social Security taxes are withheld on the employee salary reduction amounts.

Tax-sheltered annuities and other types of 403(b) plans are intended for retirement. Under certain circumstances, money can be withdrawn before retirement. Such distributions are allowed due to financial hardship, death, disability, or termination of employment.

INDIVIDUAL AND GROUP CONTRACTS

An individual contract means that each person participating in the retirement plan receives a contract that lists the different aspects of the TSA. Under a group contract, each participant receives a certificate verifying participation and indicating that the contract is between the insurance company and the employer.

Individual contracts have certain guarantees that exist until the contract ends. Group plans may have assurances that last for a certain period of time, such as five years. A major difference between individual and group contracts is flexibility. Individual contracts are portable. If you change jobs there are several options to choose from: (1) freeze the account; (2) transfer part or all of the account to a program offered by your new employer, assuming the new company has an existing TSA program; or (3) place part or all of the monies in an IRA. All three of these options allow the account to continue to grow and compound tax-deferred. If the changeover is properly made, no tax event will be triggered.

Movement of a TSA to another plan can escape the IRS penalty and taxes, but may not avoid withdrawal charges from the previous insurer. Generally, group contracts include some type of transfer fee; individual contracts can normally be moved from one employer to another without charges.

TAX BENEFITS

The major attractions of TSAs are its income tax implications. These benefits are: (1) Contributions reduce your taxable income, dollar for dollar; (2) once invested, monies grow and compound tax-deferred; and (3) when withdrawals are made, you may be in a lower tax bracket, thereby minimizing the tax consequences.

THE ACCUMULATION PERIOD

During the accumulation period, the employer is putting money in the TSA on behalf of the employee (participant). Contributions are made with before-tax dollars on a biweekly, semimonthly, or monthly basis; the monthly schedule is most commonly used. The insurer then deposits most or all of each contribution into the participant's account. How the money is actually invested depends on the options elected by the employee.

When deposits are made on your behalf, a transaction charge may occur. Additionally, either quarterly or annually, a maintenance fee may also be deducted from the account's balance. Some companies recover their expenses by charging a negligible amount during the accumulation period and a larger fee when monies are withdrawn.

THE PAYOUT PERIOD

When you are ready to receive the distribution (payout) from the contract, usually at retirement, there are several options available. You can take it all out as a lump sum, make a partial withdrawal, roll over the account into an IRA or another TSA, or annuitize the contract and start receiving a series of monthly, quarterly, or annual payments.

If you choose to annuitize, the payment will depend on the rate offered by the insurer and the annuity option selected, as well as the amount being annuitized. Annuity rates are stated as the amount of monthly income that will be paid by the insurance company for each $1000 of accumulated monies. Some insurers allow the contract owner to select either a fixed or a variable account during payout, regardless of the type of contract used during accumulation.

If a variable account is used during annuitization, there are no guarantees as to the monthly benefit. If the portfolio does well, monthly benefits will increase, and vice versa. In order for the insurer to initially select or later change the monthly benefit, it must select an assumed interest rate of return (AIR). For example, if the AIR is 6 percent and the investment return to you each year is also 6 percent, the benefit will not change. If the return is 14 percent, the monthly benefit will increase. If the return is only 2 percent, the benefit will decrease.

METHODS OF CREDITING INTEREST

The two most common methods used to determine the current interest rate to be credited to employees' accounts are the portfolio average and banding methods. The *portfolio average* method reflects the insurer's earnings on its entire portfolio during the given year. All policy owners are credited with a single composite rate.

portfolio average   determines the current interest rate to be credited based on the insurer's earnings on its entire portfolio.

The *banding* approach uses a year-by-year means of crediting accounts. Employee contributions are banded together for that particular year; each account is credited with the yield such monies actually earn. Thus, the contributed money for year X may earn 9 percent. All of the previous years' contributions may, on average, be returning only 8 percent. Part of any participant's portfolio would then, in this example, be receiving 9 percent, while the balance would be averaging 8 percent. Next year's contributions may earn an entirely different rate from the then-existing balances.

banding   a year-by-year method of crediting interest to a fixed-rate 403(b) annuity contract (offered to teachers and school administrators, hospital employees, and nonprofit employees). The concept of banding has to do with what rate of return is earned on existing money and money periodically contributed by salary reduction plans.

The banding method is advantageous to the investor when interest rates are rising. In a declining interest rate environment, the portfolio method is best. As might be expected, it is misleading to compare the current rate of return between companies using different approaches.

Current Trends in Crediting

Several companies no longer use a calendar-year approach in valuing the rate of interest to be credited to accounts. These companies now use a quarterly, monthly, or even daily method. The reasoning behind this more responsive method is to allow the insurers to be more competitive and also to move quickly to alter the credited rate if it is too high in relation to the actual yield on the company's portfolio.

A small number of insurers have adopted a provision called "market value adjustment." This method adjusts the accumulated fund balance, not the yield, upward or downward. The adjustment is in the opposite direction of the movement in interest rates. If the current rate is higher for new contributions than other monies, the value of the investor's account will decrease. Conversely, a decrease in the current rate results in an increase in fund value. In this particular situation, accumulated monies can constantly change in value, even though you invested in a fixed-rate portfolio.

Two-Tier Interest Crediting

Although the two-tier method is another method of crediting interest, it bears special mention. Two-tier policies are particularly distasteful and misleading. Two-tier policies are considered so unfair that they have been outlawed in more than one state.

The two-tier approach usually credits the contract with a lower rate of interest if a partial or total liquidation is made. Also, it often has a substantial charge for withdrawals, a charge that may never disappear. Finally, accounts are credited with an artificially low rate if a minimal payout or period is elected. These three aspects of two-tier policies allow a company to appear to pay competitive rates during the accumulation period. The rate is actually realized only if annuitization through the initial insurer is utilized. Rates of return *during* annuitization are often comparatively poor.

As you can see, transferability (a 1035 exchange) is discouraged because of the punishing rates actually received or credited. Comparing the current rate of return from a two-tier contract with rates offered from other types of contracts is misleading.

CONTRIBUTIONS

Approximately 70 percent of all TSA contributions are made by the employee, as outlined in the salary reduction agreement; the remaining 30 percent of the contributions are made by the employer. Contribution parameters are set by the insurer; total annual contributions cannot exceed IRS limitations. The amount by which the employee's paycheck is reduced may be an exact dollar figure or a percentage of pay. The investments are normally sent to the annuity biweekly, semimonthly, or monthly.

Another way to make a contribution is by transfer. The employee may move funds from one insurer to another or from one subaccount to another portfolio offered by the same insurance company. Transfers are made for one of the following reasons: (1) dissatisfaction with the current portfolio's performance, (2) change in employer, (3) change in the employee's ability to take risk, (4) change in the investor's retirement date, or (5) new employment with someone who does not offer TSAs.

IRS Publication 571 provides the guidelines by which an individual participant calculates one's maximum exclusion allowance (MEA). Contributions in excess of 20 percent or exceeding $9500 could result in audits. Additionally, in California most school districts have chosen to have the employee's retirement contributions contributed on a pretax basis, which will alter the calculation. Many insurance carriers provide software that will provide the contribution limits for your particular situation.

RETIREMENT OPTIONS

Upon retirement you have a choice of several options: (1) Leave the money where it is and let it continue to grow until a later date, (2) withdraw part or all of the account, (3) take out the account balance in a series of payments over a period of years, (4) select a fixed-rate or variable contract and annuitize, (5) transfer the balance to another insurer, or (6) move the account to an IRA rollover that is invested in another annuity or elsewhere.

Some participants will accumulate funds with one company and then elect to transfer the entire account to another insurer that offers a better annuitization schedule. If you consider such a move, make certain you are familiar with any withdrawal costs or lost opportunities.

If a participant decides to annuitize, the type of plan chosen should depend on the person's health, dependents, and expected longevity. If the employee is in poor health, a straight life annuity is probably a poor choice. A life annuity with period certain or a joint and last survivor option would almost certainly be a better choice. If you have dependents who will continue to need financial support after your death, the period certain or joint and last survivor option would again be a wise choice. Without dependents a life annuity would provide the highest periodic payouts. And finally, a retiree who does not want to outlive his or her income should look at one of the life options instead of just considering a lump sum or installment payments.

A creative retirement approach would be to use an *assumed interest rate* (AIR). All variable accounts require an AIR as the basis for initial and subsequent payments. Many variable annuities allow the participant to select his or her own AIR in calculating the initial payment level; the higher the AIR used, the higher the *initial* checks will be. Other companies offer only one AIR.

assumed interest rate   certain projections, illustrations, or examples are based on an assumed interest rate. The rate of return is assumed because the investment does not offer a guaranteed rate of return (e.g., a money market, bond, or stock portfolio) or the guarantee does not last as long as the illustration is showing (e.g., a fixed-rate annuity that has a guaranteed rate of 6 percent for seven years but the investor wants to know what the account will be worth in 20 years, assuming 6 percent is paid for all 20 years).

The AIR is an assumption, not a guarantee. Subsequent checks will vary, depending on the actual performance of the employee's portfolio versus the selected AIR. If actual returns are exactly equal to the AIR, the payment schedule will not be altered. If investment returns are greater than the AIR, payments will go up. If rates of return are less than the AIR, payments will decrease.

To illustrate the effect using different AIRs, assume someone annuitizes a $100,000 variable annuity at age 65. Further assume that the account ends up averaging exactly 6 percent. Under an assumed interest rate of 3 percent, monthly payments would be as follows: $810 (for year one), $910 (for year five), $1050 (for year 10), $1220 (for year 15), $1400 (for year 20), and $1620 (for the 25th year). If the AIR was 6 percent, monthly payments would be $1000 every month for the entire 25 years. But see what happens if the AIR is 9 percent: $1200 (for year one), $1080 (for year five), $940 (for year 10), $820 (for year 15), $710 (for year 20), and $620 (for year 25). This steady decrease would be on top of any erosion due to inflation.

As you can see, performance during the distribution period can greatly affect the amount of one's checks. The higher the investment returns, the better off the retiree will be, and vice versa.

Since annuitization under a variable contract can be risky, most companies offer a fixed-rate account. Fixed-rate portfolios do not have an AIR (assumed interest rate) to consider. The insurance company determines its current annuitization rates; these rates in turn determine the amount of your monthly benefit. Fixed contracts normally provide a minimum rate; it would be highly unlikely that the offered rate will ever be this low. That is why, when comparing fixed-rate annuitization programs, use the *current* annuity rates.

Qualified annuities are used in paying out retirement income from pension plans, profit-sharing plans, 401(k)s, IRAs, and 403(b)s. Because the dollars that purchase the annuity are qualified, the annuity income generally is considered fully taxable as it is received. If the employee or heir decides to annuitize the qualified annuity retirement plan, there may be an upfront, onetime premium tax. In California, the state premium tax is 0.5 percent. This rate is substantially lower than the 2.37 percent California charges when a nonqualified contract is annuitized.

LOANS

A number of insurers allow you to borrow a portion of your TSA, but there are several reasons why a company may not allow loans. The chief reason is probably due to concern by the IRS; they have convinced Congress to enact legislation restricting the amount and period of any loan.

The Internal Revenue Code (IRC) includes these seven restrictions:

1. A loan is taxable if it exceeds 100 percent of the employee's account or $10,000, whichever is less, *if* the account is less than or equal to $10,000.

2. A $10,000, or greater, loan is taxed if the participant's account is more than $10,000 but less than $20,000.

3. If the value of the account is over $20,000 a loan is also taxable if the amount borrowed is 50 percent of the value of the account or $50,000, whichever is less. The $50,000 amount referred to here is reduced by any net loan repayments made by the employee during the preceding 12 months.

4. Loans, except certain real estate–related ones, must be repaid within five years.

5. If the loan is not repaid in time, any outstanding amount is immediately subject to taxation. It could also be subject to a 10 percent penalty tax.

6. If a loan is in default, the insurance company involved is required to notify the IRS and the participant.

7. If the loan ever exceeds the value of the employee's account, any excess is taxed.

In addition to these outlined IRS restrictions, a number of companies require that a certain minimum be loaned out and that a certain amount remain in the investment after the loan is made.

Insurers that offer loans may also levy a fee when the loan is taken. These charges may be in the form of an initiation fee, administration fee, or account maintenance fee. Additionally, there is a special provision in the TSA contract allowing insurance companies to charge interest on the amount of the outstanding loan. The loan rate may be a flat fee or tied to some well-known index rate. Most companies also prohibit a second loan until the first is fully repaid.

LOAN PROTECTION

Due to the potential adverse tax and penalty consequences of TSA loans, prospective borrowers should contact their annuity company or investment adviser to find out about any possible safeguards. Such measures can protect you against an inadvertent late payment, also referred to as a technical default. Some insurers state that any payment due, but unpaid, may be deducted from the remaining funds in your account. This type of forced payment may be considered a withdrawal, but any withdrawal charges would be minor in comparison to a loan default.

DEATH BENEFITS

The great majority of annuity contracts do not charge any type of fee or penalty for a liquidation due to the death of the participant. If a penalty is levied it could be the reduction of interest via a lower-tier withdrawal rate.

You may wish to review the two-tier interest crediting section earlier in this chapter.

Upon death of the employee, most companies will pay out the total account value. The death benefit may be taken as a lump sum or the contract can be annuitized by the beneficiary; a few insurers offer additional payment options. Processing time for death claims, once all required paperwork has been received (e.g., certified copy of the death certificate), averages about two weeks. Sometimes, the process may take only a few days.

TSA EXPENSES

Every TSA has expenses; some of them are more identifiable than others. There are two basic approaches used by insurers in obtaining these fees—explicit and implicit. *Explicit charges* are clearly spelled out and visible; they may be applied regularly throughout the year, such as when the account is valued, a contribution is received, a loan is made, or a withdrawal occurs.

explicit charges   clearly spelled out, these may be applied when the account is valued, when a loan is made, and so on.

Implicit charges are made indirectly and can often be much higher than their explicit counterparts. An implicit charge might be the difference between the returns the insurer actually earns versus the amount credited to your account. Another hidden cost may take place if, and when, the contract is annuitized; that cost will include a profit margin (the spread between what you receive and what the account actually earns) and expense charges. It is not unusual for a participant to ignore or underestimate the number and magnitude of implicit charges.

implicit charges   indirect, hidden costs, such as the difference between returns actually earned versus the amount credited to your account.

Insurers have the right to alter or amend TSA contracts; this privilege is usually quite broad. Such alteration can affect the amount of any charges made, interest credited to the account in the future, annuity rates per $1000 annuitized, and other provisions described in the contract. For the most part, only group contracts can be altered without your permission; individual TSAs can be changed only with the permission of the investor.

Chapter

13

Your Financial Plan and Annuities

There is no single best investment. Indeed, every legitimate investment is appropriate for some investors during certain periods of their lives. A money market account or bank CD is a proper choice for an aggressive investor who needs a temporary place to park money before making an investment decision or until there is a change in the economic outlook. At the other extreme, a mutual fund that specializes in international stocks would be a good choice for a conservative investor who needed a hedge against inflation, wanted to decrease the risk of holding just U.S. stocks, and/or was willing to leave the investment alone for the next five to ten years.

If there was a best investment, there would be no need for stockbrokers, financial planners, or investment counselors. You and I would simply place all of our money in one place. Unfortunately, the world of investing is not that simple. In fact, it can be quite complex. This chapter will give you some general *and* specific ideas as to how your entire portfolio should be structured. You will also be able to determine if annuities should play a minor or major role in your portfolio. Let us begin by trying to determine what it is we are trying to do with our money.

Everyone is trying to do something with one's money. Some people need current income while others are looking only for growth. Still others need some current income but also need growth to offset the effects of inflation. Thus, the first step is to determine if you need growth, current income, or growth and some income.

RISK LEVEL

Most people have a good idea as to how much risk they can accept (refer to the risk tolerance test in Chapter 2). As a broad generalization, you are either conservative, moderate, or aggressive. To help you determine your risk profile more precisely, look at Table 13.1 and pick out the single description that best describes you.

While reviewing the expected range of returns and the probability of losing up to 5 percent of your money in any given year, keep in mind the following four points:

1. The loss during the year or at a particular point in time could be dramatically higher than 5 percent (e.g., on October 19, 1987, the stock market dropped over 23 percent, but investors who were in the market for the entire calendar year actually earned 5 percent).

2. The loss would not be permanent, assuming you did not panic.

3. The recovery time needed to make up the loss could be as little as three months or as long as three years.

TABLE 13.1 Find Your Risk Profile		
Investor Profile	Expected Range of Returns Annually	Odds of Losing 5 Percent
Very conservative	5–8%	1 in 40
Conservative	7–10%	1 in 20
Conservative to moderate	9–12%	1 in 10
Moderate	11–14%	1 in 7
Moderately aggressive	14–17%	1 in 5
Aggressive	16–19%	1 in 4

4. Returns become more predictable if the expected holding period is five or more years.

Speaking of time, let us now determine our comfort level by factoring in our level of patience and the period we are planning to own a particular asset.

TIME HORIZON

Barring an emergency, you are the only one who knows when you will need money and how much. Some investments are designed to be held for the short term (zero to three years); others work best if they are owned for an intermediate period (four to seven years); still others perform best if they are owned for a long time (eight to fourteen years). *Short-term investments* include bank CDs, money market funds, and bonds that are going to mature in just a few years. *Intermediate-term investments* include tax-free or taxable bonds that mature in less than a decade; mutual funds or variable annuities that are "balanced" or "total return" (a portfolio of stocks and bonds); a portfolio of growth and income stocks, foreign securities, growth stocks, and high-yield bonds. *Long-term investments* would include real estate; bonds that mature in 15 to 20 years; variable annuities and/or mutual funds that invest in aggressive growth, growth, and international stocks as well as growth and income securities; all-cash (non-leveraged) leasing programs; and real estate investment trusts (REITs).

short-term investments   a security that matures in five years or less (zero to three years by some definitions).

intermediate-term investments   a bond or other security that matures in five to fifteen years (four to seven years by some definitions).

One of the great benefits of investing in common stocks is that the longer your holding period, the more likely you are to do well. Not only are the returns going to be more predictable, but the chances of a loss are greatly reduced. As an example, looking over the past half century (1948–1997), the chances of making money in the stock market during any given calendar year were 80 percent. If the time horizon is extended to three or five years, the chances of making money were 96 percent. Over any 10 consecutive years (e.g., 1948–1957, 1949–1958, etc.), the odds of showing a gain are 100 percent.

long-term investments   a bond or other security that matures in sixteen to thirty years (eight to fourteen years by some definitions).

These percentage figures become even more attractive if you are invested in a variable annuity or mutual fund that has the benefit of professional management. Like other things in life, a specific risk level and time horizon may not be exact or may not apply to all of our holdings. It is for this reason that a blended approach may be needed.

BLENDING INVESTMENTS

Like most people, you may find that you do not want all of your investments to be conservative, moderate, *or* aggressive. You could also discover that the majority of your assets can be invested for a certain number of years but that some can be left in for a different period of time. There is nothing wrong with this; in fact, this approach is quite common. Often, a conservative investor wants to be a little risky with 5 percent or 10 percent of his or her portfolio. Conversely, a moderately aggressive person may need to know that $15,000 will always be available as a cushion or emergency fund.

These nuances or special considerations can be worked out with your financial adviser. But, before going to your investment counselor, take a few minutes to determine your tax bracket. Specifically, we need to find out how much of our income needs to be sheltered in tax-free bonds and annuities. After all, an overriding concern should always be what we make after factoring in the effects of income taxes.

TAX TABLES

Table 13.2 combines federal and state income taxes. This combination table, which includes California state income taxes (1998 rates), shows the full impact of taxes: how much is going to your state *and* federal governments. The state you live in may have higher or lower taxes than California. If you do not know your state tax bracket, the table will provide you with a good approximation.

When calculating your taxable income, make sure that you *exclude*: (1) any earnings or growth in a retirement plan, such as an IRA, Keogh, or pension plan, that has not yet been distributed to you, (2) interest from all tax-free bonds, and (3) growth and/or interest in your annuity that you have not yet withdrawn.

INVESTING IN ANNUITIES

Annuities are the ideal choice for someone who is in a moderate or high tax bracket and is looking for a way to shelter current income or growth. Fixed-rate annuities would be a smart alternative to CDs, money market accounts, GNMAs, Treasury bills, or other government obligations, particularly if you are the type of investor who would only need to touch such monies in the case of unforeseen circumstances. Variable annuities would be a proper choice for a taxpayer who trades quite a bit in his or her account, is in a moderate or high tax bracket, and is tired of paying taxes on capital gains, dividends, and interest from securities. They would

TABLE 13.2 California State and Federal Income Tax Tables Combined (1998 Rates)		
Taxable Income		*State and Federal Bracket*
Single	*Married*	
$25,350–$61,400	$42,350–$102,300	34.7% (28.0% federal)
$61,401–$128,100	$102,301–$155,950	37.4% (31.0% federal)
$128,101–$278,450	$155,951–$278,450	42.0% (36.0% federal)
Over $278,450	Over $278,450	45.2% (39.6% federal)

also be a good substitution for mutual funds that are highly taxed each year or an appropriate vehicle for a fund investor who makes at least a major change within a 12-month period (switches within the same or different mutual fund family).

The previous paragraph describes someone who is looking for growth and is in a federal tax bracket greater than 15 percent. But what about those investors who want current income? Do annuities make sense for these people? Yes. As you may recall from Chapter 3, annuities can be structured for current income. The checks can be automatically mailed to you on a monthly, quarterly, semiannual, or annual basis. Income can be sent to you for a set period of time or for the duration of your life expectancy (and/or that of your spouse, friend, child, etc.). You decide the frequency and duration of the distributions. And, as you previously learned, a substantial portion of these checks can be tax-advantaged for several years (if the income stream is annuitized).

The typical equity (stock) mutual fund is much more tax-efficient than most people expect. A mutual fund that is considered to be highly tax-efficient is one in which only a small percentage, roughly five percent to 15 percent, of any gain for the year is taxable. Thus, an investor in an equity fund that has a very good year and is up 30 percent will typically pay taxes on only 3 percent and not 30 percent (10 percent of 30 percent equals 3 percent). Even assuming a 50 percent tax bracket, the total tax liability would be 1.5 percent (3 percent times 50 percent equals 1.5 percent).

Dividends from an equity mutual fund would also be taxable, but the S&P 500 has an annual dividend yield of under 2 percent and a large number of funds have dividends in the zero to 1 percent range. Whatever the dividend, the actual tax liability would be very low since the dividend would still be multiplied by the investor's tax bracket (15 percent to 40 percent) and the resulting number would be well under 1 percent.

The average mutual fund that invests exclusively in stocks has a tax efficiency of about 80 percent to 85 percent; a number of great performing equity funds are 90 to 95+ percent tax-efficient. *The 100 Best Mutual Funds You Can Buy* (1998, Adams Publishing) lists the tax efficiency of the better risk-adjusted return funds each year. Contrary to what you may have read in a number of well-respected financial periodicals or books, surprisingly there is no relationship between tax efficiency and turnover. High-turnover mutual funds, such as those frequently found in the aggressive growth or small company growth fund categories, can, and often are, highly tax-efficient. Even during great years, investors in a large number of these funds get to keep almost the entire year's gain. The only way the entire gain becomes taxable is if *the investor* sells or exchanges fund shares.

You have a great of latitude in deciding what percentage of your total portfolio should be in annuities. Variable annuities often become a preferable choice for the equity portion of your portfolio if you: (1) are a market timer (someone who moves from stocks to cash and vice versa depending on market conditions or when a "buy" or "sell" signal is generated), (2) lack patience (meaning you are likely to make a large shift if a moderate or large part of your portfolio is not doing well during the course of the year), or (3) move in and out of funds or individual securities, going into the then-hot sector or buying into a category or specific stock after it has taken a beating. Patient equity investors, with the possible exception of utility stock investors, are usually better off with individual stocks or a handful of different mutual funds. Bond, CD, Treasury bill, and money market investors who keep rolling over interest each year, rarely, if ever, touching the account, are almost always better off in a fixed-rate or bond subaccount. The sheltering of current income in an annuity is very appealing in such situations.

IMPORTANCE OF FINANCIAL PLANNING

If I asked you to take a car ride with me and I said, "I don't know how long we will be, I don't know where we are going, I don't know how much gas I have, and I don't have a gas gauge," it is doubtful that you would want to come along. Yet, this is how most people plan their financial future. They have no set goals, objectives, or disciplined approach when it comes to investing and planning ahead.

Throughout this book, references and examples of the importance of having a financial plan have been given. A large number of mutual fund and variable annuity companies offer free work sheets to help you draft your own plan or help determine retirement and future education costs of your children.

If you seek outside professional help, expect to pay anywhere from several hundred dollars to a couple of thousand for a comprehensive plan. Before you pay for a financial plan, interview the planner and find out what you are getting for your money. Find out the adviser's background and ask for referrals. A good source to begin with is the Institute of Business & Finance, which confers the CFS (Certified Fund Specialist) and BC (Board Certified) designations; for a list of certified professionals in your area, phone 800-848-2029. The Institute can give you a list of qualified people who are well trained in financial planning, mutual funds, and variable annuities.

REPOSITIONING ASSETS

Often, investors see tables that list the 10 best mutual funds or variable annuities and rush out to quickly invest in these portfolios. Do not attempt to "chase last year's winners." What performed well last year may do poorly this year. In fact, extensive neutral studies show that funds and variable annuities highly rated by *Consumer Reports*, Morningstar, *Business Week*, Lipper, *Forbes*, and others often underperform their peer group during the subsequent one-, three-, or five-year period. It may surprise you to learn that future winners are frequently the previous period's losers or were at least in the second tier of recommendations. Truly, there is little, if any, relationship between past, present, and future performance.

No one knows what the next best-performing investment category will be. It might be international, aggressive growth, high-yield, or growth and income. What is a tortoise one year may overtake the hare the next year. Smart investors know that they cannot predict the future; therefore, they spread their money out among several different categories. Such a strategy reduces risk and often increases one's return.

By diversifying among several different investment categories, over any given year your "missed opportunity" could be great; but then again, so could your "avoided disaster." When you look at meaningful periods of time, I think you will discover that very little, if any, is lost by being properly diversified. What is gained is peace of mind and more predictable results. Investing should be considered a lifetime goal; gambling is a short-term proposition.

SUMMARY

As you can see, annuities can, and often should, play a major role in your investment plan. It is their flexibility and guarantees that make them an integral part of your financial security. As you and your adviser begin to look at different contracts, look for companies that have portfolio managers that have been in existence for several years, that enjoy a strong reputation in the financial services community, and that include the sub-accounts and provisions that are important to you.

Commonly Asked Questions

IN GENERAL

How do annuities work?

Fixed-rate and variable annuities have two stages: the accumulation period and the payout period. The accumulation period begins as soon as you invest. You invest with one payment if you select a single-premium deferred annuity. Or, you make one or more payments of various amounts to a flexible-premium deferred annuity. Once you make a payment, your money begins to accumulate tax-deferred earnings. Later, your principal and interest are paid out to you in the form of regular income or as a lump sum.

Are annuities a new type of investment?

No. Annuities have been around in this country for over 100 years. They have been available in other countries for several hundred years.

I read somewhere that annuities are a bad idea; is this true?

Absolutely not. However, like any other type of investment, annuities can be misused or improperly represented by an advertisement or adviser.

Equally important, just like mutual funds and bank CDs, some annuities represent a bad value or have demonstrated poor performance. If you remember hearing about annuities through friends or parents who said they were a bad deal, they were probably referring to annuities that were offered a couple of decades ago with poor rates of return and noncompetitive provisions—in short, some annuities relied on the ignorance of the investing public. Fortunately, things have greatly changed over the past 25 years.

Why should I purchase an annuity?

There are three good reasons:

1. As a safe vehicle for your money.
2. For tax-deferred growth of earnings.
3. To ensure that your resources last as long as you need them.

Is there more than one type of annuity?

Yes. Annuities can be categorized in one of three ways: (1) when they commence payment, (2) what they invest in, and (3) whether money can be added to the contract. An immediate annuity is for someone who wants to start receiving income right away. A deferred annuity would be the right choice for someone who did not need any additional income now, but might in the future, and/or who wanted a growth vehicle. The second way of categorizing annuities is by how the money is invested. When you invest in a fixed-rate annuity, the contract owner receives a set rate of return, similar to a bank CD. Under a variable annuity, the investor is not promised a set rate of return but instead chooses among various portfolios, ranging from conservative (money market account) to speculative (aggressive growth fund). The third way to categorize an annuity has to do with principal contribution(s). A single-premium contract allows for only a onetime deposit. A flexible-premium contract is structured so that additional monies can be added now or in the future.

How do I choose which type of annuity is best for me?

Your first decision is whether you want a guarantee (fixed-rate annuity) or flexibility (variable annuity) with your investment. Next, determine which contract provisions (e.g., how the free withdrawal is calculated, when the penalty period ends, expense charges, etc.) are important before comparing contracts.

How much money should I invest in an annuity?

The answer to this question depends on your risk level, how your money is currently invested, your time horizon, and current as well as projected tax bracket. It is important to see how annuities fit in as part of an overall financial plan. Like anything else in life, the answer to this question will largely depend on your comfort level and what feels right to you.

Is there an exact way to determine risk?

No. There are several different tests to help investors to determine their risk profile, but there is not one that clearly stands above the others. Defining risk in precise terms is almost like trying to find a universal definition of love that everyone agrees to—a process that is elusive at best.

Should I avoid annuities since I don't understand them?

Be patient. The first time you heard about mutual funds or bonds you probably did not understand all of the workings of such investments. Annuities are not difficult to understand.

What makes an annuity better than other investments?

Tax-deferred growth. In addition, an annuity can guarantee you an income stream that you cannot outlive. The daily guarantee of a fixed-rate annuity and the death benefit (or enhanced death benefit) in the case of variable contracts is another benefit. Finally, the ability to make changes without paying income taxes may be the biggest advantage.

What does tax deferral mean to me?

It means you pay no taxes on interest or growth, as long as such earnings remain in the contract. The money that would otherwise go to the government goes to work for you instead—compounding even more. The cumulative effect of this tax deferral can be startling. Your funds grow much faster, as shown in Figure 14.1.

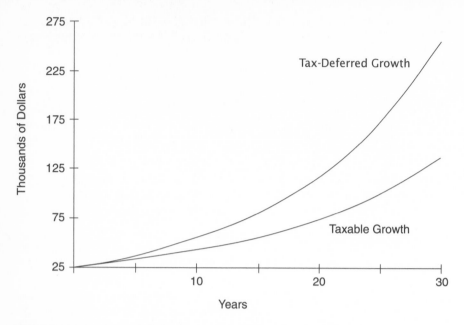

FIGURE 14.1   A tax-deferred versus a taxable investment of $25,000 at 8 percent return (assuming 28 percent marginal tax bracket).

What is often overlooked about an annuity is the income stream that it can later provide. Tax deferral results in greater growth of principal, which can be used to provide an income stream that is far greater than what would have been gained from an investment that was partially or fully taxable each year. Phrased another way, tax deferral does not have to be a ticking time bomb; there is most likely no need to liquidate the contract during your or your spouse's lifetime.

How does an annuity compare to an IRA for retirement?

Annuities and IRAs differ in a number of significant areas. Not everyone can open an IRA—only those with *earned* income. Anyone can purchase a fixed-rate annuity. When contributing, you are limited to $2000 annually with an IRA; there are no limits with an annuity.

On the tax front, IRA contributions may be deductible, although the law imposes limits based on income and pension-plan coverage. Generally, no deductions are allowed for payments to an annuity. If you are not allowed a deduction for your IRA contribution, an annuity is a smart alternative—your money still grows tax-deferred.

How important is professional management?

When you invest in an annuity you have hired professional management. Individually, you and I cannot afford to hire the top money managers, but collectively we can hire the best. By hiring professionals to manage our money we do not have to worry about the day-to-day fluctuations in the stock and bond market or wonder if the securities purchased are about to be downgraded.

Are there disadvantages to other investments?

Absolutely. There is no such thing as a perfect investment. If there was a perfect investment, you and I would never have to read the financial press or buy another book on investments. Unfortunately, there is no panacea when it comes to investing.

What does the insurance company do with my fixed-rate premium?

The company invests the funds in its investment portfolio and credits interest to your account. This is called the accumulation phase of the contract. It is important during this phase to know that your annuity company manages its investments wisely. You want to choose a company that is highly rated by independent analysts for its ability to meet its obligations. The company should have a strong capital base and a history of high ratings, preferably from at least two well–known services.

Are insurance companies the only ones that offer annuities?

The answer to this question is somewhat confusing. True, it is only the insurance industry that is allowed to create annuities for the public, but other financial institutions, such as banks, brokers, and financial planners, market these products.

Aren't tax-free exchanges oversold?

You may think that you will never want to move your money from a mutual fund, stock, bond, or bank CD, but think again. No one knows where interest rates will be in a couple of years or if a bank may become troubled or when a favored manager may leave a mutual fund. When such an event occurs, you may be reluctant to move your money either due to a sense of safety (comfort level in dealing with the same institution year after year) or because of the tax ramifications.

WITHDRAWALS

When and how can I withdraw money from my annuity?

Like all tax-qualified savings plans, annuities are intended to provide a retirement income, so the payout phase generally begins at retirement or after age $59\frac{1}{2}$. You may withdraw a lump sum, or you can annuitize. Withdrawals may be made at any time; you simply contact the insurance company.

Can I get to my money before I am $59\frac{1}{2}$?

Yes. Most annuities provide certain liquidity features, such as withdrawals of a portion of your interest, free of charge. Withdrawals in excess of that amount are possible but, in the early years of your contract, may trigger surrender charges. Keep in mind that the IRS generally imposes both ordinary income tax and a 10 percent penalty on earnings withdrawn before age $59\frac{1}{2}$.

Will I have access to my money if I need it?

Annuity contracts generally provide several liquidity features. Depending on your specific contract and how long it has been in force, you may be able to withdraw a certain dollar amount or a portion of your contract without charge. In other cases you may incur a surrender charge. If you withdraw all your money, you surrender the contract and it terminates. The surrender benefit is generally equal to your contract value minus any surrender charges.

Does every annuity impose a penalty for early withdrawals?

No, but most companies impose a penalty. The typical penalty for an annuity is in the five-to-seven-year range; the typical charge is 5 percent. Some companies offer what is known as a CD/annuity wherein the rate of return is guaranteed for only one year but the penalty also lasts for only one year.

What does "annuitize" mean?

Choosing to liquidate the contract at regular intervals and receiving tax-advantaged checks over time is "annuitizing." Most companies offer at least three annuity options, based primarily on how long you want the income to last.

When will my annuity payments begin?

In most cases, you can choose when payments begin. However, if your annuity is part of a qualified plan (IRA, Keogh, pension plan, etc.), the Internal Revenue Code generally requires that you begin taking payments by age 70½. If the annuity is nonqualified, you may never have to make any withdrawals (but your nonspouse heir will). Some companies may offer immediate annuities, for which payments begin right away.

How much will I receive in each payment?

That depends largely on four factors: (1) how much money you invest in the annuity, (2) what payout option you choose, (3) the general level of interest rates, and (4) the competitiveness of the company you have selected.

What happens if I die before receiving any payments?

If you die before annuity payments begin, your beneficiary will receive a death benefit, usually equal to your total annuity value (premiums paid plus interest earned) or the value of the contract on date of death, whichever is greater. This benefit avoids the costs and delays of probate.

What happens if money is paid out to my beneficiaries?

As a contract issued by a life insurance company, a variable annuity provides a death benefit that can pass outside your probate estate directly to your beneficiary, thereby avoiding costs and delays. The guaranteed minimum death benefit generally is the greater of either the total amount of your paid premiums less any withdrawals, or the current value of your investment.

Some companies may be more generous in their contracts, allowing a death benefit equal to the value of the contract on the most recent anniversary date. This means that if the contract has lost value since that date, the beneficiary receives a greater amount.

Are annuity payments taxable?

Partially. When the payout phase begins, you pay income tax on the interest portion of the payments only; the rest is a tax-free return of principal. If you decide to make a withdrawal of funds before age 59½, you may be subject to regular income tax and a 10 percent penalty tax on the interest/growth withdrawn. Withdrawals of principal are not subject to income taxes or the 10 percent IRS penalty.

How are payments determined if I annuitize a variable annuity?

First, the insurance company converts your accumulation units to annuity units; this entitles you to payouts that are partly a tax-free return of principal and partly taxable interest. Meanwhile, the undistributed portion of your investment continues to compound, tax-deferred.

Can the monthly payment of a variable annuity change?

Yes. The amount you receive each month can and will fluctuate with the performance of the securities portfolios you have selected.

VARIABLE ANNUITIES

What is a variable annuity?

Your premiums are invested by the insurance company in one or more securities portfolios and earn income and/or capital appreciation.

What do I purchase with my variable annuity premium?

Your premium usually purchases accumulation units in the insurance company's separate account, which is not commingled with the company's regular portfolio of investments. This separate account in turn purchases shares in securities portfolios established and administered for the variable annuity. In this sense, accumulation units are similar to shares in a mutual fund. Most variable annuities also let you allocate funds to a fixed account option that is part of the insurer's regular portfolio and guarantees a minimum interest rate.

Like mutual fund shares, each unit's value or price is determined by the value of the portfolio, divided by the number of units outstanding. Each unit represents a share of the total worth of the portfolio. For example, assume a $10 million portfolio has one million accumulation units: Each unit has a current value of $10. If the portfolio appreciates to $12 million, the unit value rises to $12 each. Divide your premium by the unit value at the time you invest to approximate the number of units you will purchase.

What happens once I have purchased accumulation units?

The underlying securities have the potential to earn interest, dividends, and/or capital gains, which are reinvested to earn still more. Gains or losses, like dividends and interest, are reflected in the price per unit; the number of units changes only if there is a withdrawal or new money is added.

What types of securities do variable annuity portfolios contain?

The majority of variable annuities provide you with a choice of portfolios of stocks, bonds, and/or money market instruments. You can allocate your money, depending on how aggressive or conservative you wish to be.

Do I have to make all of the investment decisions?

No doubt maintaining a balance between stocks, bonds, and money market instruments can be tough. If you would prefer experts to make the choices, an asset allocation subaccount might be best for you. Professional managers view current market and economic conditions to determine the best mix of investments for achieving a portfolio's objective at any point in time. The objective of an asset allocation portfolio usually is to provide a somewhat predetermined level of total return consistent with long-term preservation of capital.

What protects against loss of my initial and/or ongoing investment?

Every variable annuity has inherent features that work to lower risk and increase your return, including:

Professional management: Like a family of mutual funds, all portfolios in a variable annuity are constructed and monitored by professional investment managers. Each portfolio has a stated objective, and the professional managers—backed by education, experience, and research—are better able to select the right investments to achieve the portfolio's objective.

Diversification: Even if you invest in a single portfolio, your risk is spread among many securities, reducing the possibility of losing a substantial amount due to any one security. Furthermore, you can invest in more than one portfolio.

Separate accounts: Variable annuity portfolios other than the fixed account option are part of a separate account, established and maintained apart from the company's general investment portfolio. The safety of your investment does not depend on the performance of the insurance company's own portfolio. Only the performance of the separate account portfolio you have chosen will affect your results.

Switching privileges: Most variable annuities permit you to reallocate your money among the portfolios, generally without charge as long as you do not move the money too often. Transfers among portfolios when interest rates or market conditions change can keep your earnings high.

Guaranteed death benefit: Variable annuities generally guarantee that in the event of death during the accumulation phase, your beneficiary will receive the greater of: (1) the entire amount of your premiums, less withdrawals, charges and fees; or (2) the current value of your investment. Some annuities provide more generous options.

Should I be concerned with the "minimum guaranteed rate"?

Normally not. However, there are periods of time, such as 1992 and 1993, when the minimum rate may just happen to turn out to be a comparatively high return. There are periods of time when it seems almost impossible for CD or money market rates to fall to the 3 percent to 4 percent range, yet it has happened on more than one occasion in the past. When such an environment exists, the minimum guarantee offered by fixed-rate annuities is a good deal.

Which variable annuity is the best?

There is no "best." It may look like there is a best because a particular portfolio was up 20 percent to 50 percent last year, but this does not mean that it cannot fall 20 percent to 30 percent next year. No investment can sustain a growth rate of 30 percent year after year.

Which subaccounts should I be using?

You money should be invested in more than one subaccount. You do not have to use different annuity companies, but make sure that you are diversified. Just because you or some financial guru thinks that the stock market is going to skyrocket or that technology issues are going to double during the next year does not mean that this is going to happen. Almost everyone has an opinion about what the stock and bond markets are going to do over the next week, month, and year. At least half of these people will prove to be wrong. Unfortunately, we will not know who the losers are until after the fact.

If a fund or portfolio is hot one year, will it do will the next?

There is no way of knowing. Sometimes a subaccount does great one year because the manager was lucky and chose stocks or bonds that happened to be in what turned out to be the popular industries for the year. What can be said with certainty is that there is a very small correlation between the performance of a stock from one year to the next. In fact, there is only a 9 percent correlation between the performance of a long-term bond from one year to the next.

Everyone claims to be number one; how can this be true?

There are many ways to rate a mutual fund or variable annuity. One account may be the number one performer of "all aggressive growth funds that are at least five and a half years old for the period 3/31/92 through 9/30/97." Another fund or portfolio can legitimately call itself the best performer "when compared to all other growth and income accounts that manage $200 million or less, for the year ending 6/30/98." As you can begin to see, there are several ways an account can be classified (size, a certain period of time, category, and being in existence for at least a certain period of time).

How should I go about selecting investments (or annuity subaccounts)?

Keep in mind that investments move in cycles. What is today's darling may be tomorrow's disappointment. Do not be overly concerned as to when you get into the stock or bond markets; the most important thing is to make some kind of commitment to either invest a lump sum or slowly percolate into the marketplace by investing money on a regular basis. Stick with investment categories whose volatility you can live with, either individually or as an entire portfolio.

Can the guaranteed death benefit help me out?

Yes. As the contract owner, you are free to name someone other than yourself as the annuitant. By naming someone else as the insured (the annuitant), you may actually benefit financially by someone else's death. This is somewhat of a ghoulish thought, though not much different from buying life insurance on someone else and naming oneself as the beneficiary.

COMPOUNDING

Why is it important to learn the Rule of 72?

This rule of thumb formula is a quick and convenient way to determine how something—anything—will multiply in value over time. (See Appendix D for more information.) Most people are curious as to how many years they must wait until they have a certain net worth.

Does the Rule of 72 work for other investments?

Yes. When comparing how fast it takes an asset to double in value, keep in mind that you must take into consideration the annual tax ramifications of the investment unless it is sheltered within a retirement account or annuity. Inflation is also something that should be factored in so that the *real* rate of return can be calculated.

How long does it take for $10,000 to grow to $40,000?

This question could also be phrased a different way by asking how long it takes money to double two times (from 1 to 2 and then from 2 to 4). The answer to these questions is: It depends on what rate of return the investment experiences. An investment growing at 9 percent will double every eight years. In this particular example, this means that $10,000 will grow to $20,000 by the end of eight years and then double again to $40,000 by the end of the second eight-year period (or a total of 16 years). Bear in mind that this assumed, guaranteed, or projected rate of return is either tax-free or tax-deferred. An 8 percent return that is subject to current income taxes will have a return of something less than 8 percent after state and federal taxes have been subtracted.

COMPARISON TO MUTUAL FUNDS

Are annuities better than mutual funds?

No. Variable annuities are an alternative to mutual funds, just like fixed-rate annuities are a choice you can make instead of investing in a bank CD. It all depends on what you are trying to do with your money.

Do funds hire better money managers than variable annuities?

No. Many variable annuity subaccounts are simply "clones" of well-known mutual funds. And, just like mutual funds, variable annuities have their share of poor, average, and excellent money managers.

Why is there more information on mutual funds than annuities?

First, mutual funds are easier to understand. Because they are easier to understand, popular publications emphasize the performance and features of mutual funds with much greater frequency. Second, the brokerage industry can make more money selling you some mutual funds than annuities. Third, the insurance industry does not spend as much money promoting annuities as do mutual funds. Finally, funds appeal more to a wider age group.

STATE GUARANTY LAWS

How important is it for my state to have a guaranty law?

Probably not very. However, let me quickly add that if you are one of the comparatively few people who may someday suffer from the insolvency of an insurance company, you would certainly disagree, and rightfully so. Keep in mind that only up to 80 percent of the contract's value is protected by such laws.

Do state guaranty provisions work?

The ability of a state to levy a special tax or draw from a pool of funds has not yet been put to the test on any kind of large or threatening scale. It appears that in the worst-case situation, investors would have to wait up to a couple of years if a state's funds were insufficient and the troubled company was not bailed out by its peers. Again, this is something we have never seen before. Troubled companies in the past have been anxiously taken over by other insurers.

How do these guarantees affect variable annuities?

Up to specified amounts, all annuities, fixed as well as variable, and life insurance policies are covered by these provisions. For practical purposes, such guarantees mean little to a variable annuity owner since his or her assets are not commingled with those of the issuer. The insurance company could go bankrupt during the year and the investor in that company's aggressive growth portfolio might experience a 45 percent gain that very same year and have immediate access to all previous and current earnings, growth, and principal.

INSURANCE COMPANIES

Are household name insurance companies safer than the others?

Not necessarily. You may be surprised to learn that some of the very best known companies such as Kemper, Prudential, and Metropolitan Life do not have the same safety as some smaller, lesser known annuity issuers.

Is it important to use a large insurance company?

No. You should be much more concerned with the company's rating, the investment options, contract guarantees, features, and any penalties associated with the contract. Many people like to deal with larger firms since it is commonly believed that regulatory bodies and/or the government will not let a big company go under. There is certainly some truth to this belief, but it should not be viewed as an absolute fact.

Are there disadvantages to dealing with the biggest issuers?

Sometimes. Some large companies, well-known because of their advertising or sales force, offer less than average rates of return or high penalties, knowing that the public is still likely to buy the product because of name recognition.

How safe are these and other companies?

Extremely safe. In any given year, those comparatively few companies that face problems will, in all likelihood, work out their problems.

Do company sales figures or assets mean anything?

Probably not. The fact that a company sells a lot of product or manages huge sums of money does not mean that your investment is any safer or riskier than if it were with a small insurer.

Why mention sales figures or assets under management?

To give you an idea as to the presence and financial clout of the insurance industry. The life insurance industry of the United States, which issues all fixed-rate and variable annuities, owns, controls, or manages one-third of the world's wealth; U.S. insurers own, control, or manage more assets than all of the banks in the world combined; U.S. insurers own, control, or manage more assets than all of the oil companies in the world combined.

REPORTING PERFORMANCE

How often will my annuity issue me a report?

Fixed-rate annuities normally only send out statements once a year. These statements show you the current rate of return being credited to your account, your account's value, and notice of any rate change. Variable annuity reports are typically issued every quarter. Statements are also sent out if there are withdrawals, additions, or exchanges.

Will my newspaper show me how I am doing in my annuity?

No. Newspapers and magazines do not publish the current interest rate of fixed-rate annuities. The same thing is generally true with variable annuities. *Barron's*, a weekly periodical, publishes performance figures of thousands of the most popular variable annuity subaccounts. A small handful of publications used by the financial services community also provide on-going numbers and percentage figures.

FINANCIAL PLANNING

How important is financial planning?

If I asked you to take a car ride with me and I said, "I don't know how long we will be, I don't know where we are going, I don't know how much gas I have, and I don't have a gas gauge," it is doubtful that you would want to come along. Yet, this is how most people plan their financial future. They have no set goals, objectives, or disciplined approach when it comes to investing and planning ahead.

How often should I move my assets around?

Often, investors see tables that list the 10 best mutual funds or variable annuities and rush out to quickly invest in these portfolios. Do not attempt to "chase last year's winners."

Why is it important to invest in several different categories?

Because no one knows what the next best-performing investment category will be (it might be international, aggressive growth, high-yield, etc.). Smart investors know that they cannot predict the future and therefore they spread their money out among several different categories. Such a strategy reduces risk and often increases one's long-term return.

How much will I lose out on if I diversify?

Over any given year, your "missed opportunity" could be great; but then again, so could your "avoided disaster." When you look at meaningful periods of time, you will discover that very little, if any, is lost by being properly diversified. What is gained is peace of mind and more predictable results.

What does it cost to have a financial plan drafted?

A comprehensive plan can cost anywhere from several hundred to a few thousand dollars. Before you pay for a financial plan, interview the planner and find out what you are getting for your money. Find out the adviser's background and ask for referrals.

Do investment advisers recommend annuities for retirement accounts?

Yes. Brokers, financial planners, and investment advisers view annuities as compatible with the long-term objective of saving for retirement. Indeed, contract owners cite this reason for investing (and tax deferral) more than any other. Many types of subaccounts work best when allowed to ride out the ups and downs of market cycles over long periods of time.

What's the difference between yield and total return?

Yield is the income per unit credited to a contract owner, from the dividends and interest, over a specified period of time. Yield is expressed as a percent of the current offering price per share. Since most people do not ever make withdrawals from an annuity, yield figures are not very important.

The term "total return" is a measure of the per-unit change in any value from the beginning to the end of a specified period, usually a year, including distributions paid to contract owners. This measure includes income received (or credited) from dividends, interest, and capital gains distributions (or losses). *Total return provides the best measure of overall subaccount performance.*

Why don't more people invest in foreign securities?

Ignorance. The reality is that foreign securities (stocks and bonds), when added to domestic investments, can *reduce* the portfolio's level of risk. The stock and bond markets around the world rarely move up and down together at the same time. It is this random correlation that helps lower risk—when U.S. stocks or bonds are going down, securities in several other parts of the world are either moving sideways or going up.

Is standard deviation the correct way to measure risk?

Not necessarily. Standard deviation measures volatility (or predictability) of returns. Standard deviation punishes a subaccount equally for upward volatility (by giving it a high standard deviation figure that is then translated by most financial writers as "high risk") as well as downward volatility; no one minds *upward* volatility.

RATINGS

Is one rating service better than another?

No. The A.M. Best Company is the best-known rating service and is certainly one of the best. Ideally, when you are shopping for annuities you should look for a top rating from at least two of the major rating services (Moody's, Weiss, S&P, etc.).

How important is an annuity company's rating?

Very important if you are investing in a fixed-rate annuity. With most fixed-rate contracts, your money is commingled in with the general assets of the insurance company. If their portfolio performs poorly there is a chance, although only slight, that your principal and accumulated earnings could be tied up or somehow penalized.

Why don't variable annuities stress their ratings?

The rating of an insurance company offering a variable annuity is not nearly as important as one that sells fixed-rate contracts. Unlike almost all fixed-rate contracts, variable annuity money is not commingled with the assets of the insurance company. Investors who participate in a variable contract need only worry about how the subaccounts (growth, international, bond, etc.) are doing, not the financial solvency of the issuer.

How often does an insurance company's rating change?

Very infrequently. The vast majority of companies that have a good rating will maintain their quality standing for years to come. You will occasionally read about a handful of companies being downgraded, but this is not very common, particularly when you consider that there are well over 1800 insurance companies in the United States alone.

Should I use only companies that are AAA or equivalent?

No. There are plenty of safe companies that have a AA or similar rating that should not be excluded as potential candidates. As long as you stick with insurance companies rated AA or AAA you should never have any problems. Better yet, use companies that have a AA, or equivalent, rating from two or more rating services.

FIXED-RATE ANNUITIES

Is there a "best" fixed-rate annuity?

No. A company that provides the best one-to-five-year guaranteed rate may have lengthy or prohibitively high penalties. A good way to gauge a fixed-rate annuity is to look at its past renewal rates compared to other fixed-rate contracts and to see how long the penalty period lasts.

Are investment options important in a fixed-rate annuity?

Most annuities let you lock in a rate of return for one of several different periods of time. Obviously the more flexibility you have as to the locked in rate and its duration, the better the contract looks. If you think rates are going to go down over the next few years, opt for a five-year contract.

If you believe that rates are going to track upward, you are better off in a one- or three-year locked in rate.

Why is the bailout provision so important?

This is the only way you can take money out of a fixed-rate annuity during the penalty period if the insurance company attempts to renew your contract at a low rate. This free bailout means that money can be moved to another company, or simply distributed to you, without cost, fee, or penalty.

Are fixed-rate annuities always a better investment than bank CDs?

Not always, but usually. During most periods of time you can get a higher guaranteed rate of return from an annuity than you can from a CD. Certificates of deposit are clearly a better choice for an investor who wants to tap part of this money during the next year. CDs are also a better choice for investors who feel there is a pretty good chance of having to invade part of this account before reaching age $59\frac{1}{2}$ when the 10 percent IRS penalty disappears.

If I am not close to 60 should I invest in CDs instead of annuities?

Not necessarily. Some people feel nervous having most of their money in a bank and seek safe alternatives. Others invest some of their money in CDs and some in fixed-rate annuities with the belief that the annuity money will not be touched for at least a couple of years.

Should most people own a fixed-rate annuity?

No. These accounts are designed for conservative investors. Variable annuities are the proper choice for most investors since they offer investment options ranging from ultraconservative to extremely aggressive.

Are most fixed-rate annuities pretty much the same, like CDs?

No. There is a wide range of differences between one annuity issuer and another. You always want to compare the issuer's penalty period, the amount of any penalty, the ability to make withdrawals, the guarantee period and rate, as well as the company's rating.

Should I consider a fixed-rate annuity if I am looking for current income?

Yes. Most companies let you take out the accumulated interest, penalty-free, at least once a year. A few companies let you take out as much of your interest and principal as you wish at the end of the year without cost, fee, or penalty. Virtually all insurers allow you to annuitize your contract, thereby receiving regular income that is tax-advantaged.

Don't I have plenty of time until I retire?

If you think you have plenty of time to plan for retirement, think about this: Studies show that only about 18 percent of Americans over age 45 are saving enough income to maintain their standard of living during retirement. If you are among the 82 percent who are not saving enough, you could be short of income during retirement. Now is the time to do something about it.

403(b) PLANS

Should I invest in a tax-sheltered annuity (TSA), also known as a 403(b) plan?

First, find out if you are eligible to participate in a TSA. Not every employer offers these plans. If you are eligible for such a retirement plan, then you should strongly consider using it. Being able to use before-tax dollars is not something that comes up every day. The ability to make an investment, get a tax deduction for it, and then watch it grow and compound tax-deferred is very powerful stuff.

Are TSAs different from annuities?

No. A tax-sheltered annuity (TSA) is a type of annuity that is offered to certain employees. The performance of a TSA depends on whether a fixed-rate and/or variable account is offered as well as current market conditions and the outlook for interest rates.

What do I do if I am eligible for a TSA but haven't used one before?

First, contact your employee benefits coordinator or one of companies offering the annuity and find out if you can participate in a "catch up" (this means that you can add additional monies over the next several years to partially make up what you missed contributing in the past). Second, find out how much you can contribute during each pay period. Next, find out what investment options are available to you. Fourth, contact your financial adviser and go over the different choices in light of your other holdings, goals, and time until retirement.

How are contributions made to a TSA?

These retirement contributions are automatically deducted from your paycheck. In most cases, you will receive a confirmation each time a contribution is made. At least once a year, but usually quarterly, you are free to alter how much money is being deducted and where it is invested. As with other annuities, you are free to move part or all of your TSA from one insurance company to another, subject to those companies on your employer's approved list.

Taxable versus
Tax-Deferred Vehicles

T he following charts give a visual depiction of what happens when a single $10,000 investment is made in a tax-deferred vehicle, such as an annuity, versus the growth rate in an investment with the identical rate of return but subject to current income taxes. Figures A.1 through A.8 show the different results assuming 6, 8, 10, 12, 14, 16, 18, and 20 percent growth rates. In each of these eight bar graphs, 5-, 10-, 15-, and 20-year time periods are covered.

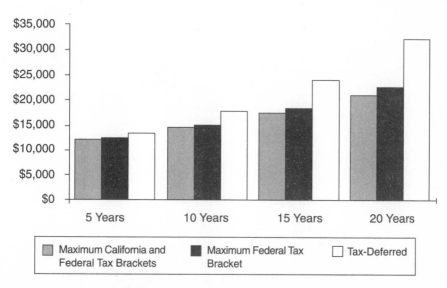

FIGURE A.1 Six percent interest rate.

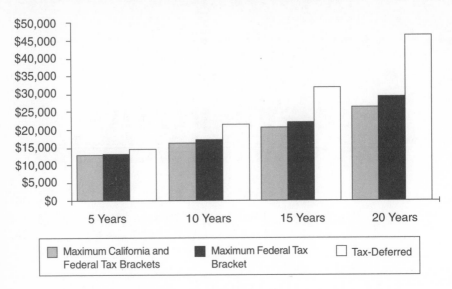

FIGURE A.2   Eight percent interest rate.

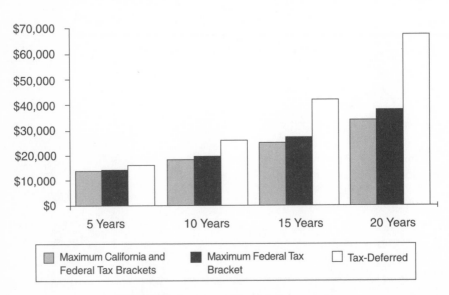

FIGURE A.3   Ten percent interest rate.

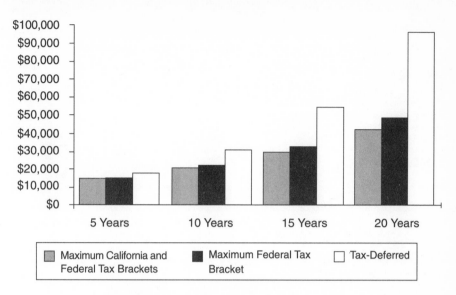

FIGURE A.4 Twelve percent interest rate.

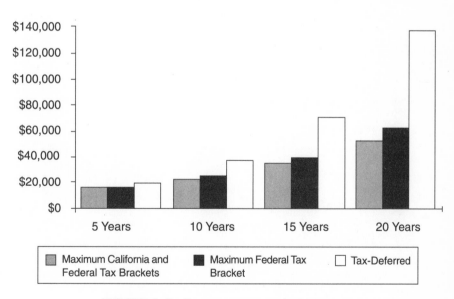

FIGURE A.5 Fourteen percent interest rate.

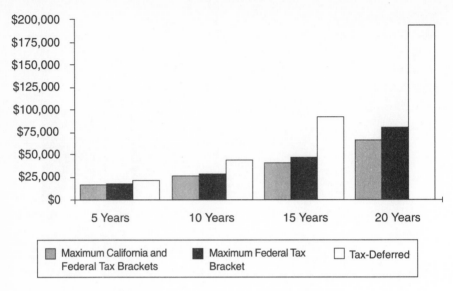

FIGURE A.6 Sixteen percent interest rate.

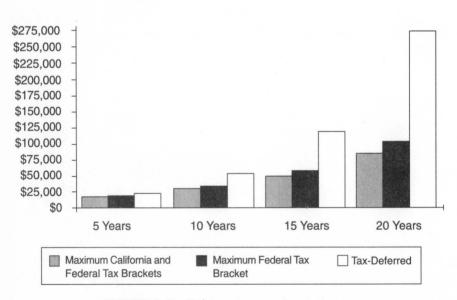

FIGURE A.7 Eighteen percent interest rate.

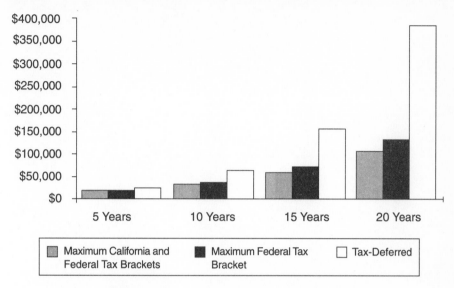

FIGURE A.8 Twenty percent interest rate.

Variable Annuity Subaccount Performance

AGGRESSIVE GROWTH

The aggressive growth subaccount category represents one of the riskiest investment options available for variable annuity investing. Although aggressive growth subaccounts have performed well over the past 10 years, investors should be aware of the volatility found in this category. (See Figure B.1.) There are over 250 subaccounts that make up this category.

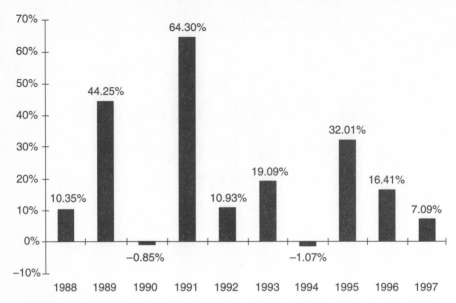

FIGURE B.1 Performance of aggressive growth subaccounts, 1988–1997.

GROWTH

Growth subaccounts are comprised of stocks whose earnings are expected to grow at a rate similar to or above that of the overall market. Appreciation is the primary objective. (See Figure B.2.) There are over 600 subaccounts that make up this category.

GROWTH AND INCOME

Growth and income subaccounts invest in stocks that often pay dividends that are higher than those found in growth subaccounts. This category tends to exhibit the same volatility and performance as the overall market. (See Figure B.3.) There are 380 subaccounts that make up this category.

INTERNATIONAL STOCK

Foreign stocks are perceived as being riskier than their U.S. counterparts because such stocks are thought of as not being as safe as their U.S. counterparts. But foreign securities diversify one's portfolio, often reducing overall risk. Global stock subaccounts, which consist of U.S. *and* foreign

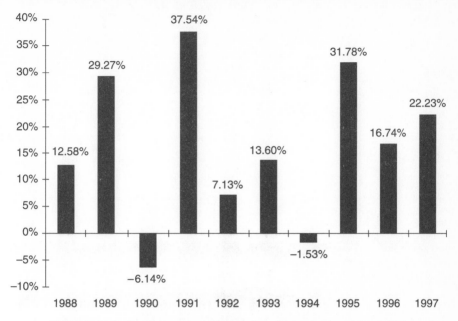

FIGURE B.2 Performance of growth subaccounts, 1988–1997.

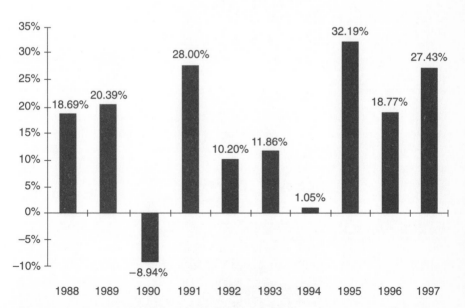

FIGURE B.3 Performance of growth and income subaccounts, 1988–1997.

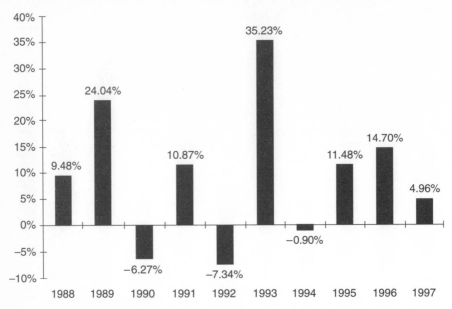

FIGURE B.4 Performance of international stock subaccounts, 1988–1997.

stocks, are included in this category. (See Figure B.4.) There are over 390 subaccounts that make up this category.

BALANCED

Balanced subaccounts invest in stocks, bonds, and sometimes preferred stocks and convertibles. Because of their greater emphasis on current income, balanced subaccounts add more consistency to their performance and are not as volatile as their equity-only counterparts. (See Figure B.5.) There are over 400 subaccounts in this category.

INTERNATIONAL BOND

International bond subaccounts invest at least 65 percent of their assets in non-U.S. currency-denominated bonds issued by foreign governments. Since interest rates fluctuate at different times from country to country, this category offers diversification benefits for the fixed-income portfolio. Global bond subaccounts, which invest in U.S. *and* foreign bonds, are included in this category. (See Figure B.6.) There are over 70 subaccounts in this category.

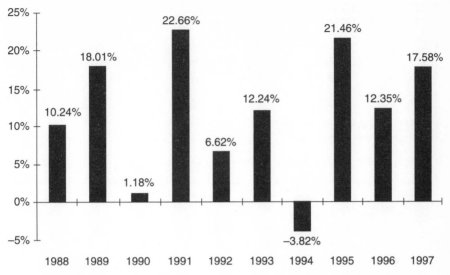

FIGURE B.5 Performance of balanced subaccounts, 1988–1997.

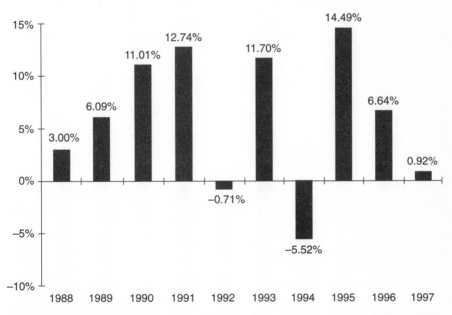

FIGURE B.6 Performance of international bond subaccounts, 1988–1997.

HIGH-YIELD BOND

High-yield corporate bonds have a greater yield and less interest-rate risk than government bonds or high-quality corporate debt. (See Figure B.7.) There are over 130 subaccounts that make up this category.

CORPORATE BOND

Corporate bond subaccounts invest in fixed-income instruments issued by U.S. companies. Corporate bond subaccounts invest primarily in high-quality (investment-grade) bonds. (See Figure B.8.) There are over 300 corporate bond subaccounts.

GOVERNMENT BOND

The vast majority of government bond subaccounts include a moderate or large weighting in federal agency issues such as GNMA and FNMA. The average maturity of the securities in these portfolios is in the seven-to-eight-year range. (See Figure B.9.) There are over 140 government bond subaccounts.

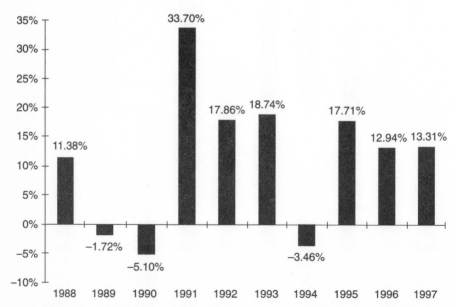

FIGURE B.7 Performance of high-yield bond subaccounts, 1988–1997.

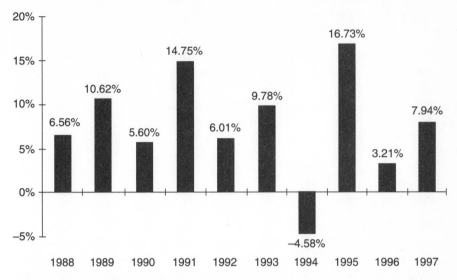

FIGURE B.8 Performance of corporate bond subaccounts, 1988–1997.

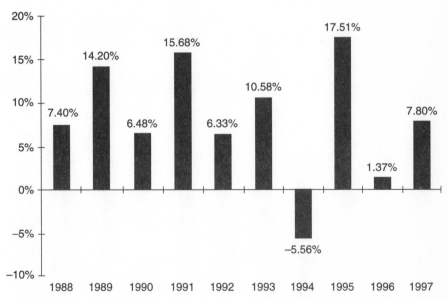

FIGURE B.9 Performance of government bond subaccounts, 1988–1997.

SPECIALTY FUND

This is a broad-based category that includes subaccounts that invest in a particular industry group, country, or region. Also known as sector funds, this category is considered to be very high-risk since management is limited to a specific theme (unlike a growth manager who can invest in any industry or region). (See Figure B.10.)

MONEY MARKET

These subaccounts invest in short-term, high-quality debt that has an average maturity of 35 to 65 days. Investors cannot lose money in this type of account. (See Figure B.11.) These subaccounts should be used only as a defensive position or a temporary parking place until a bond or stock subaccount has been selected.

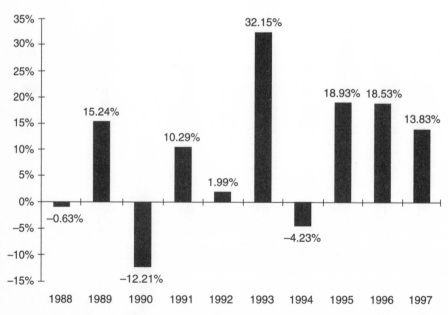

FIGURE B.10 Performance of specialty fund subaccounts, 1988–1997.

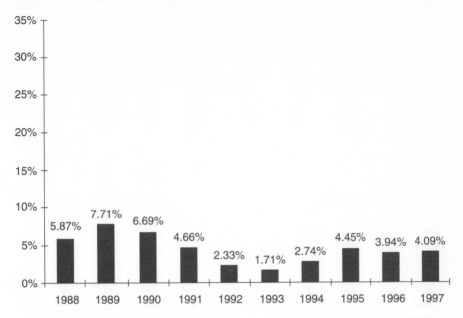

FIGURE B.11   Performance of money market subaccounts, 1988–1997.

AVERAGE ANNUAL RETURN

The vast majority of investors incorrectly go into an investment based on recent performance figures. But even though a five-year time frame is more representative than figures for any given year, there is still no relationship or correlation between past, present, and future subaccount returns. (See Figure B.12.)

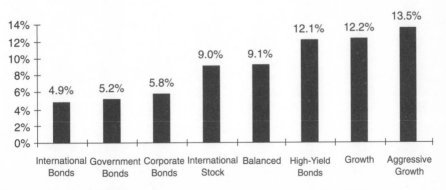

FIGURE B.12   Average annual return, 1992–1996.

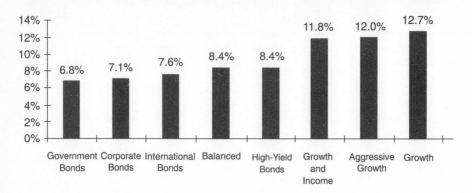

FIGURE B.13   Standard deviation, 1992–1996.

STANDARD DEVIATION

Standard deviation measures an investment's volatility. It is determined by looking at the range of returns around the investment's average return. Higher standard deviations imply greater volatility, which increases investment return uncertainty. (See Figure B.13.)

Appendix

C

Variable Annuity Performance versus Mutual Fund Performance

T he following bar graphs (Figures C.1 through C.8) compare the performance of variable annuities and mutual funds in eight categories over three-, five-, and ten-year periods, ending 12/31/97.

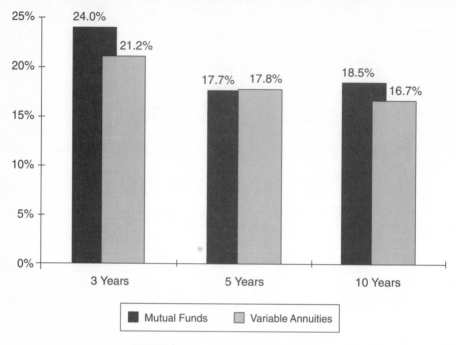

FIGURE C.1 Aggressive growth.

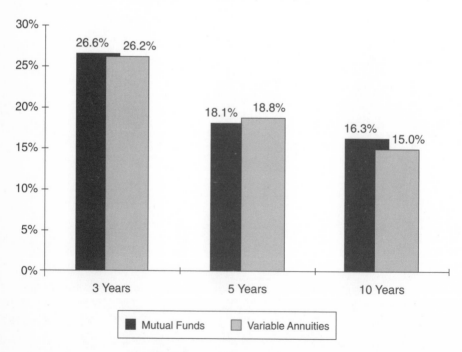

FIGURE C.2 Growth and income.

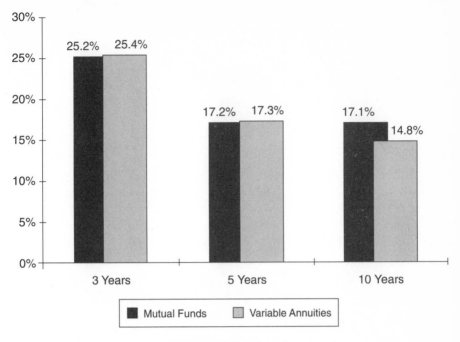

FIGURE C.3 Growth.

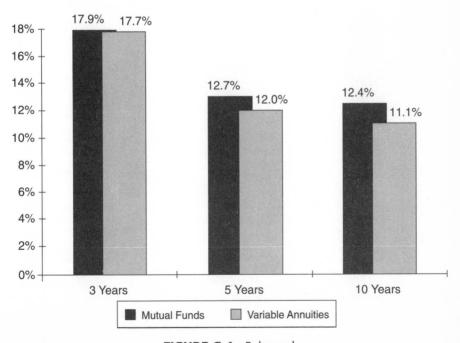

FIGURE C.4 Balanced.

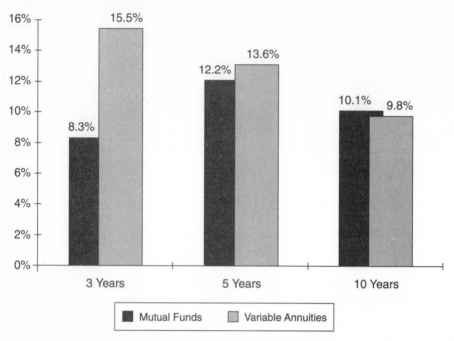

FIGURE C.5 Foreign and global equity.

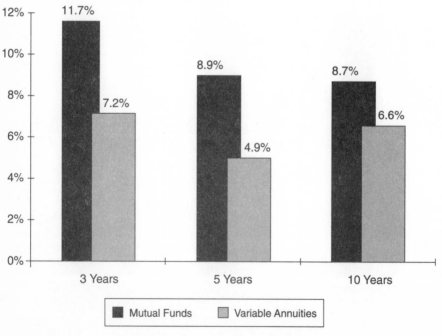

FIGURE C.6 Foreign/U.S. bond.

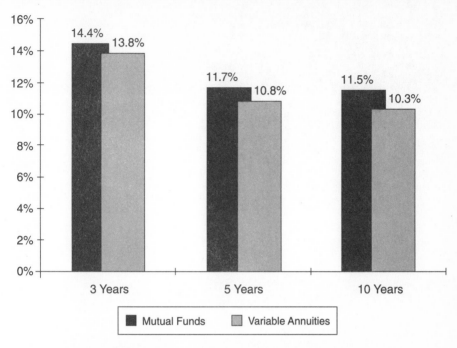

FIGURE C.7 High-yield corporate bond.

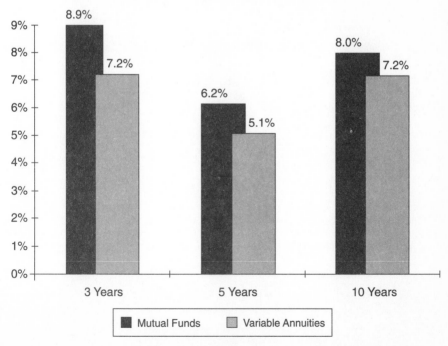

FIGURE C.8 Government bond.

Appendix

The Rule of 72

Whenever we invest somewhere we want to know what the investment will earn and what will happen if we leave the earnings and reinvest them. We know that if we do this long enough, the reinvested growth and/or income of the investment will cause it to double in value.

The Rule of 72 is an easy formula you can use to see how fast one dollar will grow to two dollars, or how quickly it will take $23,000 to grow and compound to $46,000. The equation is based on simple division. Take the assumed, projected, or guaranteed rate of return from an investment and divide it into the number 72. The resulting answer is the number of years it will take an investment to double in value.

As an example, suppose you are looking at a variable annuity that has averaged 18 percent over the past several years and you want to know how long it will take your $25,000 to grow to $50,000. To find out, take 18, the projected rate of return, and divide it into 72. Eighteen goes into 72 four times. This means that $25,000 will grow to $50,000 in four years. If the $25,000 investment grew instead by 10 percent annually for the next several years, it would take 7.2 years to double in value to $50,000 (10 divided into 72 equals 7.2).

COMPREHENDING INFLATION

What is interesting about the Rule of 72 is that it also shows us something about the terrible effects of inflation. For the Rule of 72 will also show

how quickly the purchasing power of a dollar, yen, peso, or franc will be cut in half. As an example, if you assume a 6 percent average annual rate of inflation for the foreseeable future, a dollar will buy only 50 cents' worth of goods and services at the end of 12 years (six divided into 72 equals 12). By the end of the second 12-year period, the purchasing power will be cut in half again. Thus, one dollar shrinks to 50 cents and then the half dollar drops to 25 cents in real value. Phrased another way, at the end of the first 12 years, assuming an average inflation rate of 6 percent, it will take two dollars to buy what you could have previously bought for one dollar. After another 12-year period, it will take four dollars to equal the same purchasing power of that original dollar 24 years previously.

Since it is extremely likely that inflation will stay with us for the remainder of our lifetimes, it is important that we recognize its cruel effects and try to safeguard ourselves against a declining lifestyle.

DOUBLING POWER

No matter how old you are, your investments can double in value only so many times. The younger you are, the more doubling periods you will enjoy. A primary goal of every investor should be to have the growth portion of one's portfolio double as many times as possible before a certain event occurs (i.e., death, retirement, going to college, etc.). Equally important, the money must be in investments that have an acceptable risk level.

Many people, particularly young singles and couples, postpone building a portfolio in lieu of other perceived priorities such as buying a new car, boat, or electronic equipment. Their belief is that they can begin saving "next year." Usually, next year comes and goes and still no investment strategy has been implemented. In fact, what usually happens is that five to ten years elapse before any kind of plan is put into place.

People who postpone starting an investment portfolio do not know how much even a few years' delay will later cost them. As an example, let us suppose you and your neighbor each have $100,000 to invest. With some skill and a little luck, you both feel that you can average 14 percent per year for many years to come. The only difference between you and your neighbor is that you invest your money now and your neighbor waits five years to make a commitment. At the end of approximately 20 years, your $100,000 in a tax-deferred variable annuity is worth $1,600,000. By waiting five years, your neighbor, who invested in the same thing you did, missed a doubling period. That $100,000 has grown to only $800,000. *The five-year delay has cost your neighbor $800,000.*

The calculations done in the previous example were easy to perform. According to the Rule of 72, if one averages 14 percent, money doubles every 5.1 years (72 divided by 14 equals 5.142 years). If, in this example, it takes 5.1 years for money to double, how many doubling periods are there? There are approximately four doubling periods, given a 20-year time horizon (20 divided by 5.1 equals close to four, thus four doubling periods). During the first doubling period $100,000 grew to $200,000; during the second doubling period $200,000 grew to $400,000. The third doubling period saw $400,000 grow to $800,000, and the final doubling saw $800,000 compound to $1,600,000.

Your neighbor got the same rate of return you did but for a shorter period of time: The compounding lasted for only 15 years, not 20 years. And, as the previous paragraph points out, this means receiving only three "doublings": $100,000 grew to $200,000, then $200,000 compounded to $400,000, and, finally, $400,000 doubled a third time to $800,000. There is certainly nothing wrong with $800,000, but it is only half as good as $1,600,000. It is doubtful the neighbor would have procrastinated knowing that the delay would cost $800,000.

Delaying your investment portfolio means that you will be losing out on part or all of one or more extra doubling periods. It will not be the first or second doubling period that you miss, when, say, $10,000 grows to $20,000 and then $20,000 grows to $40,000. The delay will cost you part or all of the last one or two doublings, after the $40,000 continues to compound to $80,000 and then to $160,000. It will be the jump from $160,000 to $320,000 and/or part or all of the doubling when $320,000 would have grown to $640,000.

A PERIODIC CONTRIBUTION EXAMPLE

Another way to examine the cost of procrastination is by showing what happens if you have two investors make periodic contributions of the same dollar amount. Assume that the first investor, age 35, referred to as the "early contributor," invests $5000 into a variable annuity each year for the next 10 years (a total of $50,000 contributed over a decade).

The second investor, also age 35, referred to as the "procrastinator," postpones making any investment until the 11th year (after the early contributor has invested a total of $50,000). Starting at age 45 the procrastinator, in an attempt to catch up, invests $7500 every year for 21 years. At the end of 21 years, the procrastinator has invested a total of $157,500.

Assuming both investors get a 12 percent annual compound rate of growth, the early contributor will have $1,061,726 at age 65, while the procrastinator ends up with $682,269 at age 65, despite the fact that the procrastinator made increased contributions and contributed for 11 more years than the early contributor.

A final twist on the example just given: Assuming a continued 12 percent growth rate, the procrastinator will never catch up with the early contributor. This is true even if the procrastinator continues to add $7500 each year to the portfolio; the early contributor invested only $5000 for the first 10 years, never making another contribution.

TABLE D.1 The Benefits of Tax–Deferred Investment		
12% Assumed Growth Rate	12% Assumed Growth Rate	
–33% Tax Rate	Pay No Current Tax	
= 8% Net Growth Rate	= 12% Net Growth Rate	
72 ÷ 8% = 9 Years to Double Your Money	72 ÷ 12% = 6 Years to Double Your Money	
Taxable Investment	*Age*	*Tax-Deferred Investment*
$ 50,000	50	$ 50,000
	56	100,000
100,000	59	
	62	200,000
200,000	68	400,000

At retirement, both investors can earn and spend 12 percent from each investment. However, the first investor's annual taxable income comes to $24,000, while the second can expect $48,000.

The tax-deferred investment was able to provide 100 percent more money—twice as much income.

DOUBLING YOUR RETIREMENT INCOME

Table D.1 shows two different investors planning for retirement. One investor relies on traditional investments that are fully taxable each year. The other investor gets the same rate of return, but enjoys the long-term rewards of tax deferral, rewards that continue long after retirement begins.

THE FINAL WORD

Prior to his death, Albert Einstein was asked what was the most amazing thing he had ever seen in his long career. His reply was, "Compound interest"!

 *Appendix*

Split Annuities

This is a strategy that can be used with either a variable or a fixed-rate annuity. It shows how a certain percentage of principal and interest can be withdrawn by the investor, while the remaining investment grows and compounds, eventually equaling the original amount invested.

The proper name for this concept is a *split annuity*. The contract owner simply divides the value of the account into two parts: One part is destined for complete liquidation, while the other part is earmarked strictly for replenishment (growth). The split annuity can be done with either a fixed-rate or a variable account, but it is only the fixed-rate annuity that can make the guarantee of complete restoration within a specified period of time.

 split annuity   value of the account is divided into two parts, one for complete liquidation and another for growth.

The split annuity is used as a means of maximizing income while preserving wealth. It is also an attractive consideration since, like any annuitization program, it offers a tax advantage. This concept is sometimes referred as a secured future.

HOW IT WORKS

The best way to illustrate how a split annuity works is by using an example, with rates provided by USG (800-369-3690), one of the most competitve annuity issuers, as of the beginning of 1998. Begin with a $100,000 original investment. Place $61,296 into a fixed-rate annuity that guarantees a 6 percent rate of return for the next eight years. Place the remaining $38,704 into an annuity that is immediately annuitized for the same eight years. By using guaranteed accounts, the $61,296 will be worth exactly $100,000 in eight years. The annuitized portion provides a monthly income of $487, 82 percent of which is not subject to income taxes (due to the exclusion ratio).

AN ALTERNATIVE APPROACH

Would you be interested in an investment that offers the upside potential of the stock and bond markets, and guarantees your principal when held to maturity? With the following variation, you can play the market with peace-of-mind guarantees.

For the sake of illustration, assume the same initial $100,000. For guaranteed return of your original investment in eight years, invest $61,296 in the fixed-rate account. Assuming an eight-year locked-in rate of 6 percent, this amount would grow to $100,000. For potential capital growth and appreciation, invest the remaining $38,704 in a variable account, the return on which is not guaranteed, for the same eight-year period. Based on the performance of U.S. stocks over the past 50 years (12 percent to 13 percent), a growth subaccount would grow to approximately $96,000.

WHO SHOULD USE SPLIT ANNUITIES

Splitting an annuity into a fixed-rate or variable contract and annuitizing the remaining portion is a strategy that should be reviewed by anyone who requires current income, needs a tax break, and wants a guarantee at the end of a specific period.

The Roth IRA versus Annuities

ROTH IRA

As of January 1, 1998, most people can now fund a Roth IRA; the maximum contribution is $2000 per calendar year. You cannot establish a Roth IRA if you file a joint return and have an adjusted gross income (AGI) of $160,000 or more ($110,000 for individual filers). Money that is converted from a traditional IRA into a Roth IRA is not used to calculate AGI limits just described. You or your spouse must have *earned* income (meaning money earned from salary, tips, bonuses and/or commissions). The benefits of a Roth IRA are numerous:

✔ Earnings grow and compound tax-free (not tax-*deferred* like an annuity).

✔ You do not have to start taking money when you reach age 70½.

✔ You can continue making contributions past age 70 (provided you have *earned* income).

It is important to keep in mind a few other points about the Roth IRA: (1) Growth and earnings are truly tax-free if the Roth IRA account is at least five years old and the owner is at least 59½; (2) taxation and penalty can be avoided even if the account is less than five years old if the owner dies or becomes disabled, or the money is used for the first-time purchase of a home ($10,000 maximum lifetime limit for this exception); and (3) withdrawals of principal are not taxed, even during the early years.

If you qualify for a Roth IRA and you cannot deduct the contributions to a traditional IRA, then you should fund a Roth IRA each year (and so should your spouse). Tax-free growth is definitely better than tax-deferred growth. Furthermore, just like with an annuity, you are not required to make any withdrawals during your lifetime. The proceeds of the Roth IRA account will pass income tax-free to your heir(s).

A traditional IRA that is deductible may be better than a Roth IRA only if certain assumptions are made as to the rate of growth, how long the money will be allowed to compound tax-sheltered, and one's projected income tax rate during withdrawal. Again, if you cannot deduct the IRA contribution (see next paragraph), a Roth IRA is always a better way to go.

A traditional (regular) IRA is fully deductible if you *or* your spouse is covered by another qualified retirement plan through work *and* AGI is under $40,000 (single) or $60,000 (married). Partial deductibility exists if your AGI is between $30,000 and $40,000 (single) or between $50,000 and $60,000 (joint return). If you or your spouse is *not* covered by a company plan, all IRA contributions are deductible, regardless of your level of income. Like a Roth IRA, you must have earned income to contribute to a traditional IRA.

ROTH CONVERSION IRA

If you have a traditional IRA and have an AGI of less than $100,000, you can convert your regular IRA into a Roth IRA. Such a conversion will trigger a taxable event but will not trigger any kind of IRS penalty. Furthermore, if the conversion takes place in 1998, the tax liability for such a conversion is spread out over four years. If you convert after 1998, you will be taxed on the full amount converted in the year in which the conversion takes place.

Whether you should convert an existing IRA into a Roth IRA (and thereby trigger a tax event) depends on the following factors: (1) your current tax bracket (since the conversion will add to your AGI in the calendar year in which the conversion occurs); (2) your expected tax bracket when you start taking money out of the IRA (the lower the expected bracket, the less desirable the Roth IRA becomes); (3) how many years the Roth IRA would grow tax-free (the longer the better the case for a Roth); and (4) the growth rate of the IRA account (the higher the rate, the better a Roth may look).

ROTH IRA VERSUS AN ANNUITY

The only major advantage an annuity has over a Roth IRA is that there is no limit to how much can be invested in an annuity each year or all at once. Otherwise, the Roth IRA is a better program for a number of reasons. First, a Roth IRA can provide you with more investment options. You can invest Roth money into your favorite annuities, mutual funds, and/or individual securities (such as stocks, bonds, REITs, or partnerships). Second, there are no taxes due when withdrawals take place, either during your lifetime or when an heir makes a withdrawal. With an annuity, the only part that is tax-free is the original principal; otherwise, withdrawals of growth and/or interest are taxed as ordinary income (not the more favorable capital gains rate). Third, annuity owners do not escape any IRS penalty or taxation if the money is used for a first-time home purchase. However, the Roth IRA caps such an advantage at $10,000.

Appendix

The Value of Annuities after 1997 Tax Changes

For investors as a whole, the reduction in the capital gains rate to a maximum of 20 percent was a blessing. For prospective annuity investors, the decision as to whether an annuity should be part of the portfolio becomes even more difficult.

One of the disadvantages of annuities has always been that withdrawals of anything other than principal are taxed as ordinary income, the top rate in 1998 being 39.6 percent. The only way to even somewhat reduce the sting of such taxation was (and still is) to either: (1) annuitize the contract, thereby having an income stream that provided some tax shelter (*note:* as you may recall, when you annuitize an annuity, a portion of each annuity payment to you represents income or growth, which is taxable, and a portion represents a tax-free return of principal); (2) wait and hope that your tax bracket drops and any subsequent withdrawals would be taxed at a lower rate; (3) leave the annuity to your spouse who might later be in a lower bracket; or (4) do not make any withdrawals during your lifetime or your surviving spouse's lifetime and let the kids (or whoever the heirs are) suffer by paying ordinary income taxes on the complete growth of the annuity within five years of the surviving spouse's death.

A disadvantage of most nonannuity investments is that interest is fully taxable each year, the two exceptions being municipal bond interest or where income is sheltered by depreciation from real estate, oil and gas, or leasing. Growth from any nonannuity investment is taxed only if the investment is sold for a profit. And, unlike an annuity, the sale of such an investment is never required, not even after inheritence (*note:* an annuity must be fully liquidated within five years after the death of the contract owner's surviving spouse, or the contract owner's death if he or she is single when death occurs). This then brings up a second disadvantage for annuities: no step-up in basis upon death.

Step-Up in Basis

When you die, most assets get a step-up in basis, meaning that your heirs receive the assets, *for income tax purposes*, as if they purchased the assets on your date of death for the then fair market value. This means that if an heir then sold an asset, any gain or loss would be based on the *inherited value*, not the price you had paid for the asset or investment when you were alive. A couple of examples at this point may be helpful.

Example #1: A "Profit" Suppose you bought 10 shares of IBM several decades ago and the price of all 10 shares came to $100. Through stock splits and an increase in the price per share of the stock, your 10 shares have now grown to 200 shares, and those 200 shares are worth a total of $25,000. If you sold those shares before death, there would be a capital gains tax on the $24,900 profit ($25,000 minus your basis of $100). With the new maximum rate of 20 percent, however, you would still net $20,020 ($24,900 times 80 percent equals $19,920 plus your original principal of $100). If instead you died before the sale and your spouse or children then sold the stock for $25,000, they would net the entire $25,000 (since the basis was stepped up from $100 to $25,000, the market value of 200 shares of IBM, on your date of death).

Example #2: A "Loss" To fully appreciate the one advantage of death, let us change the aforementioned example slightly. Let us continue to suppose that you paid $100 for the IBM stock and it was worth $25,000 on your date of death. Now let us assume that heirs do not sell the stock right away. Instead they wait a few weeks, months, or years and then sell all 200 shares. Unfortunately for them, the IBM stock has dropped in value from $25,000 down to $22,000. *From a tax standpoint*, this turns out to be good news! A sale at $22,000 creates a $3000 tax loss ($22,000 minus the new $25,000 basis). The $3000 loss can be used to offset any gain the heir has that year or can be used to offset what is known as ordinary income (meaning income earned from salary, tips, bonuses, or commissions).

Back to Annuities

Certain assets do not get a step-up in basis upon death. These assets include: annuities, CDs, money market funds, and qualified retirement accounts (e.g., traditional IRAs, Keoghs, pension plans, etc.). Instead, the heir must pay ordinary income taxes when such investments are liquidated. The portion that is taxable is the difference between the selling price and the purchase price (or purchase price plus dividends, capital gains, and/or interest that was automatically reinvested each year and thus subjected to taxation each year). An exception to this equation is for qualified retirement accounts: Everything in the account is taxable when withdrawn (except for those dollars that were originally contributed on an after-tax basis—meaning they were not deductible when invested).

Since variable annuities have quite a few similarities to mutual funds and fixed-rate annuities are similar to bank CDs, let us go through a couple of examples of the tax consequences of such investments. For illustration purposes, we are going to assume the following:

- ✔ The initial investment is $100,000.
- ✔ All of these investments are held for 20 years.
- ✔ The fixed-rate annuity and bank CD average a 5 percent annual return during the 20 years.
- ✔ The variable annuity growth subaccount and growth mutual fund average 12 percent per year.
- ✔ The investor's (and heir's) tax bracket is 39.6 percent for ordinary income and 20 percent for capital gains (the maximum federal rates in both cases).

Example: Fixed-Rate Annuity versus Bank CD At the end of 20 years, the fixed-rate annuity is worth $265,000. The investor's son inherits the $265,000 but must pay $65,340 in federal income taxes (39.6 percent of the $165,000 "gain"), netting $199,660 after paying federal income taxes.

The CD investor also starts off with $100,000 compounding at 5 percent per year, but the entire 5 percent is subject to income taxes each year. So, instead of compounding at 5 percent, the CD investor is compounding at 3.02 percent per year because 39.6 percent of the 5 percent is going to Uncle Sam (5 percent times 69.4 percent equals 3.02 percent after-tax return). At the end of 20 years, the $100,000 CD is worth $181,000.

As you can see, the annuity is the better investment ($199,660 versus $181,000). The $18,660 difference is not that dramatic since we are looking at 20 years—a very lengthy period of time. The difference in "real dollars" (meaning inflation-adjusted dollars) shrinks the annuity advantage by quite a bit.

The conclusion to be reached from this example of fixed-rate annuities versus a CD is that the annuity offers only a minor benefit and that it takes several years for there to be any meaningful difference. Phrased another way, tax-deferred growth is better than taxable growth but for the difference to be substantial, higher-returning investments need to be compared (see next example).

Example: Variable Annuity versus Mutual Fund At the end of 20 years, the original $100,000 in the variable annuity is worth $965,000. The investor's daughter inherits the $965,000, but must pay ordinary income taxes on $865,000 ($965,000 minus the basis of $100,000). After paying $342,540 in federal income taxes, the daughter will net $622,460.

At the end of 20 years, the original $100,000 invested in the growth mutual fund will be worth approximately $806,000. "Approximately" is used because it is assumed that the true growth rate on an *after-tax* basis each year is 11 percent, not 12 percent (*note:* the Vanguard 500 Index Fund has a tax efficiency of about 92 percent, meaning that if the fund were to return 12 percent in a year, the investor would keep 92 percent of 12 percent, which is very close to 11 percent). The daughter will inherit the $806,000 at a basis of $806,000. Any subsequent sale (which, unlike an annuity, is not required) will result in a profit or loss based on a starting point of $806,000.

Finishing up on this example, suppose the $622,460 from the annuity is invested in a growth mutual fund that averages 12 percent, the $806,000 remains in the growth fund (or is sold and the $806,000 is invested in the same growth fund as the annuity money), and these "new" investments are held by the heir for 25 years. At the end of 25 years the $622,460 will be worth $8,459,231 (we are assuming an 11 percent after-tax growth rate). The $806,000 will grow to $10,953,540 (same after-tax growth rate, but the difference is due to the extra $183,540 in the initial growth fund).

Appendix H

An Example of Bad Luck

If you are still not convinced about the long-term benefits of being in stocks, consider the story of Louie the loser. There is only one thing you can say about Louie's timing: It is always awful. So, it is no surprise that when he decided to invest $10,000 a year in the American Legacy III Growth Portfolio, a subaccount featured in this book, he managed to pick the worst possible times. Every year since the subaccount's 1984 inception, he has invested on the very day that the stock market peaked. (See Table H.1.) How has he done? He has over $339,000, which means his money has grown at an average rate of just under 15 percent a year.

TABLE H.1 Investing at the Stock Market Peak			
American Legacy III Growth Portfolio			
Date of Purchase (Market High for Year)	Annual Investment	Price per Unit (When Purchased)	Total Value (End of Year)
12/16/85	$10,000	$0.22	$ 9,790
12/2/86	10,000	0.29	22,496
8/25/87	10,000	0.40	31,443
10/21/88	10,000	0.34	45,562
10/9/89	10,000	0.47	68,211
7/16/90	10,000	0.48	72,824
12/31/91	10,000	0.54	105,456
6/1/92	10,000	0.54	125,785
12/29/93	10,000	0.68	153,967
1/3/94	10,000	0.69	161,879
12/31/95	10,000	0.89	222,076
12/27/96	10,000	0.99	257,508
8/6/97	10,000	1.23	339,790

What happened? Louie chose a subaccount managed by an organization with a consistently outstanding record. He also found that while there are good times and bad times, over the long haul any day is a good day to invest.

If, perchance, Louie had managed to pick the best day each year for those 13 years to make his investments, the day the market bottomed each year, his account would have been worth over $423,000 by the end of 1997 (18 percent per year). (See Table H.2.)

Even though his timing was terrible, Louie still fared much better than if he had done what many people are doing today: waiting for the "perfect" time to invest.

TABLE H.2   Investing at the Stock Market Low
American Legacy III Growth Portfolio

Date of Purchase (Market Low for Year)	Annual Investment	Price per Unit (When Purchased)	Total Value (End of Year)
1/4/85	$10,000	$0.18	$ 12,226
1/22/86	10,000	0.22	28,608
10/19/87	10,000	0.31	40,356
1/20/88	10,000	0.29	57,288
1/3/89	10,000	0.34	86,920
10/11/90	10,000	0.37	93,012
1/9/91	10,000	0.40	135,593
10/9/92	10,000	0.52	159,092
1/20/93	10,000	0.61	193,208
4/4/94	10,000	0.64	201,402
1/30/95	10,000	0.67	277,051
1/10/96	10,000	0.84	320,598
4/1/97	10,000	0.96	423,380

Variable Annuity Directory

Below, in alphabetical order, are the insurance company listings, and the telephone numbers of those companies that issue variable annuities.

Insurance Company	Phone Number
Aetna Life Insurance & Annuity	860-273-9105
Aid Association for Lutherans	800-778-1762
AIG Life Insurance	800-362-7500
Alexander Hamilton Life Ins. Co.	800-252-4028
Allianz Life Ins. of North America	800-624-0197
Allmerica Financial Life Ins. & Annuity	800-533-7881
American Enterprise Life Ins. Co.	800-817-4647
American Franklin Life Insurance	800-528-2011
American General Life Insurance	800-531-6466
American International Life of N.Y.	800-362-7500
American Life Insurance of N.Y.	800-872-5963
American Maturity Life Ins. Co.	800-396-5552
American National Insurance	800-899-6806
American Partners Life Ins. Co.	800-297-8800
American Republic Insurance	800-367-6058
American Skandia Life Assur.	800-541-3087

American United Life Insurance	800-634-1629
Ameritas Life Insurance Corp.	800-255-9678
Ameritas Variable Life Insurance	800-634-8353
Anchor National Life Insurance	800-445-7862
Annuity Investors Life Insurance	800-789-6771
AUSA Life Insurance	914-697-8000
Canada Life Ins. of America	800-905-1959
Charter National Life Ins.	800-225-2470
Chubb Life Insurance of America	800-251-7202
Citicorp Life Insurance Company	800-497-4857
Connecticut General Life Insurance	800-628-2811
Cova Financial Services Life Insurance Co.	800-343-8496
CUNA Mutual Life Insurance Co.	800-798-5500
Equitable Life Assur. Soc. of U.S.	800-789-7771
Equitable Life Ins. Co. of Iowa	800-344-6864
Farm Bureau Life Insurance	800-247-4170
Fidelity Investments Life Ins.	800-544-2442
First ING Life Insurance Co. of N.Y.	800-249-9099
First Investors Life Insurance	800-832-7783
First SunAmerica Life Ins. Co.	800-996-9786
First Variable Life Insurance	800-996-9786
Fortis Benefits Insurance	800-996-9786
General American Life Ins.	800-800-2638
Glenbrook Life and Annuity Company	800-622-3699
Golden American Life Ins.	800-425-4299
Great American Reserve Ins.	800-237-6580
Great-West Life & Annuity Ins.	800-342-6307
Guardian Insurance & Annuity	800-468-8661
Hartford Life Insurance	800-468-8661
Horace Mann Life Ins. Co.	860-246-4819
IDS Life Insurance	800-231-5453
IL Annuity and Insurance Company	800-521-0538
Integrity Life Insurance	800-231-5453
Jackson Nat'l Life Insurance Co.	800-437-0602
Jefferson-Pilot Life Ins.	800-325-8583

John Hancock Mutual Life Ins.	800-634-0142
Kansas City Life Insurance Co.	617-572-5666
Kemper Investors Life Insurance	617-572-5666
Keyport Life Insurance	800-554-5426
Life Insurance of Virginia	800-554-5426
Lincoln Benefit Life	800-628-2238
Lincoln Life & Annuity Co. of N.Y.	800-352-9910
Lincoln National Life Ins.	800-352-9910
London Pacific Life & Annuity Co.	800-248-0838
Lutheran Brotherhood	800-341-0441
Manulife Financial	207-770-2211
Massachusetts Mutual Life Ins.	800-557-2223
Merrill Lynch Life Insurance	800-234-5606
Metropolitan Life Insurance	413-788-8411
Metropolitan Tower Life Ins.	800-535-5549
Midland National Life Ins.	800-492-3553
Minnesota Mutual Life Ins.	605-335-5700
MML Bay State Life Insurance	605-335-5700
MONY Life Ins. of America	605-335-5700
Mutual Benefit Life Ins.	800-362-3141
Mutual Life Ins. of New York	800-362-3141
Mutual of America Life Ins.	800-328-9343
National Integrity Life Ins.	800-272-2216
National Life Insurance Company	800-468-3785
Nationwide Life Insurance	800-325-8583
Nationwide Life & Annuity Insurance	800-451-0070
New England Life Insurance Co.	800-545-4730
New York Life Ins. & Annuity	800-777-5897
Northbrook Life Insurance	800-598-2019
Northern Life Insurance Co.	800-598-2019
Northwestern Mutual Life Ins.	800-654-2397
Ohio National Life Insurance	800-870-0453
Pacific Life Insurance	800-366-6654
PaineWebber Life Insurance	800-722-2333
Penn Insurance and Annuity Co.	800-800-7681

Penn Mutual Life Insurance	800-800-7681
PFL Life Insurance	800-766-7366
PHL Variable Insurance Company	800-548-1119
Phoenix Home Life Mutual Ins.	800-766-7366
Principal Mutual Life Ins.	800-843-8348
Protective Life Insurance	800-892-4885
Provident Mutual Life Ins.	800-247-4123
Providentmutual Life & Annuity	302-452-4989
Providian Life & Health Insurance	800-654-7796
Pruco Life Ins. Co. of New Jersey	302-452-4000
Prudential Ins. Co. of America	888-778-2888
ReliaStar Bankers Security Life Ins. Co.	800-445-4571
Reliastar Life Ins.	800-437-4016
SAFECO Life Insurance	800-456-6965
Security Benefit Life Ins.	800-426-7355
Security First Life Ins.	800-426-7649
Security Life of Denver Ins. Co.	800-888-2461
Southland Life Insurance Company	800-933-5858
Sun Life Assur. of Canada (U.S.)	800-933-5858
Sun Life Ins. & Annuity of N.Y.	800-752-7216
Teachers Ins. & Annuity Assoc.	800-752-7216
Transamerica Occidental Life Ins.	800-752-7216
Travelers Insurance	800-447-7569
Union Central Life Ins.	800-842-8573
United Investors Life Ins.	800-334-4298
United Life & Annuity Insurance Co.	800-334-4298
United Life & Annuity Insurance Co.	800-842-9368
United of Omaha Life Insurance	800-842-9368
USAA Life Insurance Company	800-825-1551
VALIC	800-998-2542
Valley Forge Life Ins. Company	800-453-4933
Western National Life Ins. Co.	800-448-2542
Western Reserve Life Assur. of OH	800-448-2542
Western-Southern Life Assurance Co.	800-851-9777

Glossary

A shares charge an upfront commission.

accumulation units similar to shares in a mutual fund; price per unit will depend on performance of portfolio.

annual high-water mark with look-back credit on an equity-indexed annuity is calculated by using the highest anniversary value.

annual reset used to determine annually how much is credited to the equity-indexed annuity investor's account, based on beginning and ending values of the S&P 500.

annuitant the "measuring life" of the annuity contract; similar to the "insured" in a life insurance policy. Every annuity contract must include an annuitant. The annuitant has no voice or control over the investment or its disposition. The death of the annuitant may trigger certain insurance company guarantees if the money was invested in a variable annuity.

annuitant–driven for a majority of annuity contracts, provisions come into being if the annuitant dies, reaches a certain age, or becomes disabled.

annuitization the even distribution of both principal and interest over a period of time.

annuity aggregation rule distributions are combined for tax purposes if a person owns two or more contracts from one insurer.

annuity contract an investment in an annuity represents a contractual agreement between the investor (who is usually the contract owner) and the insurer (the insurance company that issues the agreement, known as the annuity contract. The annuity contract contains certain guarantees, assurances, descriptions, terms, and potential penalty provisions.

annuity unit annuitizing a contract converts accumulation units into annuity units, which are used to calculate the amount of income to be paid out.

asset allocation subaccount part equity and part debt, has a tendency to emphasize stocks over bonds.

assumed interest rate certain projections, illustrations, or examples are based on an assumed interest rate. The rate of return is assumed because the investment does not offer a guaranteed rate of return (e.g., a money market, bond, or stock portfolio) or the guarantee does not last as long as the illustration is showing (e.g., a fixed-rate annuity that has a guaranteed rate of 6 percent for seven years but the investor wants to know what the account will be worth in 20 years, assuming 6 percent is paid for all 20 years).

B shares charge a back-end sales fee.

back-end load *See* **contingent deferred sales load (CDSL).**

bail-out owner can liquidate the annuity without fees or penalties if the interest renewal rate is lower than the original rate by 1 percent.

banding a year-by-year method of crediting interest to a fixed-rate 403(b) annuity contract (offered to teachers and school administrators, hospital employees, and nonprofit employees). The concept of banding has to do with what rate of return is earned on existing money and money periodically contributed by salary reduction plans.

beta a measurement of a mutual fund's or variable annuity subaccount's market-related risk.

C shares no upfront or back-end commission; 1 percent is debited annually.

call option there are two types of options: call options and put options. Both types of options usually expire (meaning they become worthless) within a year. You can also buy options that expire in just a few days, weeks, or months. When you buy a call, you are betting that a certain stock (or stock index such as the S&P 500) is going to increase in price within a certain period. There is a great deal of leverage going on when an option is bought. Purchasers of options can end up making a small gain on their money, or they may end up making 100 percent, 200 percent, or even more. You can also lose part or all of your money.

cap rate the annual maximum percentage increase allowed for an equity-indexed annuity.

CD/annuity a contract with a one-year life.

coannuitant a second "measuring life," somewhat similar to a second-to-die life insurance policy. Naming a coannuitant means the death of one annuitant will not trigger a possible forced distribution of the annuity. Only a small number of insurers include a coannuitant option as part of the annuity application.

compound interest interest already earned is reinvested so that a larger amount is earning interest.

consumer price index (CPI) the mostly commonly used yardstick to measure the rate of inflation in the United States.

contingent deferred sales load (CDSL) a commission incurred by the investor when liquidating part or all of an investment. Also known as a *back-end load* or *surrender charge*, a CDSL can be avoided by withdrawing less than a certain amount each year (usually 10 percent of the money invested), death of the annuitant or owner (in the case of annuities, depending on how the contract is worded), or by keeping the money with the insurer for a specified number of years, which can range from one to 10 years but is usually in the five-to-seven-year range.

contract owner the person or entity that owns the annuity. Most of the time, the contract owner is the one who made the investment. The annuity contract is between the insurer (the issuer of the contract) and the contract owner.

contract termination if the contract is "annuitant–driven," the death of the annuitant may require liquidation within five years.

convertible subaccount allows owner to convert or exchange securities for corporations' common stocks.

coupon rate part of the description of a corporate, municipal, or government bond (the name of the issuer and the bond's maturity date are the other ways in which one bond is distinguished from another). The coupon rate represents how much the issuer—the corporation, municipality, or government—is paying in interest each year, based on the bond's $1000 face value (what the bond will be worth at maturity). Thus, a 5 percent bond pays 5 percent of $1000 each year ($50), a 6.5 percent bond pays $65 in interest each year, and so on.

debt instruments IOUs of an individual, partnership, company, municipality, or national government. Examples of debt instruments include trust deeds, notes (short-term IOUs), and bank CDs, as well as corporate, municipal, and U.S. government bonds. When you buy (or invest in) a debt instrument, you are lending your money to an entity or a person. In return for the use of your money, the borrower (the bank, corporation, government, etc.) agrees to pay you interest plus your principal at some future date.

deferred annuity there are two types of annuities, deferred and immediate; deferred annuities are the more popular of the two. Under a deferred annuity, the investment grows and compounds tax-deferred. Income, growth, and/or principal are withdrawn at some time in the future by the contract owner or heirs.

disposition the power to decide the distribution of the investment.

diversification choosing a mix of conservative and aggressive investments to balance market highs and lows; the policy of all variable annuities to spread investments among a number of different securities to reduce the risk inherent in investing.

dollar-cost averaging investing a fixed amount of money in a given subaccount at specific intervals to average out high and low unit prices.

enhanced death benefit minimum benefit equals original invested compounded by 5 percent or value on date of death.

equity vehicle all investments fall into one of two categories: equity or debt. When you own an equity, you own part or all of the asset. Examples include real estate, common stock, preferred stock, variable annuity subaccounts, and mutual funds that invest in stocks, as well as collectibles (rare coins, stamps, etc.) and metals.

exchange privilege the ability to move assets among subaccounts.

exclusion ratio the proportion of an annuitized payment that is a return of capital and therefore not taxed.

expected return the projected or assumed rate of growth.

explicit charges clearly spelled out, these may be applied when the account is valued, when a loan is made, and so on.

first-auto correlation the relationship, correlation, or predictability of an investment's return from one year to the next. A high first-auto correlation means that the investment's return for the next period, which could be a day, week, month, quarter, year, or multiple years, will most likely be very similar to its return for the most recent past period (e.g., a money market account or bank CD). A low correlation means that there is little, if any, relationship or likelihood that the past return will be similar to the future return (e.g., common stocks and real estate).

fixed-rate annuity investor receives a set rate of return.

flexible premium when you invest in an annuity, the money being invested is sometimes referred to as the premium. A flexible premium means that additional monies can be added at any time in the future to the same annuity contract. Flexible premiums are extremely common with variable annuities but rare with fixed-rate annuities.

floor the minimum amount credited to the investor, regardless of the index's performance.

forced annuitization some contracts require distribution or orderly liquidation once the annuitant reaches a certain age, typically 80 or 85.

fund expense the fee paid to the mutual fund or management company overseeing the investment portfolios.

general account pool of money from fixed-rate annuity investors and other sources.

guaranteed death benefit the beneficiary receives the greater of the principal or the value of the account as of the date of the annuitant's death.

hot new issue stock offered by a company going public for the first time for which there is great demand.

immediate annuity a type of fixed-rate or variable annuity wherein money starts to be paid to the contract owner or annuitant either right away or within a month, quarter, or year. Immediate annuities are designed for people who need income on a regular basis.

implicit charges indirect, hidden costs, such as the difference between returns actually earned versus the amount credited to your account.

income tax event when a sale of a security or other asset is made, there is a potential income tax event since the item is usually sold for either a profit or a loss. In the case of annuities, any withdrawal of income or growth is reported to the IRS, and taxes are due on the gain.

index benefit how much an investor actually earns.

intermediate-term investments a bond or other security that matures in five to fifteen years (four to seven years by some definitions).

investment adviser organization or individual that provides professional advice on a wide range of investments, including annuities.

investment objective goal (e.g., long-term capital growth, current income, etc.) that the investor and subaccount pursue together.

liquidity the ability to get back all, or almost all of your investment at any time. Money market funds, certificates of deposit, passbook savings accounts, and U.S. Treasury bills have a great deal of liquidity. Whereas long-term bonds, real estate, collectibles, and stocks may be quite marketable, their liquidity can range from excellent to poor (since value can fluctuate quite a bit in a relatively short period of time).

long-term investments a bond or other security that matures in sixteen to thirty years (eight to fourteen years by some definitions).

mortality fee an annual percentage of the total value of the annuity contract, used to pay for the guaranteed death benefit.

no-load an investment that does not charge the investor a commission fee.

owner–driven for a minority of annuity contracts, the policy stays in force until the contract owner dies.

participation rate also known as the index rate; refers to the percentage increase in the S&P 500 that the investment (equity-indexed annuity) will grow by.

point-to-point used to determine the account's credit by subtracting the value of the S&P at the end of the term from the beginning value.

portfolio collection of securities owned by an individual or institution (such as a variable annuity *subaccount*).

portfolio average determines the current interest rate to be credited based on the insurer's earnings on its entire portfolio.

price/earnings (P/E) ratio a measurement of the selling price of a stock in relation to the company's earnings for the year.

probate a term that means "prove the will." This legal proceeding takes place even if the deceased did not leave a will. Probate can be an expensive, time-consuming, and frustrating event. The typical probate takes well over a year; the cost of probate is based on the value of the decedent's gross estate and can be tens of thousands of dollars, or more. Annuities, qualified retirement accounts (i.e., IRAs, Keoghs, pension plans, etc.), and assets held in joint tenancy with rights of survivorship pass free of probate and are not considered part of the probatable estate.

prospectus outlines the different subaccounts, their performance, and any charges.

reserve pool system of insurance companies that assumes the liabilities of a defunct member company.

seven-pay life insurance a whole-life policy that is structured so that the contract owner can make tax-free withdrawals (policy loans). "Seven-pay" refers to IRS regulations that require premium payments to be paid in over at least seven years so that the life policy maintains its integrity as insurance and not just an investment that can produce tax-free income each year.

short-term investments a security that matures in five years or less (zero to three years by some definitions).

single premium a lump sum of money that is used to purchase an annuity. Most fixed-rate annuities have a single premium since the contract owner is locking in a set rate of return for a specific period, similar to a bank CD.

single-premium variable life a type of whole-life insurance wherein the policy owner can select how the cash value of the policy is to be invested. Investment choices are similar to those found in a mutual fund family and range from conservative (money market) to aggressive (small-company growth stocks). "Single-premium" means that a lump sum is invested, a single investment.

split annuity value of the account is divided into two parts, one for complete liquidation and another for growth.

standard deviation volatility of return.

step-up in basis the unrealized appreciation on an inherited asset is not taxed.

step-up in principal a death benefit feature found in many variable annuities. When the annuitant dies, the beneficiary(s) receive the greater of: (1) the value of the contract on the date of death, or (2) the original principal plus any additional contributions.

subaccount variable annuity investment choice(s), may include a combination of stocks, bonds, and money market securities.

surrender charge *See* **contingent deferred sales load (CDSL)**.

tax-free exchange *See* **1035 exchange**.

tax-sheltered annuity a retirement plan for school, hospital, and nonprofit employees under Section 403(b) of the Internal Revenue Code.

1035 exchange also known as a *tax-free exchange*, the transfer of an investment from one annuity company to another; such a transfer is not taxed.

universal life a type of whole-life insurance. Whole-life insurance can be described as term insurance with a forced savings plan (what is called the "cash value" of the policy). This means that part of each premium payment goes toward insurance (paying the insurance company to take on the risk of someone dying) and part goes toward the cash value. With traditional whole-life insurance, the cash value grows at a set rate of return. With universal life, the cash value is invested in a money market account, wherein the interest rate is constantly changing, reflecting the then-current level of short-term interest rates. Universal life also allows the contract owner more flexibility in premium payments and loans.

variable annuity no set rate of return, but choice of one or more *portfolios (subaccounts)*.

vesting schedule outlines the amount that can be withdrawn yearly without penalty.

wrap fee account instead of commissions, an annual fee is billed quarterly.

Index